WHAT A RIDE, MATE!

Peter Leitch with Phil Gifford

WHAT A RIDE, MATE! THE LIFE AND TIMES OF THE MAD BUTCHER

HarperSports
An imprint of HarperCollins*Publishers*

National Library of New Zealand Cataloguing-in-Publication Data

Leitch, Peter Charles.
What a ride, mate! : the life and times of the Mad Butcher /
Peter Leitch with Phil Gifford.
ISBN 978-1-86950-689-6
1. Leitch, Peter Charles. 2. Butchers—New Zealand—
Biography. 3. Businessmen—New Zealand—Biography.
I. Gifford, Phil. II. Title.
381.4160883092—dc 22

Harper*Sports*
An imprint of HarperCollins*Publishers*

First published 2008

HarperCollins*Publishers (New Zealand) Limited*
P.O. Box 1, Auckland

Copyright © Phil Gifford 2008

Phil Gifford asserts the moral right to be identified as the author of this work.

All rights reserved. No part of this publication may be reproduced, stored in a retrieval system or transmitted in any form or by any means, electronic, mechanical, photocopying, recording or otherwise, without the prior written permission of the publishers.

ISBN 978 1 86950 689 6

Cover design by Astred Hicks, WideOpen Media
Cover photograph by David Roberts
Internal photographs from Peter Leitch's personal collection
Typeset by Springfield West

Printed by Griffin Press, Australia

79gsm Bulky Paperback used by HarperCollins*Publishers* is a natural, recyclable product made from wood grown in a combination of sustainable plantation and regrowth forests. It also contains up to a 20% portion of recycled fibre. The manufacturing processes conform to the environmental regulations in Tasmania, the place of manufacture.

This book is dedicated to Janice and
our family for their love and support.

To my mum and dad, who were always
behind me in everything I did.

To my brothers and sisters, who
have always been special to me.

To all the Mad Butcher customers:
Without you the Mad Butcher
would not have been possible.

And to all my mates in sport, charity
work, and life: I hope the ride has been as
much fun for you as it has been for me.

Phil Gifford would like to thank David Kemeys
for his invaluable help with research, and his
wife, Jan Gifford, for so often asking 'When
are you going to work on Peter's book?'

Contents

Foreword 9
Introduction 11
1 A very good butcher 17
2 Childhood 35
3 Auckland 57
4 Radio 89
5 Business 111
6 Mangere 151
7 Television 169
8 Charity 191
9 Sponsorship 215
10 Speeches 253
11 The Warriors 269
12 Touring 305
13 Kiwi manager 327
14 Sell 377

Foreword

I HAVE KNOWN Peter Leitch, aka the Mad Butcher, through my associations with rugby league for many years. Peter's contribution to the sport has been phenomenal. He has always shown his passion for rugby league and his total commitment to the sport, the players, and the fans.

Peter's unshakeable support and backing for the Warriors is legendary. At the best of times, and in the worst of times, he is still there helping the team, hosting events, finding sponsors, and using his Mad Butcher's radio advertising slots to promote the games and the team, win or lose.

Peter has made the unique transition from Team Mascot to Team Manager — from individual mentor to financial supporter. But it should not be overlooked that he is also a successful self-made businessman, who started from scratch and now has a multi-million-dollar business.

Peter is a great networker: not only do I have a direct line to him, but he also has one to me!

I wish Peter every success with this book — he deserves it for all the work he's done for sport and charity over many years.

HELEN CLARK
Prime Minister

Introduction

WHEN THEY MADE the Mad Butcher, they threw away the mould. He is unique, distinctive, different and indescribable. An amazing mix of ego and humility, shrewdness and naivety, intensity and relaxation, intelligence and ignorance, arrogance and humanity — the Butcher is, quite simply, all things to all men.

Peter has never heard of the proverb, 'Fools rush in where angels fear to tread'. Immediately after the 2007 Rugby World Cup loss by the All Blacks in Cardiff he rang me to announce, 'Graham Henry's all right, mate. I've just phoned him.'

When the New Zealand media attacked me for a drug report I released in 1990, my phone rang. 'Mate, you don't know me, but you're right, and those stupid dickheads in the media are puffing the shit anyway. Now, when you've fixed that drug problem, I want you to sort out this graffiti. The little pricks are even writing on my Mangere shop.'

As a friend he is all-embracing, demanding, loyal, genuine, sincere and, at times, hilarious. The Butcher once gave the most entertaining speech I have ever heard, and it was off the cuff. The scene was the eve of a Bledisloe Cup game in Sydney, and, since it didn't involve his beloved Kiwis, the Butch was out of his comfort zone, if that was possible.

Half the audience were Aussies, and the guest speaker didn't turn up. Peter didn't know he was the replacement until the master of ceremonies had finished introducing him. Undeterred, he jumped up and all the old lines flowed. 'Aussie mongrels, sons of convicts . . . do you always bring your daughter with you, sir?' (this to an interjector who had obviously married his secretary the second time around) . . . and, of course, 'Listen, you mongrels, I've got 500 readies here on the mighty All Blacks. Put your bloody money up or shut up.' He concluded by getting all the Kiwis to sing the national anthem, followed by a rousing haka.

The man is all about belly laughs, and in the main it is harmless stuff that is often at his own expense. He's an entertainer, who has lived the role of the Mad Butcher full-time. It's hard to tell where Peter Charles Leitch stops and the Mad Butcher starts — not that it matters, because either way it is great fun.

Peter's generosity is legendary. He is not as wealthy as some think, because he is always giving stuff away. He drives around with a car boot full of sausages, meat, gadgets, photos of the Warriors, posters, books, dolls, jerseys, jackets and other assorted giveaways. He's not happy unless he is loading you down with a load of junk you don't want. Nor can you give it away, because it is all branded. More important, though, are the charities he's involved in.

When the Butcher gets involved, he takes over. And why not? As he so politely puts it, 'the dickheads wouldn't know what they're doing. They couldn't run a piss-up in a brewery.' If they're especially incompetent, they are categorised as 'not being able to get a root in a brothel'. Once he's taken over though, the show rocks.

How much has he raised for charity? It must be millions — a brilliant effort.

Throughout all the highs and lows (and they have been steep highs and deep lows) the Butch has been supported, advised, cajoled, lectured and loved by the three women in his life — wife Janice and daughters Angela and Julie.

Janice has given him his head while riding the highs and surviving the lows. He must be very nearly impossible to live with, but publicly there has never been a chink in the Leitches' combined approach. Angela is reserved, polite and courteous, qualities she obviously inherited from her mum, because her dad missed out on all three. Julie is a chip off the old block, and there is little doubt that she will provide great support as her partner, Mike Morton, the new owner, continues to build The Mad Butcher dynasty.

It seems incredible that I've written this much without mentioning rugby league. It's widely known that the Butcher loves the sport and the people in it. His success as Kiwi manager, and the trust that was built up between him and coach Bluey McClennan, led to one of the most successful campaigns the Kiwis have ever had.

What is not known is that the Butch knows nothing about the game. How could he? He's on the phone right through the game — not that it matters. He has become as much a part of the game's history as Ces Mountford, Stacey Jones or Mark Graham. Just don't ask him what happened, because, outside of the score, he doesn't know.

Why has he been so successful? It is his energy, enthusiasm and passion, his street cunning and intuitive ability to pick the good guys from the pricks (there are only two types of people in the Butcher's categorisation of humanity) and his basic honesty that mark him out as different, as hugely successful.

Ours has been an unusual friendship. At times the Butch has almost jeopardised his status as 'Mister Ambassador for All Things Rugby League' when his 'bloody mate on the radio' has been bagging league. He reckons he has stopped hundreds of blokes from knocking my block off. We all know how much he exaggerates — I'm sure there were no more than a dozen.

Through it all we have remained good mates, even confidants. I trust him implicitly. My life has been richer for him being in it. There are times when I wish he wouldn't try to take it over!

Finally, there's no one better to write this biography than Phil Gifford. Peter and Phil have been friends for many years, and only a man with Phil's sense of humour should attempt the task. What has been a rich, full life will certainly be portrayed by a writer capable of bringing it to life in prose.

Murray Deaker

1

A very good butcher

Peter Leitch, the Mad Butcher, has lived a life he finds hard to believe himself. He left school at the age of 15 with no qualifications, having struggled with dyslexia, yet went on to build a meat empire that on any given week will see 200 tonnes of chicken sold, and on a big day 23 tonnes of sausages made — enough, laid end to end, to stretch from Auckland to Dunedin. Every week around 145,000 New Zealanders will walk past his red and black caricature into a Mad Butcher shop, part of a chain that encompasses 34 stores from Whangarei to Christchurch.

Embracing rugby league when he was in his twenties, the fervent fan who lived on the sidelines of suburban Massey

Park in South Auckland rose to the heights of managing a Kiwi team that thrashed the Australians 24–0 in a Tri-Nations final.

In New Zealand he's a household name. In league he's a worldwide household name. Trying to get a phone number to wish Wally Lewis well when Lewis was recovering from brain surgery, Peter called Lewis's close friend, Gene Miles, whom he'd never met. 'Christ,' said Miles, 'I've got to help the Mad Butcher. Here's the number.'

Those who have the good fortune to know Peter will know that not only does he never lose sight of where he's going, but he's never lost sight of where he's been. Bob Lanigan, an Australian who became the trainer of the Warriors in 1994, says he never ceased to be astounded by the range of Peter's friendships. 'I remember when [former prime minister] David Lange died and Peter got all the barbecues out and put on a feed for everyone at the Big Top over at Mt Smart for the service. Peter had known David for many years because he used to come into his store. Peter had never forgotten that and I remember him telling me Lange was a good mate because he had time for him when he was just starting out as a butcher.

'He has an incredible circle of friends. He took me to the Mt Roskill Cricket Club in 1998 because he was sponsoring something, and Helen Clark was there. She wasn't the prime minister then — she was the opposition leader. He introduced me to her and we got chatting, and it was obvious that she genuinely admired him. Her praise for him was amazing.'

If there's a single word hammered home by Aussie league players and coaches, it's 'mate', and it's become Peter's calling card. There's another word too, but we'll come to that.

Colin McKenzie, one of the best New Zealand league callers, has a very personal theory as to why Peter has won the right to use 'mate' as much as he does. 'We're all friendly with the Butch for different reasons, and it's not some kind of competition, but I have to say that he's been the best kind of friend since I stopped my radio work after I had a stroke. He has shown me enormous kindness ever since, and two weeks wouldn't go by without him getting in touch with me to have a chat and to see how I'm getting on. I suppose it's a friendship that was born of laughter and rugby league, which has been my life. But when my life changed, that friendship didn't.

'I had a stroke in 2006, and when Peter found out what had happened, he was on a plane to Christchurch a couple of hours later. He just walked into the hospital and he had all sorts of signed gear and best wishes cards and the like.

I know he got on the phone and basically told all sorts of people in Christchurch they had to come up and see me. He's a very, very kind friend. People give him stick for using the word "mate" all the time, but I reckon he has the right. He understands what being a mate is really about, and it's certainly not just about the good times.'

In naming Peter one of New Zealand's 50 most influential people in 2006, *New Zealand Listener* said: 'He might be Mad, but his chain of butcher's shops and passion for rugby league have made him a working-class hero. The suggestion to include him in the list came out of the blue, and the selection panel immediately agreed the dyslexic kid who left school at 15 had a huge, warm following among "little Kiwi battlers". Fronting his own slightly manic ads, Leitch is a man-brand and a voice for the ordinary bloke — some might even go so far as to describe him as a Marc Ellis for an older, humbler generation.' 'That retail chain has created a culture through the sheer force of his character,' says Russell Brown, one of the first and most successful online media commentators in New Zealand.

Through it all Peter Leitch has never deviated from his

solidly blue-collar roots. 'I'm the worker's friend. I'm not up myself. I still talk to the ordinary person,' he says. He's never removed the tattoos of his youth — a dove on his left hand, and a skull and a snake on his right arm — which he describes as a boy thing he did just after he left school, admitting that his father wasn't too happy about it.

His fingers are festooned with six or seven rings, which all tell different stories for him. 'One is an inheritance from my mother and father, one is a Mad Butcher's ring which my daughter Julie gave to me, and one is a Warriors ring. Another one is a 19th Vodafone Warrior, when they retired the jersey in my honour — a mate, Terry Baker, got that made for me. There are two rings I bought in Dubai: one is modelled on a Rolex watch, and the other is for horse racing, because I used to like the old racing; I rotate the two Dubai rings. In 2007 the Warriors brought in a ring for every player who had played 100 games. The club decided to give one to me for the work I'd done, and they engraved it with PCL on one side and QSM on the other.

'I like to be a bit different. I've worn a lot of rings for a long time. I wore them when I was working full-time in the shop, and it built up over time. I take them off every night, but so far I've never had to take them off through airport security.'

He's achieved everything without moderating what you might call his 'colourful' language. In the 1980s, when he helped sponsor the University Club in Auckland, an elderly club member looked down his Remuera-bred, patrician nose at Peter and drawled, 'We don't use bad language at this club.'

Replied Peter: 'You do now, mate.'

He'll cut to the heart of any discussion with breathtaking honesty. Yachting commentator Peter Montgomery tells the story of how he was chatting to the Butcher, musing over possible reasons for the decline of sales at his car dealership. At the time, in the 1980s, Montgomery was becoming a regular international traveller, calling yacht races all over the world. The Butch listened for a few minutes, then said, 'You know why it's not working so well? You're never bloody there.' Several years later, Montgomery would still laugh and say, 'You know, he was dead right.'

Along the way the number of people and organisations the Butcher has helped staggers the mind. Jim Ruka, from the Pakuranga rugby club in Auckland, where Peter has been an active sponsor for years, spoke for many when he mused that 'New Zealand used to be one of those places where people mucked in for each other. I think for Peter it still is. He believes — well, I think a lot of us believe it really — that it's a better place when it's still like that. I don't think you'll ever change him and I can't think why you'd want to.'

One of Peter's close friends is Dave Roberts, a former police photographer who has lived in Canada for 27 years. In his view, while success hasn't changed Peter, it's made him more of what he already was. 'I mean, one day we are sitting in a pub in Vancouver, having a couple of beers, and of course his mobile goes — I swear he's had that thing surgically attached. Anyway he answers it, and it's all: "Hello, dear . . . what's that? You need a pair of league boots for a charity auction? Leave it with me and I'll make a call." He hangs up and then he dials someone — I have no idea who it was to this day — and he tells them this lady needs the boots and they need to get them round to her right now because it's for charity. Then, as quick as a flash, he's off that call and on to the woman again to let her know the boots are on the way. Then he finishes the call and just carries on like nothing has happened.

'It's not that sensational a story, but when you think about it, there is really quite a talent in getting people to do what you want them to do, especially when you're on the other side of the world — and it's especially hard to get them to do it when you want them to. You could say he's a master manipulator, but that's got a negative connotation. He manipulates people, sure, but almost always it's a win-win situation. It's not anything he would do in any kind of bad way.'

A man with an astounding work ethic, if there's one regret Peter Leitch has, it's that he was so busy as a young father making a living that he didn't spend enough time with his daughters, Angela and Julie. Angela says that her father often says he was away from the house too much when they were children, but that it's not something she recalls. 'I can't remember him not being there. When we were at college he was always there to take us to our sports, and if he wasn't around a lot when I was smaller, it certainly hasn't scarred me.

'From childhood, you can only take the memories that are clear. I would have thought we did spend a lot of time together, back in the old days. Sometimes it was at the shop on Massey Road at the weekend. We'd all be out the back, counting the money, putting newspaper on the floor. As a child that was fun, a good time. Or we'd go to Carlaw Park with him on a Sunday — we'd go to the tuck-shop and roll down the bank while he watched the game.

'It was a happy time. He can rest assured he hasn't hurt his children. He's been very good to us, and we'd be lost without him. He's a wonderful dad and Poppa we all love and admire.'

Those sentiments are echoed by younger daughter Julie. 'If he was away a lot, it didn't really bother me. It just seemed the normal way things were. He was a very firm dad, but he was my dad. I don't have any bad memories from when I was a young child. I know that he'd take me to netball and always watch the games whenever he could. He might not have said it a lot, but you knew he loved you, and you could always rely on him, and that's what counts, isn't it?

'No matter what I did, he might tell me off but he'd always support me and be in my corner. If I was ever at a party or somewhere and I felt I needed to be picked up, he'd be there in a flash. What more can you want?'

Through Julie's college years there were times when people might say something smart about her father, but it was water off a duck's back to her. 'I'd ignore it, or just give it back. With my friends, Dad being the Mad Butcher was virtually never discussed. If it ever came up, a lot of my friends would comment on what a good guy he was.'

For both Angela and Julie, adulthood was a time when

they grew to admire their father's principles, realising that he wasn't like every other dad. 'Not many people are that driven,' says Julie. 'I'm really proud of him, because he's so giving of his own time and energy. He can be hard, but he can also be very compassionate.'

For Angela, who does wonder about some people who will introduce her or Julie not as themselves but as the Mad Butcher's daughters, it's not a lot of bad to take with a large amount of good. 'And Dad's done a lot of good. I've always been really proud of what he does, and I think people don't fully realise how much of his time he gives to charity.'

She was sometimes amazed at how people would ring her father and ask for money, for no reason she could discern. When someone would call him to say their daughter was going to Australia and could he pay for it, she often felt like suggesting a part-time job might be a good idea.

For Julie, her father's work ethic is something she's grateful for, and the way he passed it on to her and Angela. Both have worked with their father, and as a teenager Julie would voice radio ads if Peter was unable to. 'One of the things I like about my dad is that you can have a disagreement, but you get it out, and then you move on,' Julie says. 'I suppose as I grew older I actually admired him more. When you're a kid, you tend to think he's full of opinions, but as you get older you see it more from his point of view, and understand where he's coming from. When I became an adult, we became friends. Now I can go to the Mad Butcher's Lounge and have a great time with him, while he's swigging away and dancing to Elvis. But he's still my father, and can keep us in line.'

One of the greatest sources of delight for Peter is his four grandchildren, Angela's Vincent and Reuben, and Julie's Kristin and Matthew. Being related to a public figure can be a burden, but for Angela's children it hasn't been that way. 'Kids at school come up to Vincent all the time and ask if his Pop is the Mad Butcher, and say how cool that is, and tell him they saw his Pop on TV in a chicken suit, or in the paper or heard him on the radio. They tell him his Pop is famous.

'Vincent just informs them that yes, it is his Pop, and, yes, he is the Mad Butcher. Even Reuben gets a wee bit of it at kindy, kids telling him that they have seen his Poppa. One kid even came up to me and asked how Reuben's Poppa got in the radio!

'I think my boys love it, and there are experiences for

them that they really enjoy. Vincent got to go on *What Now* with his Pop, and they have both been on the radio with him as well. Reuben plays at being the Mad Butcher. He'll say to Dad, "You're the Mad Butcher, and I'm the Mad Butcher Junior, aren't I, Pop?"

'Both the boys get their Mad Butcher dolls and play at being Mad Butchers. How does that game go? They say "Mate" a lot, and they talk about the Warriors, especially Ruben Wiki. If it's not the Warriors, they sometimes take off the radio ads.

'Dad is very good. He'll go to their sports days, or go to a play they're in. You know that it might not really be his thing, but he's always there.'

Selling the business to Mike Morton, Julie's partner, has given Peter more time to reflect on his life and his family. 'For me, the grandchildren have been a learning curve. It's been a mind-boggling experience for me about how bright kids are. When it suits him, Reuben, who's four, wants to be the Mad Butcher. And everyone who says g'day to me is my mate. "He's your mate, isn't he, Pop?" he'll say. "She's your mate too, isn't she?" He's like a pirate too. Sometimes he'll be talking about us and say we cut people's heads off!

'I went to pick up Vincent, who's seven, from school the other day, and I had his brother in the car with me. I said we'd better keep an eye out for Vincent, to make sure we didn't miss him. Reuben said he'd be easy to find because he had a Spiderman knapsack. When Vincent arrived, I said, "You'd better turn round so I know it's my Vincent, the one wearing the Spiderman knapsack." He said, "Don't worry, Pop, you know it's me. I'm the only one in the class wearing freckles."

'Julie's little bloke, Matthew, who's two, starts calling out, "Pop, Pop," as soon as he comes in the door — it's great.' When Julie's 16-year-old daughter Kristin was made a prefect at her college, it's doubtful there was a prouder grandfather. His affection for his grandchildren is so patent you could almost touch it.

Waiheke Island is a place that features increasingly in future plans for Peter and the family. The Waiheke car ferry is close to Peter and Jan's house at Bucklands Beach. The ferry's a place where, as odd as it may seem, Peter does actually relax and unwind, and then there's only a three-minute drive to their holiday home.

Jan's grandparents used to live on Waiheke, and she has always loved the island. 'I have really fond memories of my grandparents, and my Nan's brothers and sisters, when I was a kid out there. It was like my second home.'

Peter too has grown to love the peace and tranquillity Waiheke offers. He started a kayaking club, and they now have several great friends there.

While Peter's certainly not famous for being a wine connoisseur, he does enjoy the meals at Te Whau, one of Waiheke's award-winning winery restaurants. 'I'm a member of both the RSA and the Surfdale Bowling Club, which I really enjoy going to. They're good people and good company.'

It's likely they'll see a lot more of Peter, and his grandkids, at the Manukau Live Steamers miniature railway in Mangere. Peter helped the club offer free train rides and lunch for special-needs children and their families, with over 600 families enjoying the day last year.

In the process of working for what he saw as a good thing for the community, Peter says he 'fell in love with the place. All boys love trains, don't they?'

If his family see the softer side of Peter Leitch, a side that may not be so obvious behind the 'true blue, macho league bloke' public persona, he suggests there's often a misunderstanding about his working career too. 'Where people get it wrong is that I'm not a shit-hot businessman. If I was, I'd be a multi-millionaire. I'm not poor, but I'm not rich list either. I was a very good butcher. That's what I'd like to say.'

2

Childhood

Peter Charles Leitch, the seventh and last child in his family, was born on 8 May 1944 at St Helen's Hospital in Wellington. He was healthy, he was happy, he was fussed over, he was cuddled and, according to his brothers, he was spoilt rotten. His parents, Myrtle Phoebe Evelyn and John Leitch, brought him home to a house they'd bought just a year or so earlier, at 17 Horner Street, Newtown. Still there today, it fits between two similar bungalows in a staunchly working-class area.

John (known to his mates as Bluey for his ginger hair) and Myrtle had four girls and, when Peter arrived, three boys. Peter grew up in a time when family was king, and in his mother's family — the Herfields — brothers, sisters, uncles and aunties all lived nearby in a network based on constant contact.

His oldest living sister, Dorothy, remembers how on most summer weekends an uncle would arrive at Horner Street, red-faced and puffing from a pushbike ride, to organise a family day out. There were no phones, so once a time had been set to meet at the tram stop down the road, the uncle would carry on to other relations' houses, and within an hour or so they'd all meet and travel to Worser Bay, or catch the ferry to Days Bay for a day together.

The most exotic home appliance was a little radio. Dorothy remembers silence descending on a Sunday night when her father's favourite programme, *Dad and Dave*, was broadcast. Oldest brother Jack suggests that Saturday afternoon was pretty quiet too, when their father took a keen interest in how certain horses were running at Trentham. Their sister Edna (who passed away in early 2008) agreed: 'It was always, "Sssh, the races are on."'

Bluey was a lively, feisty man. 'You look at Peter and you see Dad,' says middle brother Gary. 'Every time we went camping with Dad, he'd get up early in the morning, go out to have a shower, whistle all the way, and he'd chat up all the old girls in the cookhouse.'

Family legend says Bluey left his Blackball home on the West Coast at 15, having already worked in the local coal mine, and stowed away to Australia. Bluey's father was apparently once banned from league fields on the West Coast. 'Gummy' Leitch, as he was known, was a fan with a difference. 'He used to trip up players with his walking stick,' says Gary.

Landing in Sydney in the late 1920s, Bluey worked on the harbour bridge, which would open in 1932, before returning to New Zealand during the Depression years of the 1930s. He had a number of jobs in Wellington, working on the wharf, in a clothing factory, and at the Wellington paint slip at Evans Bay, where they brought boats up for surveys.

Gary worked with his father there for a time. 'We weren't cleaning the hulls — they did that on the floating dock. On the paint slip we'd do repairs on the plumbing, that sort of thing. We'd sail with the ferry boats, to do the repairs on board.' When Peter was a child, he remembers his father working at the Tramways workshop.

One thing remained constant — Bluey was a staunch unionist, with deep-seated socialist beliefs. Jack recalls his father buying *The People's Voice*, the weekly newspaper of the New Zealand Communist Party, and how Bluey's stand in support of the 1951 waterfront strike cost him a job at the Rembrandt clothing factory. 'He found out that some of the material coming into the factory had been unloaded from the wharves by the soldiers who were filling in for the strikers,' Jack says. 'He told the management he was sorry, but he couldn't work when he knew the picket lines had been breached. It can't have been easy at home for a while, but I do remember that a parcel of food for the family arrived from the management at Rembrandt.'

Bluey was no fan of organised religion either. Jack says that when he and some mates signed up together with the Marist league club, Bluey was deeply unimpressed. It would have been the same if the club had been run by Methodists.

While there was never violence in the home, parents were there to be totally respected. 'We were brought up in a house where everybody was taught to speak to anyone who came in,' Dorothy says. 'And most of all, you didn't answer your parents back.' Dorothy has a suspicion the usual rules might not have fully applied to Peter. 'When he was at intermediate school, Dad had retired, and they never had afternoon tea until he came home from school.' And if there was one member of the family who could challenge Bluey, it was Peter. In his teenage years he hit an Elvis phase, which was expressed, sister Edna remembered, in an obsession for getting every strand of hair oiled and in place.

Gary says rock 'n' roll, and the jive talk that went with it, had other effects too. 'Pete used to say to Dad, "Come on, crazy Daddy-o," and click his fingers and give a bit of a wiggle to taunt Dad a bit. Alan [Dorothy's husband] reckoned that Dad would murder Pete one night.'

Today Peter realises that the fact the Horner Street house was owned by his parents was unusual for the time and the area, when many of his friends lived in rented or state-owned houses. 'I was close to my parents, but not like you are today with your kids, where you talk as friends. Dad worked hard, and we'd sit down together for tea every night. We had what I'd call a good upbringing. We always got a feed. I have no complaints. My memories are all of it being a close family, and a happy family.'

Talking of meals, at Horner Street it was never a surprise to the Leitch kids to see one or two or more visitors at the dinner table. There wasn't much room, but Bluey and Myrtle had a cast-iron rule that anyone who visited was welcome to stay for a meal, and if they needed a bed for the night, that was found too.

'Dad was always a sociable man,' says Gary, 'always inviting people into the house. He met up with a league team from the Coast, and they all ended up at our place for a beer. You could always have a party at home, have a few beers, then doss down on the floor.'

That hospitality could go even further. David Sims, who now lives in Napier, was a young man in the big city when he met Peter. They became friends, and before too long he was invited to become a boarder at the Leitch home. 'Bluey was a great guy. He got me a job at Wellington Paint and Slip where he was a boilermaker, and got me out of a few scrapes too. Those boilermakers are a pretty hard sort of men, by and large. But he was one of those guys who basically never had a bad word to say about anyone. He'd help people out before he'd do anything else. Peter's mother was a terrific person too. I think much of Peter's generosity comes from his parents.'

Like a lot of people from the West Coast, Peter's father was a bit of a character. 'I say the "f" word a lot, and Dad taught me that,' Peter says. 'A lot of parents frown on the use of that word, but Dad was big on it, and so am I.' Peter's sisters say they can't remember their father swearing, but suggest that to brother Jack and he roars with laughter. 'I think Pete's got it right.'

If the social side of Peter's nature echoes his father's, it was something reinforced by his mother. 'My mother was a very good talker. She could sit down with a drink and talk all night. She wasn't a boozer, but she liked a social chat. Jack and Gary have it a bit. But I suppose if they were giving out a gold cup for talking, I guess they would have to give it to me.'

As well as the talking, Myrtle's sense of fun could appear at unexpected times. 'One night,' remembers Gary, 'my sister Edna and her friends had been telling ghost stories. Edna left to walk one of her friends home, and while she was away, Mum climbed under her bed. When Edna put the light out and got in, Mum reached up and grabbed her leg. She nearly hit the ceiling.'

As well as saving enough to pay cash for the house in Newtown, Bluey and Myrtle also had a wooden bach, in what was then rural Tawa. The bach was just one room, with bunks on the wall, a kerosene lamp, and a little wood-burning stove. 'You had to catch the train and get off at

Tawa,' says Dorothy, 'then you walked along the railway lines to get to the bach.' A grocery van and a butcher's van would call there a couple of times a week during the school holidays. The boys would go eeling, and all the family would play cards and swap stories.

Back home, the greatest source of entertainment for the younger kids was an abandoned brickworks, off Horner Street behind the Maple furniture store, left behind when Amalgamated Brick and Pipe moved operations to Miramar. As a playground for kids, the old tunnels that ran beneath it made it risky, but in that more self-reliant age, that never stopped the Leitches and their friends.

'It was out of bounds,' says Jack, 'but we all used to play in there. We'd go over and make forts. One guy who was about my age, who called himself the Masked Avenger or something like that, would wreck our fort. So then we'd go there and have fights with bits of brick. If one had hit you in the eye, it would have done some damage, but nobody was ever badly hurt.

'The fights weren't the danger anyway. The place was all a big rusting metal frame, with bits of tin flapping around. Many a time the police would come up there and tell us to keep out. How nobody ever got hurt I'll never know. We had a lot more adventures in those days.'

A few minutes' walk away was Newtown Park, now a headquarters for sports clubs, but then mainly a large open space. 'They used to have trenches up there,' says Jack, 'that had been dug in the Second World War by the Home Guard. Pat, myself and Gary, with Pete tagging along, would go up to the park with a tomahawk, knock the pine cones off the trees, and bring them back for the fire. We'd do that on a winter Sunday to get out of Mum's way.'

It was a neighbourhood where you were never without company. 'Where we lived, there were miles of kids,' said Edna. 'Every family in the street seemed to have a swag of kids.'

Peter, Jack and Gary all slept in the same room. Like most younger children in a family, Peter could be a target for his brothers, but not one who suffered silently. 'We'd been to see *The Wizard of Oz*,' says Gary. 'I'd torment him and say I was the wicked witch. Straight away he'd call out to Mum, "Gary's teasing me again."'

The only real drama when Peter was a toddler came when he broke his leg in a fall. While he thinks the accident happened when he slipped on cat's pee, Edna thought he wriggled out of someone's arms, while Dorothy remembers him in hospital, but can't recall how the accident happened. One thing Gary is very certain about is that however the accident happened, it cemented Peter's place as the golden child, and not just with his parents. 'There was a woman next door called Mrs Moffett, and she thought Pete was just the bee's bloody knees. She fussed over him even more when he had his broken leg.'

In 1949, when his mother walked him to Newtown school on his first day, Peter soon discovered that school would be hard for him, suffering as he does from a degree of dyslexia, a condition barely recognised, if at all, in the 1950s. 'I doubt it was in the dictionary when I started school,' he says. 'I was always in the low classes, and we had the worst teachers.

'I'm bitter about the education system because it hasn't changed. The dumb kids still get the worst teachers and the bright kids get the best, where I think it should be the other way round. Most of the teachers I had always gave me the impression they were just seeing it out to the end of the year. But the last year I was at school we had a teacher called Mrs Main, and if I knew where she was, I'd like to go to her and say thank you for the effort she put in for me, because without it I would never have got to where I am now. I think she just cared about us, which was important to someone who struggles.

'I wasn't a good learner at school, and I didn't really realise how much reading meant until I was an adult. Don't get me wrong — I can read and write — but I don't absorb things easily.'

It was a holiday in Cuba in 2005 that Peter and Janice took with me and my wife Jan that really brought home to him what he'd missed out on by not being able to read easily. 'I was blown away by what you and Jan knew about the place,' he told me. 'That was the time when it really hit home. I genuinely mean that.'

The most tangible product of his schooldays — in addition to the friends he still keeps in touch with — was a wooden half-moon table he made in woodwork class. He gave it to his sister Dorothy, and it's still in use at her house, where it sits in the hallway, decorated with a plaster swan for flowers.

One of Peter's classmates from intermediate and high school, Les Webb, also suffers from dyslexia, and has vivid memories of what it was like not being able to understand what was being written on a blackboard. 'It was very hard. I used to dread all my days at school, especially when you had to write something down. I'd have to find someone to let me copy it down. Some people use that sort of thing as an excuse — you see people who end up in trouble with the law using it. For Peter to do what he's done has been fantastic, because I know just how hard it was.'

Paul Turner started school with Peter and he remembers Peter trying hard in class. 'He'd really concentrate, but back then nobody had heard of dyslexia. He was just considered a dumb bastard — they made him sit at the back of the class.'

If the academic work was a battle, making friends wasn't. Les Webb describes Peter as an outgoing boy, with a great deal of confidence. 'We were in the low class, and both suffered with our learning abilities. But he had plenty of energy and was always bright and breezy. I don't remember him telling a lot of jokes as such — in fact, he still doesn't — but he always had a ready quip.

'I think it's Peter's ability to talk to people — to get along so well with them — that's been the reason why he's done so well in his life. He has incredible energy. I don't know how he manages to keep going at the pace he does. He's always been someone who gets bored quickly. He has to keep moving around.'

Peter Leitch the schoolboy was also a stirrer — not a malicious one, but certainly mischievous. 'There wasn't much of him at school,' says Webb. 'I was a bit more thickset and solid than Peter then, although he's probably bigger than I am today. He was a devil for starting a lot of scraps, but then he'd step back and let me and other guys take over. He was good with the talk, good at getting the other guys toey — he always loved what followed.'

Gary says that the ability to talk got Peter out of scrapes at home, although sometimes it was just sheer good luck. 'Our neighbour's house had an overflow pipe coming out from the toilet. It used to drip, and the houses were so close together that the water would run into our place, so one day Dad decided he'd plug it. He goes up there and he plugs it with a potato. Next thing the house next door is flooding, so I go up the ladder to try to get the spud out.

'Meanwhile, Pete's gone out for a drive, having borrowed Dad's Morris Minor. When he comes back, he calls up to me, "Gary, come down. You'll have to tell Dad I've had an accident in the Morris Minor, but it wasn't my fault. Some clown came through a light at an intersection."

'I said, "Aw Jesus, is that right?" Dad comes out and, being quite short-fused, begins to give Pete a hard time. But then I manage to pull the spud out, and the water pisses out. Who's the big idiot then? Me! And Pete gets off the hook!'

It may surprise many people who know how passionate he is about rugby league that Peter was never that infatuated with sport when he was a child. 'I didn't do a lot of sport at school. People think I'm a fanatic, but the reality is that I played a little bit of softball for a couple of years for Island Bay and a bit of indoor basketball, and I did a bit of wrestling, and that was about it. I've never played a game of rugby league in my life. Sport is very much something that's grown on me with the years.'

The sports fans in the family were Edna, who played everything from basketball and netball to softball, and Jack, today a golf enthusiast, who as a young man was the only brother to play a substantial amount of rugby league. However, Peter did spend a lot of time at Athletic Park, the old rugby ground in Wellington, which was close to Newtown. But it was not as a player or even a huge fan. Schoolmate Paul Turner got him there, largely on a commercial basis.

'Opposite the Tramways there was an old guy who would sell souvenirs for the rugby,' Turner recalls. 'You'd go in and buy four or five cartons off him for ten bob each, and sell

Peter Charles Leitch, born 1944, happy, healthy, fussed over, and, according to his brothers, 'spoilt rotten'.

Pre-school days with Pamela Cook, 'my first girlfriend'.

Smiling and safe in the arms of his mother, Myrtle.

Peter's first year at Newtown School, 1949. That's him on the far right of the middle row

Newtown School, 1953, with Peter second from the right in the middle row. One of his best mates, Paul Turner, is in the same row, fourth from the left.

Peter was an adult before he realised the fact his parents owned their house at 17 Horner Street, Newtown, was unusual in the neighbourhood.

Street photography thrived in New Zealand towns in the 1940s. Peter and his parents in downtown Wellington.

His school report for his last year at Wellington Technical College, and his form teacher suggests Peter's future is as 'a reliable worker'.

Form 4B4   **Dept.** BUILDING   **2nd Half Year, 1959**

Subject	Exam. Mark	Av. of Form	Quality of Work	Remarks	Teacher
English	42	45	D	Peter generally works very well, but it must be more consistent	
Social Studies	20	50	O	Has applied himself well.	P.J.
Biol.	62	47	D	Work has improved this term	
Gen. Sc.	32	49	E		
Woodwork	52	50	C	Has shown much improvement this term	
Technical Drawing	50	44	C	Works very hard	
Woodwork Theory	40	38	C	An excellent book. Showing diligent work	
Mathematics	25	40	D	Sometimes Peter does good work but examination was disappointing	

Music
Phys. Educ. Keen and interested
Conduct Very good.
General Remarks— Peter shows interest in his work and is a reliable student. Always willing to help and please. He should be a reliable worker when he leaves school.
Absent 2½ days

FORM TEACHER
HEAD OF DEPARTMENT
SEEN BY M Leitch   PARENT OR GUARDIAN

DEPARTMENT OF EDUCATION

LEAVING CERTIFICATE

Wellington Technical College School

This is to certify that Peter Leitch

left this school on 8th December, 1959.

The records show that on leaving school at the age of 15 years 7 months he/she had been in Form 4 for 1959.

Principal or Head Teacher.

Date: 8-12-59.
E.—19/14   50,000/1/57—73540 J

The Leitch family in the late 1940s. From left, Edna, Dorothy, Patricia, mother Myrtle, Jack, Peter, father Bluey, Gary, and Edith.

In the early 1950s, Gary, Peter, Myrtle, Edna and Patricia.

A love of noise began early.

So, apparently, did
another interest.

A schoolboy visit to the studios of 2ZB in Wellington. Peter thinks he was there with a school group to sing.

Exactly what the impressive cup was won for remains a mystery. Peter suggests it was for 'the bullshitter of 1948'.

The infamous donkey ride on Brighton Beach during a family holiday in Christchurch (see chapter nine). Brother Gary looks happy, but Peter's mother is at his side in both photos to make sure he would not dismount until his time was up. 'I was crying but she wouldn't let me off.'

them for three times that. You'd have rosettes, streamers, cards, and you'd go down and sell them at Athletic Park. A couple of times I took Pete, because you could make a few dollars. We'd go down to the park, and you'd get in for nothing, because you were selling stuff. So we saw a lot of games. You'd go to the guy, hand all your money in, get paid, and then you'd be off.'

While it didn't turn him into a rugby head, Peter clearly remembers the trips to the park, and adds cushions to the list of goods being sold.

A purely rugby memory that does stick with him came in the 1956 Springbok–New Zealand University game, which the NZU team won 22–15. Ron Jarden, a great local hero, streaked 70 metres for what was called 'the greatest try that never was'. Right at the start of the run, unnoticed by the referee, the players and most of the crowd, a touch judge had detected that Jarden had put his foot in touch.

Childhood memories are always hard to be certain about, but when you read Peter's school reports from Wellington Technical College, it seems his own recollection of not being as perky as others recall him is accurate. In 1958 his first report from the third form is summed up by the head teacher saying, 'Peter always tries hard, and sometimes does well, but lacks confidence in himself.'

He would leave at the end of his fourth-form year in 1959, after a series of reports that consistently rated his conduct as 'very good indeed', while academically he was complimented for working hard. The only suggestion that anyone realised he was dyslexic comes from his fourth-form English teacher, who wrote that 'Peter works well, but does not find this subject easy'.

When Peter left school as a 15-year-old, the senior master wrote a brief reference that said Peter had impressed him as an earnest and interested boy. 'He has behaved in a manner that would bring credit to himself and his school. He is a reliable and responsible boy and, as such, would possess qualities which should be acceptable to an employer.'

It remains an odd fact that while family and friends recall Peter as a confident, talkative young man, his memory is the opposite. 'In my early days I lacked a lot of confidence. I wasn't a big, good-looking guy. I wasn't a big tough bastard.' His sister Edna confirmed that, like his brothers, Peter was never keen on scrapping. 'He wasn't a naughty boy. Kids respected the police in those days. Peter knew that if he got into trouble, he'd get it from Mum and Dad as well. I can remember Peter coming out to Naenae to babysit for me. He came out once and some local kids accosted him. He reckoned he wouldn't come out again.'

So how did he get involved in a macho sport like wrestling? 'My brother Jack played indoor basketball at the Kilbirnie gym,' says Peter. 'I played some basketball with him there, and really enjoyed it, although I wasn't very good at it. How I got into the wrestling I can't really remember. I didn't wrestle for long — maybe a couple of seasons. I didn't have the confidence. I'd make a great professional wrestler now, where there's plenty of talk, but this was the amateur stuff.'

At the time it wasn't easy to get into a sports club unless you had a connection, so Jack arranged for his younger brother to play basketball, and before too long the Kilbirnie Wrestling and Sports Club became his home away from home. While the gym is no longer active, Jack is one of a group who pay $5 a year to keep the club going to support kids from Wellington's eastern suburbs in a range of sports. 'We sponsor girls' wrestling, rowers, cyclists . . . any number of sports,' he says. 'Back then a mate of mine was in the wrestling club, and talked me into going over there. I got into softball and basketball as well.

'The big trip to Christchurch was for the Wellington

rep team, although I think we were all from the Kilbirnie club. We had some hard-case wrestlers, and a lot of them were good too — they'd represented New Zealand or won inter-provincial titles.

The Christchurch trip started with a bit of trouble on the way down. The gym uniform was a nice blue blazer, but it had a massive crest, like the old American ones. We were in this bar, and these guys were giving cheek about the crest, and next thing it's all on. Our heavyweight, John Harris, who was a national champion, and little Joe Frost — both Pommies — weren't putting up with that. We had the police waiting for us in Christchurch. One of the cops came over, and it could have been tricky, but when he gets to us, he turns out to be an ex-Kilbirnie gym man, so we were fine.'

Ronnie Butts, twice a New Zealand champion in 1963 and 1964, had become Peter's coach while he was still in the midst of his own career. 'We had a lot of kids who wanted to wrestle,' Ronnie says, 'and Bob McColl, who was my coach, couldn't take all of them, so he broke all the kids up with all the senior wrestlers that were there, and I won Peter. He was just a little, harum-scarum sort of kid, but he showed a bit of promise.

'When we knew we were going to Christchurch, Bob

said to me, "We haven't got a bantamweight. What about that boy Leitch?"

'I said, "Gee, he hasn't been wrestling long. I don't mind taking him as long as you don't throw him in against someone that's a champion." Bob said he'd sort it out when he got down there.

'When we got to Christchurch the only wrestler the South Island had was a wrestler who had just won the New Zealand title. I said, "We can't put Peter in against this guy." Bob agreed, but later on he came back and said we had to put someone in, so it was decided to give Peter a go.

'I didn't want to tell Peter who he was wrestling — that the bloke was a national champion — so all I said to him in the corner was, "Just go in and do what I taught you." Anyway, he went out and shook hands. He was as nervous as hell, and back in the corner he told me he was a bit worried as the other guy looked pretty good. All I could do was tell him not to worry and I suggested he went out and picked the guy's legs up. So he walks out, and tries to do just that, but the guy beat him to it, and before long he had Pete pinned.'

Peter was distraught he was beaten so quickly, and by the time he made it back to the changing room he was nearly in tears, feeling completely worthless. 'Ronnie came in, and he said to me, "Leitchy, you're a bloody champion! That guy you fought was the New Zealand champion — he should have got you in the first seconds. It took him 38 seconds to get you. You're the winner, mate!"'

Ronnie will never forget the change those words made to the young Peter. 'I've never seen a bloke change so quickly. A big grin came over his face, his chest went out, and he was so happy you'd think he'd won a national title.'

Peter agrees. 'I felt great. I went from really depressed to feeling wonderful. That's what a good coach can do for you. One thing I've learned in life is that you must believe in yourself, or you're wasting your time. To live in the house I do now and look out at the water was beyond my wildest dreams when I was a boy.'

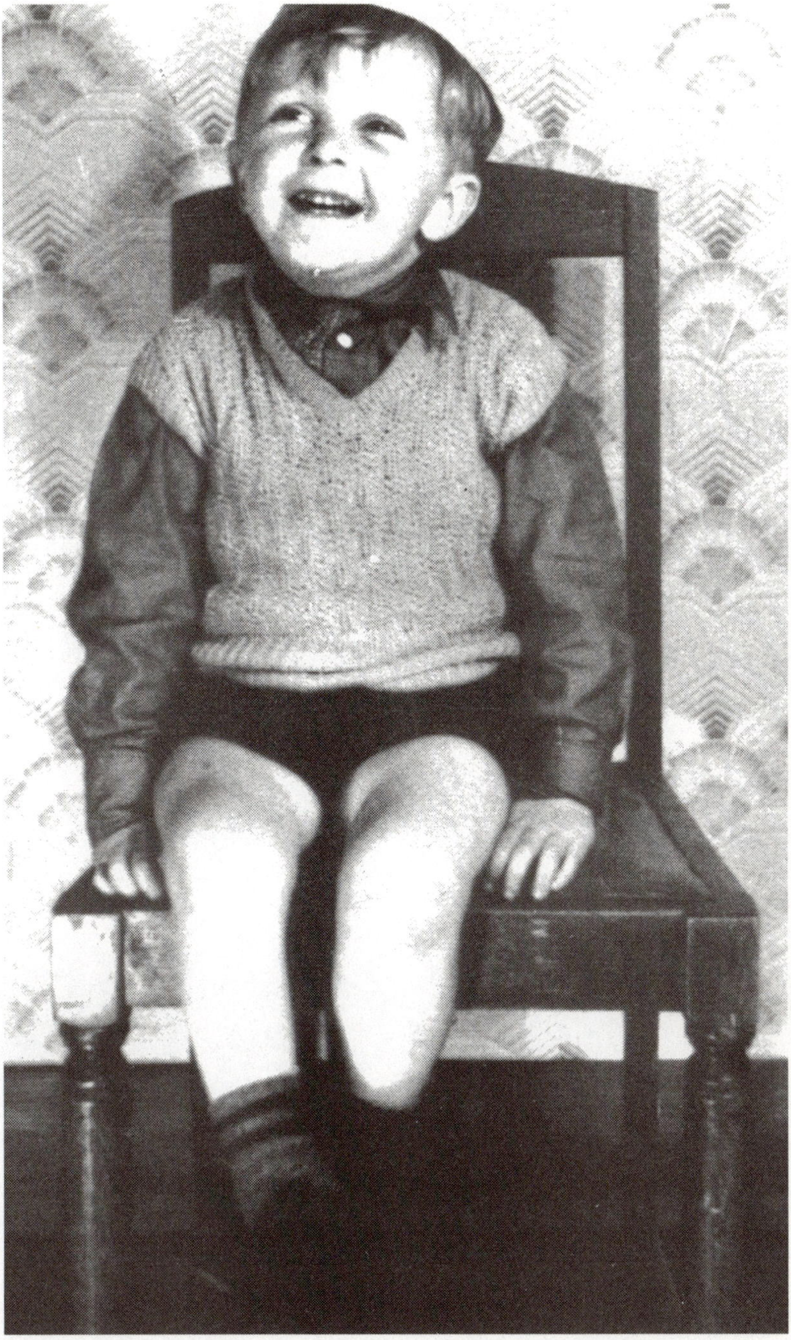

3

Auckland

Working life began at 15 for Peter Leitch, and it began in the Post Office. In 1960 the government owned the Post Office, which was nearly 30 years away from being split into Telecom and New Zealand Post.

Labour's Walter Nash was the Prime Minister, and the hand of the welfare state was everywhere. The government was loaning money for new house owners at three percent, and you could cash in the family benefit to buy a house. All radio stations were government owned; in Auckland the first experimental television programmes were being broadcast, and a former bank clerk from Wanganui called Johnny Devlin, the country's first rock-and-roll star, had the sleeves of his shirt ripped off by an hysterical crowd in Christchurch.

Peter's first job was delivering telegrams in Wellington, and then he progressed to working in stores for the New Zealand Post and Telegraph Department. In the stores, bureaucracy reigned: 'To send a couple of toilet rolls to Auckland, you had to get about ten autographs,' Peter recalls.

How did a teenager with dyslexia cope? The best he could — Peter wasn't aware that his problem had a name, so he dealt with things like delivering telegrams to the right address by double-checking everything, and taking the time to carefully dissect every invoice or order he struck in the stores.

After six months it was time for a change, and butchery called, if faintly. 'When you don't have great results from school, there are not a great number of jobs you can choose from,' says Peter. 'You couldn't be too fussy — you really had to take what came along. At first I chose to be a butcher for no other reason than to make a living. I was always keen to work, and I grew up in a home where I was used to seeing my father work hard. The only time he wasn't at work was when he was on strike.'

Charlie Yeoman was offering a job for a butcher's boy

at his shop in Seatoun, and Peter was grateful when he got it. He can't remember the wage he received, but agrees it would have been very small. Of course, there was no apprentice scheme then. Today, a young butcher will aim to complete a three-year course, which will include not only time in a shop, but also classroom instruction at a technical institute.

It's a matter of some amusement to Peter that, with the exception of a food-handling certificate he obtained later in his career, he has no formal qualifications as a butcher. Like all the others of his era he learned by watching and listening.

It didn't begin swimmingly. 'The first day I started, I was too scared to hop in the fridge in case someone shut the door. They wanted me to get some liver, and I wasn't too keen to pick the liver up. I didn't like the feel of it. As a boss, Charlie wasn't the most humorous guy in the world, but he was fair, and he gave me a job.

'The butchery was something you learned yourself. You didn't go to tech — you just picked it up. There was no structure for learning. You learnt as you went along. They just gave you a knife and gave you all the shit jobs. You cooked the fat and made the mince, and it didn't start out sensationally well.

'Cooking the fat to make dripping was a prick of a job. When I started, you cooked it up in a big copper, like your mother used to boil water for washing before they had washing machines. It was greasy, it got into your skin, and felt terrible. If you overcooked the fat, it spilled on the floor, and it'd be your job to clean it up. Later on they had a machine called a clarifier. You'd load up chopped-up fat before you left for the night, and it'd melt down. But if you forgot, and left the tap open after you'd loaded it, you'd arrive in the morning and the back room would be chocker with bloody fat.'

Even the thought of cooking fat makes Peter shudder to this day. How much did he hate it? Years later, in Mangere, when he reached a stage in his own shop where he could afford to give up making his own dripping, he actually took an axe to the fat machine, shattering it into shards of metal.

But the young butcher soon found other aspects of the job in which he revelled, and quickly developed a passion for butchery that has never wavered. 'Once I got the chance after a couple of months to get out of the back room, into the shop, and talk with the customers, I loved it. Working on the counter, dealing with people, is something I've always loved. To be fair, most butchers then were big talkers. An old butcher said to me once, "We're like dentists. The only difference is that we're not extracting teeth, we're extracting money out of people. So if you keep people smiling, it doesn't hurt them as much."

'He's right. Most people hate parting with their money, so you make it sweeter by being pleasant to them. When I started out I was polite, but as my confidence grew, I started to make the odd quip and pay the odd compliment.'

With time Peter also came to relish the satisfaction of using a boning knife well, and swiftly. It's true that injuries were always a possibility. Today there are metal mesh guards to protect fingers, and to wear over your groin. When Peter began, hands were bare, and there was only an apron between a knife and your body.

A few years into the trade Peter was breaking down a beast when he stabbed himself in the thigh. The cut itself was bad enough, but the razor-sharp boning knife flashed within an inch of his groin. 'To be blunt, I nearly cut my dick off. I wasn't happy about that idea, I can tell you.'

But on most days, breaking down a carcass was a task in which he took real pride, and something at which he was very good. 'It's really an art, although not many people would recognise that. If you get it wrong, you'll lose money on the carcass, so someone who can work quickly and cleanly is very valuable. I got a lot of pleasure from the work.

'Butchers were a hard-case bunch then too. You had a lot of laughs, a lot of fun. We weren't politically correct, but we enjoyed ourselves. There were tricks and jokes going on all the time. I remember once running into the shop after I'd been to the toilet, terrified, because I'd had a pee and it was bright pink. I thought I had some terrible sickness. The other guys were killing themselves laughing. One of them had some pill that he'd slipped into my tea and it turned your piss pink.'

The next step was to work for Whales Bros., at 126 Cuba Street in the city, a big name in the meat business. Ian Taylor would become one of Peter's workmates, and he recalls clearly the day a teenaged Peter bowled into the shop. 'There were about three or four of us standing at a butcher's block, and in came this young fellow, full of cheer and business, who said, "G'day boys, any jobs going?"

'It was a period of time then, in the early 1960s, where in the butchery business if you could stand up and say, "Give us your money please," you could get a job. They were almost leg-roping anyone who could work as a butcher and dragging them into the shop. We had a chat, then packed him off across the road to speak to the proprietor. He came back, and he was employed. He was an absolute riot from that moment forward, an absolute pleasure to work with.

'He was always very humorous — that's what made him so different. One day he was serving a rather heavily pregnant Samoan lady, whose stomach was protruding to the counter. As he was serving her he reached over, patted her on the stomach, and said, "How's my boy today?"

'Those were the sort of antics he got up to. He always used to address me as Taylor, never as Ian. One day I was writing "ox tongues" on the window with the old shoe whitening, as we used to. You couldn't get rid of ox tongues for love nor money. He came bouncing over and said, "Hey Taylor, I can do that. What do you want me to do?" So I told him, and went back inside, because we were pretty busy. Then a few people started coming inside with a bit of a grin on their faces. When we looked up he'd written "Oxe Tonges" on the window. From that day on in the shop we always called him Oxe Tonges.

'About the only time I ever saw him embarrassed was when we sent him up to a flat that was rented by some Polish girls who were on the game. One of the guys, who had a particular leaning towards the girls, used to deliver the meat on a regular basis, but he was sick. We sent Peter up. He came back into the shop at about 1000 mph, with his face as red as a beetroot. All he'd say was, "I'm never going back up there again, Taylor."

'There was a pub we all used to drink in where all the local crims and so on would hang round. We used to watch Pete — he'd stroll in, and he knew all these guys. He was always on the right side of the law, but from a very early age he was street savvy. On the day he left to go up north, he told us all that one day we'd all be working for him, which proved to be quite prophetic. It was his typical sort of banter, but I thought from the start he was very skilful at promoting himself. He was a tremendous salesman. A woman would come in basically for a look around, and he'd be chatting away to her, then she'd walk out with a basketful of meat.

'I worked with a few butchers who academically were well qualified, but for sheer nous he'd leave them for dead. You underestimated him at your peril.'

Entertainment for the teenage Peter and his friends was pretty basic. A highlight was going hunting on an isolated farm inland from Wanganui, not far from the Jerusalem commune that was established by the poet James K. Baxter.

'We'd go up on a Friday night,' says Peter's friend from school days, Paul Turner. 'My brother Bob, who was also a butcher, and Peter would take up a load of meat for the farmer, who being in the backblocks didn't have ready access to fresh sausages, saveloys and luncheon sausage.' In exchange for the meat, the farmer would let the boys go anywhere on his land. The only warning they ever had was when he told them: 'You shoot any of my prize bulls, and I'll shoot you.'

He'd also give the boys a packet of shot, and tell them he wanted 50 possums. 'We'd go up to an old hut, and opposite it was a big tree,' Paul recalls. 'Bob had a semi-automatic, I had a .303 and Pete had a .22. We'd blast the tree and get our possums out of that. We'd bunk down in the hut, which was pretty ripe, with the sort of stuff you were eating up there.' Eventually the farmer would come along in his truck and pick them up on a Monday morning to take them out.

While Paul remembers them getting a couple of deer and a pig, he also remembers how the two young butchers narrowly avoided being taken out by their prey. 'They were walking along a track beside a bank that was about two metres high, and could hear grunting in the bush above them. Next thing a wild boar charged, and it came out in such a hurry that it didn't realise there was a drop there. It flew straight over the track and disappeared into thick bush where the land dropped away on the other side.

'Bob said, "Shit, I'm glad that missed me!" I think Pete might have been lost for words for once. It was pretty big, and it just shot over the top of their heads.'

The boys had to rally round to help Paul on another occasion. 'I fell down an old well. We were chasing deer through the valley, and Bob says to me, "There's one over there, take a shot." I took two steps and disappeared. I landed in water that was about a metre deep, and bloody freezing. The well was about three metres deep. Bob chucked a torch down and I could see the water was putrid. They had to go away for about an hour and get a rope to haul me out.'

In the city, on the weekends, the likely lads followed the age-old pursuits of drinking and trying to charm girls. 'On Saturday,' Paul Turner says, 'we'd sometimes go to the Tramway Hotel at 9 o'clock in the morning, knocking on the door, and we'd end up boozing most of the day. We'd go on to the New City, where we'd also go on a Sunday, when it was supposed to be closed.

'We used to go to Garlands restaurant for lunch on a

Saturday, where you could get a five-course meal for five shillings. It was quite reasonable. Pete would try to chat the waitress up — he was a real charmer. You'd go to parties then where you didn't really know the people. As long as you brought some beer with you it was okay.'

Late one night, long after closing time, the lads were at a party when the beer ran out. One of the partygoers collected some money from them all and disappeared, coming back at about three o'clock in the morning with a load of Chinese beer. Paul asked him where the hell he got it from, and the man said he was a customs agent. 'He told me to shut up, and gave me my money back.

'Another place we'd go to was the Regent pub, which was a bit rough. We were sitting round at Pete's place one Sunday and another mate came in. He said an argument had started at the Regent the previous night, and a seaman had been stabbed. When you're young and bullet-proof, you didn't realise how rough some of those places could get.'

A massive turning point in Peter's life came at the start of 1964, when he moved to Auckland — not the huge, sprawling city it is now, but still by far the biggest in New

Zealand. It wasn't a calculated decision, or something he had dreamed of for years. It was an adventure, pure and simple. He was young, single, and without a mortgage or a contract to tie him down.

Another Newtown teenager, Colin Armstrong, was in the same boat. They hadn't gone to school together, or played sport in the same team, and in fact the two can't really remember when they first met. But in a part of town where people made a lot of their own fun, it was probably through mutual mates.

Colin remembers spending a lot of time with a bunch of Newtown boys by the end of 1963, often at Peter's place, yarning inside, or taking mudguards on and off cars a few of them were lucky enough to own. Probably on a lazy Sunday afternoon, wishing they had more money to buy petrol, they hatched a plan to travel together to Auckland.

Peter doesn't remember any concerted effort by his family to talk him out of going. With hindsight he believes they didn't really expect him to stay long in a city where essentially he had no relatives and no long-term friends.

The trip would eventually revolve around a 1934 Plymouth truck. Peter and Colin had advertised for a truck or a bus, and the flatbed Plymouth came up for sale. Colin was a mechanic, and they put a canopy on the truck, with twin wooden beds. 'We had a canopy lying around that had been on a milk truck, so we adapted that,' says Colin. 'We wouldn't actually sleep in it a great deal, but it was okay to stay in.'

The trip to Auckland took four days. 'We went looking for work straight away,' says Colin. 'We didn't have any money, so we both went to work in a graveyard when it came up.' They found a place to board in Mt Roskill, where they shared a house. Peter remembers that, at the time, a lot of people thought that, with him coming from such a big, close family, he'd return home very quickly. 'But I never went back.'

In the 1960s in Auckland, unskilled work was extremely easy to come by. At this stage in New Zealand history, the Common Market in Europe was still only looming as a possible threat to our massive exports of meat and wool to Britain. It was 1973 before Britain joined the European Economic Community, and only then New Zealand access to the huge market of the UK would be seriously squeezed.

For New Zealand in the early 1960s, farming export earnings continued to flood the country with money. As well as the traditional dairy and sheep exports, huge mills to process timber had recently been opened in Kinleith and Kawerau. If you were prepared to work, there was always an opening. You could walk down the Great South Road at Penrose in Auckland, and take your pick from job vacancies listed outside factories. There were massive freezing works at Otahuhu, and the railway workshops — government-owned like the Post Office — offered plenty of work for good keen men.

Peter found himself digging graves, at Purewa cemetery in Meadowbank, a job that lasted just a few months but made a deep impression on him. Unlike other periods in his life, which he readily recalls with humour and a light-hearted comment, he never jokes about this time. Recalling it brings out a reflective side that would surprise many who only know his public persona. 'It was an interesting job. It taught you humility, and respect for life. When you're burying a little baby, it sets you back on your heels. When you're a young man, you think you're bullet-proof, you think you'll never die. So it was a job that was quite humbling. We dug every grave by hand — there were no mechanical diggers. It was hard work.'

After Peter and Colin had been in Auckland for a couple of months, Queen's Birthday weekend rolled around. The

Newtown boys loaded up the Plymouth truck and headed south to catch up with friends and family.

South of Lake Taupo, the motor started knocking. The boys kept driving down the Desert Road, hoping that if they didn't get to Wellington, at least they'd get to a town. But just north of Waiouru, a rod smashed through the side of the engine block. 'We knew straight away we couldn't do anything with it,' says Colin. 'We were able to get a local mechanic in Waiouru to tow us in, and we sold the whole thing to him — all our gear, the lot — then we hitchhiked on to Wellington.'

Colin stayed on in Wellington, working in a garage with his brother, while Peter took the train back to Auckland early in the weekend. Peter would never leave Auckland, while Colin would never go back. Since 1976 Colin has lived, and run a small car repair business, in Levin.

As happens when young men, a group not famous for writing letters or even sending Christmas cards, live in different towns, there was very little contact until, to their mutual pleasure, Peter contacted Colin for details used in this book.

Before the end of 1964 the chance for Peter to get back into a butcher's shop arrived, first at a small shop in Newmarket for several months, and then at Newton Meats in Karangahape Road, next door to the Pink Pussycat Club, the city's best-known strip joint.

'The girls would come in and we'd give them a discount,' Peter recalls, 'then we'd get a discount when we went to their shows. There were a lot of cocky young butchers in there, and I wasn't cocky in those days, so I was usually pretty quiet.

'Then one day I had a boning race with another guy, who thought he was pretty good, but then I beat him, and I was amazed to realise I was better than him. When I look back I was a good butcher, although I had some weaknesses. I wasn't very good at sharpening knives, which is unusual for a butcher — there were guys that were better. But that boning race turned my life around, and I started to get some self-belief.'

And soon Peter found there were strong personal reasons for staying in Auckland. 'I was boarding with a lady, and I was going to take her sister out. But her sister got a better offer from a bloke with a convertible. I didn't even have a car. Instead, the sister offered to tee me up with her girlfriend on a double-date.'

Her girlfriend was Janice Granich, who at that time was working at the Aulsebrook biscuit factory with Peter's landlady's sister. Janice was asked if she'd like to meet this guy who was boarding with her colleague's sister. When she asked what he did and was told he was a gravedigger, she replied, 'Aw God, I'm not into gravediggers. Don't think I'm rude if I don't stay long.'

Travelling in style in the convertible with the top down, the two couples went to a party together. Cruising back after midnight, with the top still down, it was a bit chilly, and Peter offered Janice his jacket. He had a plan. 'I left Janice with my jacket so I could ring her the next day to get it back. When I rang I invited her out to the pictures.'

Several months later the relationship moved to another stage. It was a time when engagements almost always came before a wedding, and young men with marriage on their minds asked fathers for permission to marry their daughters. Janice's parents, George and Gladys, lived in a state house in Remuera. Peter made sure he did the right thing by asking her father, who most people knew by his nickname of Dutchy. 'Her father was a hard case,' Peter says. 'He was a character and known to enjoy a few beers. I got on extremely well with him, although I have to admit that when I asked him if I could marry Janice he was lying on a couch and I think he jumped six feet straight up in the air.'

When they married in 1965 it was agreed the wedding would be at St Mark's Church in Remuera, and the reception at the Tamaki Yacht Club on the Auckland waterfront. 'The week before the wedding,' says Peter, 'Jan fell down the stairs at the yacht club. I thought she might have broken her back.'

Although a little battered and bruised, Janice was okay by the day of the wedding. Her cousin Zeta was her bridesmaid, and Peter's nephew Ken was his best man. The reception, for about 100 family and friends, was fine, but the honeymoon in Rotorua, spent with Peter's brother and his wife and three children, wasn't quite so perfect. 'I don't think Jan was very happy,' says Peter.

Back from their honeymoon they settled close to Eden Park, in a house that was theoretically divided into two flats, without any real dividing wall. 'The other couple were nice people, but different. I remember they bought a new oven, and they had it for about a year without ever switching it on,' Peter recalls.

If her workmates saw Janice with a black eye at the time, it wasn't any sign of problems in the new marriage. 'One night my brother Gary and his wife were up from

Wellington to see us,' says Peter. 'I was working long hours, and the three of them went out to the movies. By the time they got home I was sleeping on the floor on a mattress, because we'd given them our bed. Janice thought for a bit of fun she'd jump on me while I was asleep. I came up fighting, thinking it was a burglar, and hit her in the eye.'

Peter still recalls himself as a much quieter, less confident person than he is now, but he had enough self-belief to move from Newton Meats to Michaels Avenue, in Ellerslie, to manage a one-man shop. 'I had no real idea what I was doing, but it went okay.

'A big help to me was a gentleman called Tom Cowley, who lived across the road from the shop, and worked at the freezing works as a night loader. This man had great qualities, and was a very calm character — he made sure I never let my emotions run away with me too much. He was a great, steadying influence.

'He was a real outdoors man too, and when my daughter Julie was about 12 he took us out tramping in the Kaimanawas. Tom and one of his mates loaded my knapsack with rocks just before we were going to ford a river. They thought I'd stop and complain, and were horrified when I plunged in and crossed over. They were worried I could have drowned.'

If there were Zen-like qualities to Tom, Peter did manage to accidentally awaken some inner anger. 'The only time I ever heard him raise his voice was when I helped him trim a hedge and he left me by myself. I accidentally cut it lopsided, and basically ruined it. When he got back, he went berserk. His sons say it was the only time they could ever remember their dad losing his temper. From then on I was only allowed to mow lawns.'

Oddly enough, for such an even-natured man, Tom had a bull terrier that could be very fierce. One hot summer's day Peter saw the dog asleep in the middle of the road. Concerned for its safety he walked out with a broom, and gently prodded the dog. The reaction was volcanic. Within a second, Peter bolted for the shop, slamming the shop door behind him, with a slavering, snarling bull terrier flinging itself at the glass. For about an hour Peter couldn't leave the shop, and no potential customer was game to come near it either.

Working at the Michaels Avenue shop would eventually lose its charm. 'I could see no future there. At one stage I was so sick I ended up in hospital, and the boss didn't bother to come to see me,' Peter says. It was a moment that would cement itself in his mind. The shop owner had one other shop, with just two staff members. His lack of interest contrasted sharply with Peter's attitude when he became an employer himself.

'It became impossible as we got more shops,' says Peter, 'but when we had one shop I would never have treated someone that way. It's just not the way you should treat anyone who has been loyal to you, and worked hard for you.'

As an example, Peter Steele, a long-term worker for Peter at Mangere in the 1990s, remembers a crisis in his life when a nervous breakdown landed him in hospital. 'Peter was about to give a big speech in town, but when he heard I wasn't well, he raced out, got me into hospital, and saw me through until I was able to get back to work.'

The idea of owning his own shop was growing stronger with Peter all the time, and in 1967 came the breakthrough. 'The first car Jan and I ever owned was a 1950 Morris Minor, and at the weekends we used to drive around Auckland. We'd look at the odd butcher's shop, and on one particular day we saw a shop in Rosella Road in Mangere East that was for sale. It was closed, but the owner was there with the land agent.

'We talked for a bit. I told him I'd looked at the shop, and he asked me what I thought. When I said I thought it could be all right, he asked me if I would take it. I said, "Mate, I've got no money — look at the car I drive. My wife's just had a baby, and we've just moved into a new home." He said to leave my name and number. I cringed a bit at that — the only people who'd ever asked me for a phone number before had been cops who'd stopped my car.'

The owner was Harold Hill, the managing director of Hancocks Wine and Spirits. Hancocks was a firm that had been built up by Sir Ernest Davis, a man who was a legend in the hospitality world, and a mayor of Auckland. Gifts from his massive personal fortune ranged from donating Browns Island in Auckland's Waitemata Harbour to the city, to a champion racehorse for the Queen Mother.

If Harold Hill, solidly built and quietly spoken, didn't have quite the clout of Sir Ernest, he still exuded the confidence of a successful businessman. The man Peter still refers to as Mr Hill lived at 1 Haast Street, Remuera, in the heart of Auckland's blue-blood territory. The furnishings were plush, the table settings solid silver, and at the back of the house was a tennis court. Hill had begun at Hancocks as an accountant, and by the time he was managing the firm it was a major player in the New Zealand hotel business, owning 140 hotels.

A former colleague, Murray Brown, now 91 years old, recalls how Hill, although well liked by his fellow workers, most of whom loved nothing more than a loud, raging party, was a conservative man, both with expenditure at the firm and in his personal life. 'Family meant a lot to him,' says Brown. 'At that time in the hotel industry we were a pretty lively bunch of people, but Harold was one who preferred to spend time with his wife and children. I suppose you could call him a homebody.'

Two or three weeks after Peter had met him at Rosella Road, Hill rang and asked Peter to see him. 'So I went in this night to his office opposite the Railway Station, a big flash joint compared to what I was used to. There was a big long corridor, and the girl at the front desk looked me up and down — I was just in my butchery gear. When I said I was there to see Mr Hill, she said, "I beg your pardon; *you* want to see Mr Hill?"

'I said, "Yeah, Mr Harold Hill. He's asked me to come and see him."

'She buzzed the secretary, and she puts her head out of

her office and looks at me, and then she goes back inside, and Mr Hill comes out and calls, "Ah Peter, come on down." He was a beautiful man.'

What happened next astounded Peter. Hill had a proposition to make: 'What if I lend you the money? I sent my wife down to buy meat at the shop in Ellerslie, and she thinks you're a lovely young man.'

'Aw, she must have gone to the wrong shop,' Peter blurted out.

Hill just laughed, and made it clear the offer was serious.

It was something that Peter is grateful for to this day. 'I know he wanted to sell the shops, and without a tenant he was never going to sell them, but he treated me very, very fairly. I was young and green, and he could have taken advantage of me, but he was an absolute gentleman. It impressed him that I was honest. I remember him telling me everybody else who had looked at the shop had tried to make out they were millionaires. He said to me, "Look, you're the only one that has been really honest with me. All the rest said they were big time, and nobody who is big time would be looking at that shop, because it's on a side street."'

That night Peter went home and told Janice that Mr Hill

was prepared to loan them the money to take over the shop. 'She said that if that was what I wanted to do, I could. So we ended up with the shop. He basically gave me a blank cheque and said, "Go and use it to get what you want."'

Hill also told Peter to get his refrigerated equipment from the company Hancocks used, which Peter tried to do. 'I went in and saw this upstart sales manager, who didn't want to know me, and was very uncooperative, saying it'd be months before he could get the job done. That night I rang Mr Hill and told him I was happy to go and see people, but I didn't want to be treated like a dog. When I told him what had happened he told me to go back again at 9 o'clock the next morning, and if I got the same treatment, I could go and get the refrigeration wherever I liked.

'Well, the next day it was, "Mr Leitch, what can we do for you? You tell us and we'll make sure it gets done."' It transpired that Hill had rung the head of the refrigeration company after getting off the phone to Peter and told him how he had sent 'his partner' in to see about some new refrigeration and he had not been well looked after. He also reminded the man that Hill's company had over 140 hotels, and if they didn't want to work with 'his partner', then they wouldn't be getting any more work from Hill.

'They started the job immediately. That was a real

learning curve for me — how much money talks. We then got the shop set up, and called it Rosella Meats, because it was in Rosella Road — a very creative bit of thinking, that.'

The new business brought some new headaches, and Peter's lack of management experience made life difficult. 'At the shop in Ellerslie, I'd done the ordering as I was the manager, but when I bought my own shop it was a major learning curve. I had no idea — I was a duck out of water. Managing and owning are as different as black and white. At Ellerslie, my boss basically told me what to order and who to go to, but when I went into business myself, hook, line and sinker, it was very different.

'I've always had an ability to do a deal, and I can say I've always had integrity in my business dealings, so people like dealing with me. So I was able to do a few little deals.

'There were two ways you bought in those days: you dealt with wholesale companies, or you dealt with livestock companies. On the livestock side, I had an agent called John McIlroy who used to go to the sales and buy for me. He lived round the corner from me. The stock would be killed at the abattoir, and delivered to the store. When you bought at the sale there was an element of risk. The animal could get condemned, or the stock agent might pay too much for it. On the other hand, you could get a good buy. Eighty per cent of the time you got a good buy, and saved a bit of money.

'Buying from a wholesaler, on the other hand, you knew where you stood. You paid the price per kilo, and if you could do your costing, you knew exactly where you were. I was actually never very good at costing, because I wasn't very good at arithmetic. What people don't really understand is that to this day I don't know all of my alphabet, or my times tables, which is not a good thing if you're in business.'

By some miracle he survived, kept his head above water and learned what he needed to know the hard way. 'I had a very simple way of doing it. If you bought a body of beef, the rule of thumb is you lose a third to bone and fat. If you bought it for a dollar you can take a third off that, so the kilo cost about $1.30. Then you could work from there. I always worked on low margins. My mother used to shop at Self Help, because it was where you got a bargain.

'That was how I developed my business, and that's the way we've tried to continue to the present day. I was very lucky I had a very supportive wife. The Rosella Road shop was never going to be a humdinger, because it was in a side street. I battled on, but it didn't go that good. I had to work at night and from very early in the morning to pay the rent.

'The deal I had with Mr Hill was that if it wasn't working, I could give him the keys back and he'd take it over. So I duly went to him and told him it wasn't working. He said, "No problem, just give me the keys. If it's not working, you can walk away." He was an absolute gentleman — a lovely, lovely man.

'When I said I didn't want to leave him in the lurch, but that I just couldn't make the payments, he said to carry on and just to pay him when I could afford it. His aim was to eventually sell the whole block of shops, which I think had been a nightmare for him. As time went on the shop started to fizz a little bit, and I was just making a living.'

Hill eventually sold the shop in 1969 to a guy who in Peter's colourful opinion was 'as mean as cat shit'. 'The first thing he did was put the rent up. The first thing I did was to go to his accountant and him, told them I couldn't pay it, and showed them the books. I remember his accountant saying, "Look, I know you can't afford it, but he insists the rent must go up."

'I went home, virtually in tears, and said to Jan, "We're

going to have to close the shop, because this guy wants to put the rent up." I didn't want to go back into a situation of losing money, and that's what would have happened.

'At the same time the shop on Massey Road, where we are today, was vacant. The rumour was that it had been condemned. Me being not too bright, I didn't believe it, so I went ahead. It was owned by a guy called Keith Smith, who had another couple of butchers' shops, and was doing very well in the meat industry. He sort of didn't want the shop, but didn't really want anyone else to have it. I used to ring his wife and him, and I pestered them until they let me have it. We called it Rosella Meats, because I'd been advertising under that name for a while — I didn't really know what a brand was in those days.

'One of the biggest shocks I got when I moved around the corner was that customers weren't loyal. I thought they'd follow me around, but they didn't. I had to build a whole new base of customers. That was a learning curve — that people won't automatically be loyal to you.

'What would prove to be one of the biggest lessons I got from moving was position, position, position. You can try as hard as you like, but if you don't have the right position, you're wasting your time. It turned out that for all the hard work I did at Rosella Road, I might as well have been pissing in the wind because its position wasn't right. I might say that the guy who bought Rosella Road lost a lot of money when he sold it some years later.

'In the new shop at Massey Road I utilised the side of the building for advertising, like a giant billboard, and I'd put the specials and the bargains on there. It absolutely proved to me how important a good buy was. They'd flock in if there was a good bargain on the wall. There was a dramatic difference if we had a red-hot special.

'We're still there at the same store today. That was when I learned how much position matters, because I went from making a living to making money.'

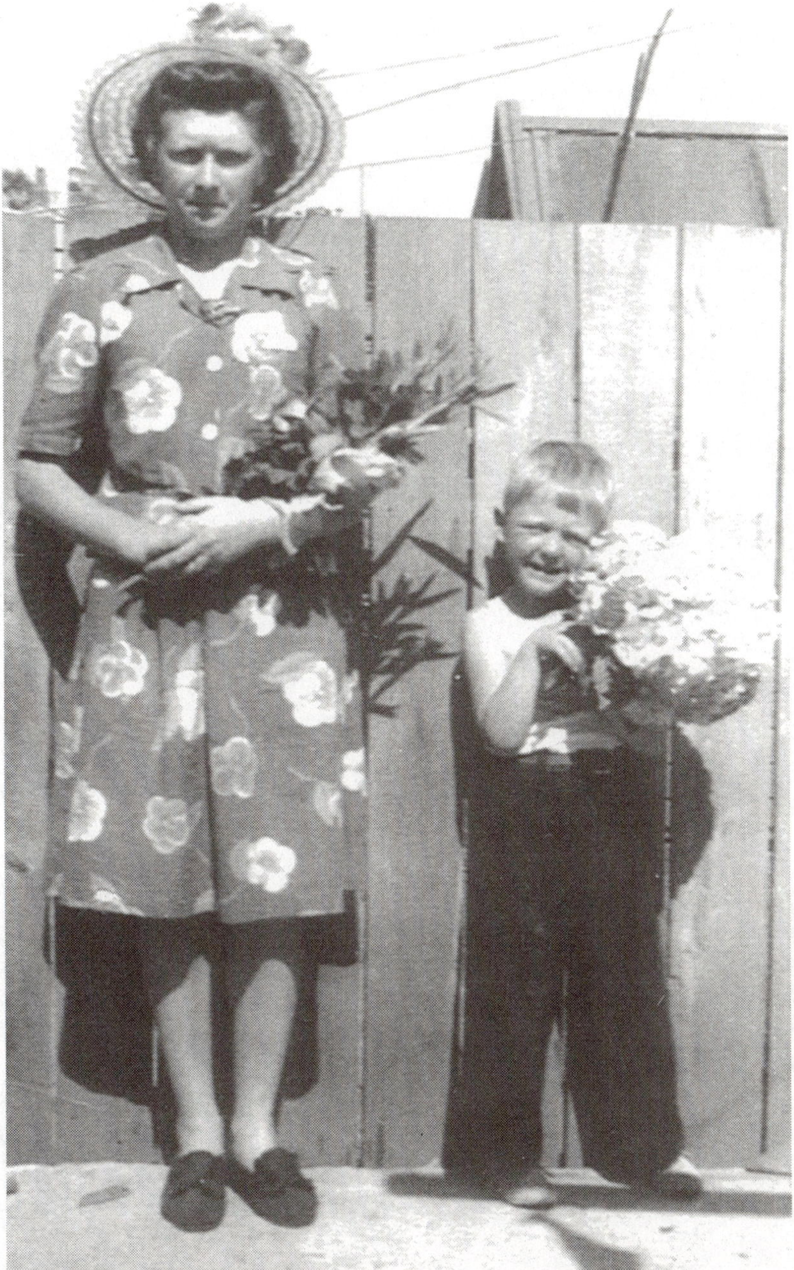

4

Radio

In the 1970s Tim Bickerstaff was the king of sports radio. Big, bold and a natural-born stirrer, he attained worldwide attention in 1972 when All Black Keith Murdoch was sent home from Britain after a late-night scuffle in a Cardiff hotel.

Bickerstaff promptly began his now notorious 'Punch a Pom a Day' campaign that drew personal threats, caused an English woman to burst into tears on air, and made him a household name in Auckland. He ran big-money quizzes on air, challenged the hierarchy of major sports, ran a competition for his listeners to select the 15 worst-ever All Black players, called international league players fat, suggested wheelchair sport wouldn't be popular because nobody was interested in spastics, and reached a stage where he was so controversial that he stopped going out at night for fear of physical violence.

On Auckland's Radio I, one of his regular listeners was a sports-mad butcher in Mangere. 'I made the fatal mistake of ringing Tim one night, about how he had bagged the mighty Mangere East Hawks,' Peter says. 'While still on air, Tim said, "Do you want to have a bet on the game?"

'I said, "Yep." But what I didn't realise was how big Tim gambled. We had a couple of bets, and I lost plenty.'

Bickerstaff, who now lives in Whitianga and runs a mail order business for Ignite, a product he promises will improve your love life, remembers the occasion differently. 'In my memory,' says Bickerstaff, 'we had a bet on the air, Glenora against Otahuhu. I was working with Geoff Sinclair then at Radio I. I usually never took a bet on air because people never fronted up when they lost. The next day this guy turned up at the studio in Newton Road, and said, "Mate, I'm Peter Leitch, I had that bet with you, here's the $100 I owe you."

'I said, "Fine, you're covered." We became a bit friendlier after that. He invited me to Mangere East for a function, so I got to know him a bit better. At the time we both lived in Pakuranga, and we saw each other there as well.'

Peter remembers how he always had to do business with Bickerstaff in the Wiri Trust hotel, and one day Bickerstaff suggested to Peter that he advertise with them. 'I said I couldn't afford to. But that night I was driving home, and I thought to myself, "If I knocked off the gambling with him, I could afford to advertise." So I stopped gambling, and started doing phone-outs with Tim.'

Bickerstaff says the association began in 1979, not long after nationally syndicated Radio Pacific had started up, with a trial for a month of advertising for $200, at $10 a phone-out. Peter says, 'We came up with the idea that we needed a nickname. A Maori guy had walked into the pub at Wiri one time and said, "Hey, there's that fuckin' mad butcher." We dropped the first bit, because that wouldn't have gone down too well on the radio, and we called ourselves "Rosella Meats, home of the Mad Butcher".'

When Gordon Dryden, another guru of radio, made the comment that Peter really only needed one name, the decision was made to drop Rosella Meats, and he became the Mad Butcher. 'The reality is that it was a fairy tale. Working with guys like Tim, who were off the wall, my personality worked, and the business grew. There was no question that the radio advertising helped.'

At the time no other individual butchers were advertising and offering specials on air. Nevertheless, Peter realised that just talking about meat wasn't all that interesting for listeners, so he used some of his street smarts and his unerring commercial instinct and included a bit of comment about the footy and other sporting events of the day. Suddenly meat wasn't so humdrum. 'If you just talk specials, it gets boring. From day one I added a bit of the community stuff, then threw the specials in.'

To Bickerstaff one of the remarkable aspects of the humour that emerged between himself and the Butcher was that nothing was prepared. 'It was all ad lib. His thing was that he didn't want it to sound like a commercial. I thought he'd be plugging the prices and the specials, but while he did that, it was never a major part of the ad. I used to wonder if the ads would ever work for him, because most of them were about rugby league, or other sport, and I'd tell him so.'

Peter laughs. 'We had a few blues on air, but it never lasted. Tim's a character, and that was how he built an audience.'

The ads worked because radio suited the Mad Butcher. Live radio demands quick thinking, a ready wit, an ability to sum up a situation in one telling phrase, and, for real success, a cheerful, likeable nature. You could say that all the things that made an old-style butcher popular with his shoppers applied perfectly to radio, and Peter Leitch was more than able to transfer his in-shop skills to the airwaves.

'He was the voice of the working-class man, which, especially when he started, was exactly what his customers identified with,' says Bickerstaff. 'He had the best grip by far on call-outs of anyone I've ever worked with. He knew when he'd said enough, he knew when we were running out of time, and it took him no time to learn.'

It was a relationship that showed a different side to Bickerstaff's hard-nosed public image. 'Tim was a hard man,' says Peter, 'but he would always ring and ask how the ads were working. If I said I hadn't been that busy, he'd throw in a dozen extra ads for free.'

Business boomed, and Peter's distinctive raspy voice proved to be a real asset — a calling card that quickly became well known. 'It amazes me sometimes how many people recognise the voice all over New Zealand. Nobody ever taught me radio — I was just a natural. You could call it the gift of the gab. You could call it bullshit, but in fact it's not. Under the Fair Trading Act you can't say she's your daughter if she's not. You have to make sure the prices are what they are in the stores.'

As well as having a distinctive voice, Peter's lively mix of business, sport and social commentary soon began including glimpses of his personal life, and gradually his listening audience came to feel they knew him. He was one of them, a real guy, not some slick media image created by a poncey advertising agency.

Bill Francis is general manager of talk for the Radio Network, a role that has seen him supervise the biggest names in talk radio, including Newstalk ZB's stars such as Paul Holmes, Leighton Smith, Murray Deaker, Larry Williams and Kerre Woodham.

To Francis, Peter's landmark radio advertisements made him an instigator. 'He was the first guy who made an impact as a personality in that genre of ads. He was the first who made an impression, because he was the first who didn't only talk about the product. There were shopping reporters before he came along, but Peter was successful because he didn't just do a hard sell. Going off on a tangent about his special interests would drag the audience in for the final message about his specials for that week.

'When that voice appeared on the radio, the listener

would be straight away tuned to what he was saying that day, other than his steak or sausages. That larger-than-life persona meant that he leapt out of the speaker — you were immediately captivated by this personality.

'Why was it special? I think it was because Peter's wasn't a trained, radio voice, and when you think about it, it was probably a start to New Zealand voices being acceptable on the radio.'

Peter's unique home-grown way of communicating was never about correct pronunciation or grammatical exactitude, but was instead the result of someone who spoke naturally about how they felt, and it hooked the listener in. 'People felt they knew him,' Francis says. 'He also had a performer's attributes — he could put on a great act if he wanted to. He has the X factor, the ability to connect. He's never been coached. He made it up as he was going along.

'Over the years since there have been a number of pretenders who have all tried to copy what he's done, but nobody has been able to deliver what Peter has.' According to Francis, listening to Peter on the radio and meeting him face to face, 'it's one and the same person. In essence, the way he acts on the radio is no different from his everyday persona. If that seems easy, it's not. The ability to be yourself when performing is actually rare.'

The late Bruno Lawrence summed it up after critics had suggested he was only playing himself in movies like *Smash Palace* and *Utu*. He said, 'It's easy to say that if you've never done it. But it's actually bloody hard to be yourself when cameras are rolling and lights are shining on you.' The great performers in radio are those who can listen, adapt and ad-lib when the occasion demands. Some of the most academically gifted can be wooden and boring on air, but to pick up a suggestion and run with it is when the best moments occur. Peter, a man with a mind as sharp as a boning knife, has never missed a cue, no matter how subtle it may be.

'Dead air, or an obvious lack of understanding between an announcer and the person being interviewed, is painful to listen to. The reason so many in radio love having Peter on air is that he'll never let you down,' says Francis.

He can also take direction. In the mid-1980s I was running a Saturday sports programme on Radio Hauraki, and was keen to include Peter as a regular guest. The manager at the time, John McCready, who would later be programme director at TVNZ, was reluctant. Peter was too over the top, he felt: 'People don't want to hear someone screaming their head off at 8 o'clock on a Saturday morning.' Peter and I talked. He understood exactly what was required, and for the next three years we chatted exactly as McCready wanted. Peter was still lively — he still had strong opinions — but he wasn't raucous.

The great beauty of radio is that technically it has none of the time restraints of newspapers, and needs nothing like the equipment required to get a television report on air. One man or woman on a phone is all you need for live radio.

A golden invention for Peter has been the mobile phone, and for dozens of New Zealand radio stations, from the powerhouses like ZB to the likes of Coromandel FM, Hokonui Gold, Central FM, or Foveaux Radio, Peter has been a touchstone.

Bill Francis commends Peter's ability to perform on air at any time of the day or night, and in whatever the circumstances. 'He's done live crosses from all over New Zealand, and overseas. Any time of the day, he can be on the phone and do what he needs to do. He's developed an incredible sense of timing, and how to deliver. He can do the Warriors bit at the top, then mention he's had a great function on for charity, and then, at the end, he can still deliver the specials in a totally professional way, within the time frame. He really knows how to do it.'

Given the sense of ownership many listeners and viewers feel about people on air, to the point where a change of hairstyle for Judy Bailey could ignite several hundred angry phone calls, it's almost a surprise to learn that a talent as raw as Peter's has received little, if any, negative feedback from radio fans.

'I won't name them,' says Francis, 'but over the years there have been a number of people who have done similar things to Peter, and I would get regular phone calls from listeners asking why I don't take that person off the air. I've never had that with Peter Leitch, which is amazing. I think it's because people can identify with him — they see him as real. They know that a lot of what he does on air is about helping other people, so they connect with that. They know that he's genuine when he does charity stuff, and they like him.'

Peter started on ZB with sports announcer Barry Holland, and has worked with many others on air, including one of his close friends, Murray Deaker. 'I've enjoyed working with so many different radio people,' Peter says. 'People like Barry Holland when I started out, Mark Bennett, Geoff Sinclair, Alice Worsley, Tony Amos, Doug Golightly, Geoff Thomas, the boys at The Rock, the morning pirates at Hauraki . . . so many have been great to work with. I've been very blessed that I've had some really good friendships with radio people.'

It was radio that nearly 20 years ago helped make Peter as much of a household name in Southland as he was in Auckland.

The *Southland Sports Sunday* was a show world famous in the south, its mix of wild humour and serious sports talk winning an audience first on Hokonui Radio in Gore, from 1988, and then, from 1990, on Foveaux Radio in Invercargill.

It was radio the way it used to be, with no pre-recorded interviews, and no dump button, which meant some close shaves, as callers sometimes forgot they weren't at a pub talking to their mates.

Hosted by Pinky (Mike Hughes, who owned the Pink Bike Shop), Fast-track (racing expert Ken Dixon) and Podge (Roger McPherson), there were two regular guests who, for no pay, did not miss a show for more than ten years — Peter and television commentator Grant Nisbett.

Grant Nisbett could be on the phone from South Africa

in the very early hours of the morning, or, on one famous occasion, Peter was on the line from England in the middle of a very liquid celebration of a Kiwi win.

'Even today when I return to Southland,' says Hughes, who now lives in Christchurch, 'people still talk about *Southland Sports Sunday* and the Butcher taking the piss out of the three of us. For a long while he's been a huge celebrity in Southland.'

The first visit Peter actually made to Southland was in 1992, when he and Janice were invited as guests of the Invercargill Harness Racing Club to an April race meeting.

He was asked if he'd mind bringing a few sausages for a barbecue. When a long black limousine met them at the airport, the driver and Peter loaded on board 2000 sausages that he'd brought from Auckland.

At the course Peter, darting between three barbecues, cooked what the harness club proudly claim as a New Zealand solo record, 1875 sausages in 1 hour 35 minutes.

In 1995 Bluff publican Murray Flynn invited Peter to the second Stabi-Craft fishing tournament in Southland, an event that over 14 years reached a point where more than $30,000 worth of prizes was offered.

Peter was the MC for the contest, and it was quickly

obvious that the match of an Auckland butcher and good keen southern men was made in heaven. Peter would return for several years, and the tournament's publicity officer, Lindsay Beer, says his input went far beyond the good humour on stage.

'He has such vast experience of events and public occasions,' says Lindsay, 'and with his instinct for promotional opportunities he made many suggestions to improve the event.

'His huge national profile put us on the national stage as he tirelessly promoted the tournament in the national media.'

Peter brought guests like Marc Ellis and veteran radio star Kevin Black too, and when Warriors commitments made it hard for him to travel south, kept supporting the contest on air and in print.

'He's always thought of with great fondness in Bluff,' says Beer. 'It was thanks to his time and energy that the event got a national profile so quickly.'

A friendship between another Southland man, Invercargill real estate agent Tim Frampton, and Peter started ten years ago, when Frampton answered the phone one day at the Yunca company, where he was then working.

Down the line he heard a barbed-wire voice saying, 'It's

the Mad Butcher here, mate. I'm in town and I want to buy 30 barbecues.'

Thinking it was a mate having him on, Frampton stalled until Peter growled, 'Mate, if you want the order, get round here now.'

A quick trip to the hotel Peter was staying at and a deal was signed. Thirty Southland-made barbecues were shipped off to Auckland.

'It was great to deal with Peter,' says Frampton, 'as we soon found that when he used our barbecues, he gave a big plug to the firm wherever possible.'

The relationship quickly grew, and when Frampton moved into the real estate area, Peter would soon use his auctioneering skills.

A great day for the southern man came when Peter asked him to fly to Auckland and take over the charity auction that was a feature of a Melbourne Cup party Peter was running at a South Auckland community centre. 'There were league stars and other celebrities there, and the sausages were being cooked flat out.'

Frampton will never forget the Butcher's parting words to the crowd: 'Now, don't take the fuckin' furniture with you, it belongs to the community.'

Another phone call and Tim and a mate were on their

way to Auckland where they were to be barmen at Peter's daughter Julie's 21st.

Arriving early they were shown the bar at Peter and Janice's home, better stocked, they felt, than any bar in New Zealand.

'Mate,' Peter said, 'these young pricks think they are going to drink my bar dry, but no one has and no one will.' There would have been a few sore heads the next day, Frampton believes, but despite the consumption the bar was drunk barely half-dry. 'Peter's a very generous man.'

For Bill Francis, the way the relationship between morning announcer Leighton Smith and Peter really clicks, despite the fact they are two very different personalities, is probably the most fascinating. 'Leighton's the wine connoisseur; Peter's the Lion Ice man. They have one thing in common: Leighton loves rugby league, so that could have been the initial connection. And they have a huge respect for each other.'

But it is Murray Deaker that has been an especially loyal friend to Peter, to the point where Peter has had to talk him out of action that could have damaged Murray's own career.

For a time Peter was on air in the weekend doing crosses to ZB's *Scoreboard* shows run by Murray. It was decided by the ZB hierarchy to replace Peter. 'Murray was prepared to go to war with management, because he thought it was unfair,' Peter says. 'I didn't worry. My attitude with radio was that I'd always be prepared to take what came along. I was able to talk him out of having a bust-up with his bosses.'

The most extraordinary public moments with Deaker came by accident when, at very short notice, Peter agreed to replace Frank Endacott as a guest on Murray's Sky television show in a pre-recorded interview. When Greg Billings, Murray's producer, rang him, Peter had just been giving details to the police of a burglary at one of his stores that appeared to be an inside job. Peter was hurt by the revelations, and was still emotional when he drove to the studios.

'I only had about ten minutes to prepare a question line for a half-hour interview,' says Deaker, 'and no time to brief him or prepare him. The result was the most talked about television programme I have ever been involved with. It was vintage Mad Butcher — the genuine article. He was totally himself. Halfway through he broke down — probably the emotion of what he'd just been through with the police got to him as he started to talk about the debt he owed his family, particularly his wife, Jan. He began to sob, and I tried to get him back on track by talking about the fistful of rings he wears. Fortunately it worked, and a couple of minutes later he was telling me he'd drop me if I referred to him blubbing.'

When the interview was over, with both men exhausted, Murray offered Peter the chance to can the interview. 'Mate, that was me,' replied Peter. 'If they don't like it, that's their bloody problem.'

Later Peter would tell Murray he had considered asking him to drop the interview. 'Fortunately he did what he has successfully done for most of his life, and went with his gut instinct,' says Deaker. 'The public loved it. For once the façade of madness was totally stripped away, and Peter Leitch, family man, butcher and league mate, was exposed. For weeks afterwards he received letters, cards, faxes and messages telling him how much the programme meant to viewers.'

In 1988, when ZB changed from a music station to talkback, the ratings went into free fall, and as Francis describes it, the station was bleeding terribly, with clients walking out the door. From commanding the number one spot in Auckland, ZB plummeted to sixth place.

Manager Brent Harman called a meeting of major advertisers, including Peter. At the meeting, where some of the clients attacked Harman for what he'd done, Peter stood up and said, 'Well I'm sorry, but the change has not affected my business one bit, so I'm backing Brent.' When some of the other clients accused Peter of sucking up to Harman, he denied it and said he was just stating a fact.

Being the astute businessman that he is, he also went on to say that if the station was losing listeners, there should be a change in the rates. Harman listened, and the rates were lowered. As Francis describes it, 'The thing was that his sense of loyalty to people who he liked and respected, and who had worked for him, was paramount in those situations. He's one of the biggest clients we have, up there with the corporate giants. Like any good client, he's someone who has to be looked after. He works through Steve Charnley, but he knows all the managers of all the stations, and he has a good relationship with John McElhinney, chief executive of the Radio Network.

'Quite a few years ago, we gave Peter a swipe card so he can walk into any floor on this building 24 hours a day. We've built various charitable partnerships with him. He did the prostate campaign for a couple of years. He instigated it, but we've got right in behind it. We've been very happy to go along with some of his projects because of his loyalty to us. He's built a number of very special relationships with people in radio. If he heard that something was going wrong — anything at all — he'd always call.

'I was over at Waiheke with him one time, and we had my 90-year-old mother-in-law in the car with us. We stopped and had a chat. He leaned in and said to my mother-in-law, "You know, Bill's a great guy, but you want to know something? He's always bagging you behind your back."

'That's him. He'll give you a spin and then take the piss.'

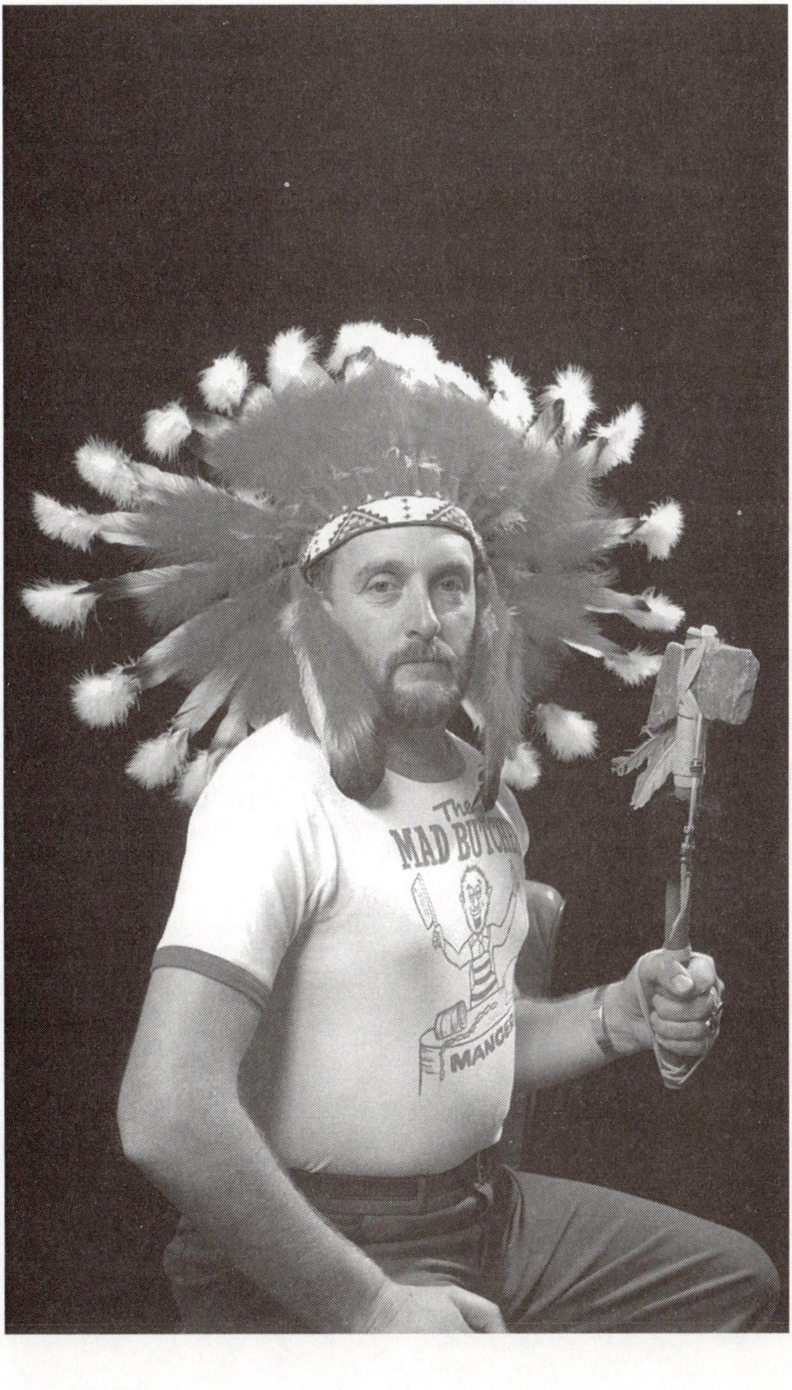

5

Business

'People ask me if I had a vision when I got my first butcher's shop,' says Peter Leitch. 'No, I didn't have a vision. I could get up now and say I did — pretend I was Martin Luther King, and say, "I have a dream!" But that's bullshit. I went into a butcher's shop, and all I wanted to do was pay the rent and survive. That was it. I didn't set out to build a huge brand, but that was what happened.'

When Peter first went into business, his mother had some advice for her son, telling him always to treat people the way he would want to be treated himself, and it was something he has never forgotten. 'That was a big issue for me with my own business. I love the job, and I love meeting people. It's a fact that money hasn't been a driving force for me — I've never invested my money, I've never tried to grow it. If I had, I'd be worth $40 million today. We just leave money in the bank.'

The expansion of The Mad Butcher brand may seem to have exploded, which would suggest it was driven hard by an ambitious man, but the reality is that for many years Peter didn't actively seek partners. When he started at Massey Road he was working so hard that there wasn't much time for dreams.

'At the start it was full on — I was working from 5 a.m. to 7 p.m. When you first arrive, you set the shop up, plus spend some time out the back, boning out, that sort of thing. I used to open the doors when I got to the shop. If someone wanted to come in at 5 a.m., they could come in. I'd get the odd taxi driver coming in to get meat. Once I had a couple of guys come in who tried to rob me. I chased them down the road with a chopper. They didn't have guns or anything — they were just a bit out of it on drugs, I think.'

The most serious robbery was in 1999 when three men came into the back of the Mangere store all armed with handguns, threatened three of the staff, and got away with several thousands of dollars. The robbers were captured the next day in Thames, after a tip-off from a woman whose marae had benefited from the Mad Butcher's generosity.

Fortunately, although the experience was horrifying, nobody was physically hurt. Shaken staff members were shouted a lavish meal at a licensed restaurant by Peter. Picked up by taxis, they had a huge night out. The homespun counselling worked perfectly — for some it was the first time at a restaurant, and one young man was able to take home food for the other six members in his family.

Cashflow was something Peter initially looked after in a very home-made fashion. At the time, his friend Dave Roberts, who now lives in Canada, was a policeman in Auckland. The two men have been friends since the days when Dave's wife worked next door to the butcher's shop that Peter managed in Ellerslie. 'Early on in the piece,' says Dave, 'when Pete was beginning to make money from his shop, he used to bring the cash home in a bag. If my wife and I were visiting Peter and Jan, we would all sit around and count the cash. If he'd had a good day, it could be a considerable amount of money.

'In case he was robbed, Pete carried a baseball bat alongside the seat in his car. One night, he came in, ashen faced, and when I asked him what was up, he told me he'd nearly come to grief. Pete had locked up the shop and started his journey home when he noticed a car keeping pace with him. He sped up, and so did his follower. If he slowed down, so did his follower. He turned left and right, only to be accompanied by the car behind as though glued to his bumper.

'Eventually, very apprehensive, Pete pulled in to the side of the road, and so did the other car. Out got a large figure, not clearly recognisable in the gloom, and Pete white-knuckled the baseball bat, ready to defend his hard-earned cash.

'A face appeared at the window — it was a traffic officer, who said, "Did you know your rear left light is burned out?" We all had a laugh, but that traffic cop never knew how close he was to getting an earful of baseball bat.'

The hours of work and the pace Peter maintained were extraordinary. 'When he first went into business he had three jobs,' says Peter's wife, Janice. 'He butchered, he cleaned South Auckland Motors in the morning, and then he'd bone meat after work.'

It wasn't long before Janice was working in the shop as well. When their youngest daughter, Julie, turned five and things got so hectic he could no longer cope on his own,

Peter rang Janice and said, 'Just get a taxi and come out here.'

One of the things he was never able to get to grips with was bookkeeping, and Janice took over that role. 'For 25 years I did the books,' she says. 'I worked every day at the shop and then went home at 3 p.m. when the girls finished school. I only stopped working full-time a few years ago when my mother got ill, and I wanted to look after her.'

When she began caring for her mother, Janice still had the bookwork sent home to her, and she would physically check every cheque butt. When the business moved to computers, she checked the printouts. 'The people who came into the shop wanted a good deal, and I could relate to that,' she says. 'That was the upbringing I had.'

The Leitches also stuck to what they knew. One of the few occasions when Peter looked to invest outside the meat business was in 1972 when a good friend suggested he have a look at putting money into a booming investment company called JBL.

There was $100,000 sitting in the bank, and before long a keen salesperson from JBL was sitting across a desk from

Peter, painting a glowing picture of the 47 companies under the JBL umbrella.

However, instead of signing over a six-figure sum, Peter invested in a block of flats in Remuera, where a land agent was also promising stellar returns.

Buying property, not shares, was a wise move. 'It wasn't that the flats were such a great deal,' says Peter. 'It was about ten years before we even got our money back on them. But it was better than being with JBL.'

Just a couple of months after he'd been urged to buy into it, the JBL empire collapsed. It took up to 17 years for debenture holders to get even a proportion of their money back.

Peter claims that the worst decision he ever made was asking Janice to work with him in the shop. 'She was a real shy girl when we were first married — wouldn't say boo to a mouse. Now I can't get a word in edgeways.' The truth, he concedes, is that she was shy, but the work she did was invaluable, and she did gain confidence. 'You had to learn to stand up for yourself,' says Janice, 'especially when the boys put a pig's eye in your cup of tea.'

In the early days, Peter and Janice operated their business from a tin shed in the backyard at Mangere. 'That was our office for many years,' Peter says. 'Even in the later stages of the business, we never got into the flash offices, the bullshit stuff. Believe me, a lot of people came into the shed at Mangere and their eyes popped out.'

In 1985 Don Graham was national sales manager for chicken at Harvey Farms. 'I used to do the deals for what were then Peter's five stores in an old container at the back of his Mangere store,' Graham recalls. 'Janice and Peter would always make you welcome with a coffee. Janice would work out the deal and Peter would then put 110 per cent effort behind the promotion by thrashing it out on the radio. He was so successful that we soon had to gear up a special production run just for him.'

Another significant factor behind the success of the Mad Butcher is the special regard given to him by Polynesian Aucklanders. Peter puts it down to the time he spent working in Karangahape Road, where he first got to know their traditions and culture. 'I knew they loved their meat, and that put me in good stead when I started at Massey

Road. Brisket on the bone was a special favourite. I knew what they wanted — I wasn't formally trained, but I could sense what people were after. It's no good putting out what people don't want.'

One of New Zealand rugby league's greatest players, Olsen Filipaina, still has vivid memories of going to the Massey Road shop when he was a local primary-school kid. Now living in Sydney, Filipaina says, 'I used to go with Mum and Dad when they were shopping, and they'd go to The Mad Butcher shop. One day, instead of waiting in the car, I went in with them, and the Mad Butcher started calling Mum "Big Mamma" in that distinctive loud voice. He was joking with her, saying Big Mamma this and that, asking, "What can I do for you today, Big Mamma?" and I was wondering, "Who does this guy think he is, calling my mother that?"

'My mother actually was really big back then, and I was thinking to myself, "You just wait until I get bigger, I'll give you a hiding for being cheeky to my mother!"

'I remember asking her after we left the shop, "Mum, why did you let that fella call you names?" She just laughed — she wasn't upset at all. Of course they'd known each other for a while because she shopped there all the time, but for me it was my first impression of the Butcher.

'With my mother shopping there all the time, I'd go in with her more often, and he started to give me a bit of cheek as well. After a while I got to know him as a real top bloke. He'd give me free cheerios when I came in, and I quickly changed my tune.' Laughing at the memory, Filipaina adds, 'I guess I thought he was okay. I told him to call my mum what he liked.'

In the late 1970s Peter began to notice how supermarkets were increasingly moving into the meat trade, and he feared that independent butchers like himself were going to be gobbled up. He saw growing the business as the answer.

But while Peter, who thrives on pressure, was in favour of expansion, Janice didn't want the stress that would be associated with it. 'My wife is more conservative than me when it comes to business, and she didn't want to expand,' Peter says. 'Jan always worried about going broke, things like that. She certainly wasn't keen on the idea, but I could see that to stay in the business we had to grow.' But when the opportunity to expand occurred, it came from an unlikely quarter.

Rod Slater, now chief executive of the New Zealand Beef

and Lamb Marketing Bureau, first bumped into Peter at meetings of the Auckland Master Butchers' Association in the mid to late 1970s. There was a strong mutual antipathy. 'We were both establishing our own businesses and, to be frank, we didn't like each other,' Slater says. 'He saw me as a smooth-talking, silver-spooned guy. My father had a butcher's shop — it was just a one-man operation — but Peter saw me as a guy who had made it the easy way. I saw him as brash, crude, whatever — dislike is probably the best way of describing it.'

Peter's memory is the same. 'I didn't like him much, and he didn't like me much. We came from different backgrounds. For example, he was an only child, and I was one of seven.'

By 1980, the retail industry in New Zealand was at a stage where there was considerable industrial unrest, much of it to do with the recent advent of Saturday trading. 'We had strikes where shops were closed down for days on end,' Slater recalls. 'It was a real problem.'

A meeting was organised in Wellington, with people like trade union leader Ken Douglas attending. 'Unbeknownst to each other we decided, "Bugger this, I'm going to go down and see what this is all about,"' Peter says.

The two men were on the same plane and, coming back,

they began chatting about the meeting and their respective concerns and philosophies, which led on to where they saw themselves going from there on. 'I said that I'd often thought about having a chain of shops, but I wasn't sure I wanted to do it on my own,' Slater says. 'Peter said he felt the same, that he'd like to open another shop, but that his wife, Janice, would never let him because there was enough drama and pressure with just the one shop.

'By then he was well known as the Mad Butcher. Tim Bickerstaff had already coined the phrase, so it wasn't as if I was saying I could make something for him — he was already well on the way. The more I talked to him, the more I thought, "God, there's an opportunity here." We got off the plane as quite good friends.'

A couple of weeks after the plane flight, a chain of takeaway places called the Chicken Spot, owned by Ballins Industries, closed down. Rod called Peter and said he thought one of their sites in Onehunga could make a pretty good butcher's shop. The two men had a look at it, and went and had a talk with the people at Ballins, where they found out that there were a few other sites also on offer.

'I'll always remember that this was the first time I saw Peter's business prowess in action,' Slater says. 'We decided to have a crack at a shop at Hauraki Corner in Takapuna.

Peter had decided he wasn't interested in the Onehunga shop, because it was too close to his shop in Mangere. We went over and had a look at another site in Mt Roskill too. It was close to where my parents lived, so I knew it well. It was on the corner of White Swan and Richardson Roads and he told me he thought we should have a crack at this one as well. I wasn't sure about the location, but in the end he got his way, and that proved to be one of our trophy shops over the years — it went from day one. That was my first taste of seeing how Peter may not know the alphabet or times tables, but that he has the street smarts in business.'

After negotiations the two partners got a sweetheart deal from Ballins, who were keen to get out of the sites. 'They left all the shop equipment in there and gave us a rental for the first two years at a fraction of what they'd been paying. It was one of those deals from heaven.'

The two set up a new company called Rodpete Enterprises, and would eventually open shops at Takapuna, Mt Roskill and Papakura, all operated by Rodpete, but trading under the brand of The Mad Butcher. The Mad Butcher Company remained 100 per cent in Peter's hands, as it did until 2007. Only the shops were jointly operated.

'I will always remember when we first got together, going to meet the new bank manager.' Slater says. 'We did a divvy:

"We'll go with my lawyer, your accountant, my bank," sort of thing. We ended up going with his bank, which in those days was CBA, which became Westpac, at Otahuhu. Peter told me he hadn't met the manager, who had just started, but we should see him and arrange an overdraft, so off we went.

'The guy turned out to be a very devout Christian, and you know what Peter's language is like. In the first two minutes of the introduction, Peter used the 'f' word about ten times, and this guy was curling up. Every time Peter swore, you could see the guy flinch — I wanted the ground to swallow me whole.

'But we still got the deal — it didn't damage that at all. You see, coming from Peter, it's just a natural part of him — he's not being abusive, and it's not offensive.'

The first two Rodpete shops were in Takapuna, which opened on 15 March 1981, and then in Mt Roskill, which opened on 15 June 1981. 'That was when I really got to know Peter the entrepreneur, Peter the promoter,' says Slater, 'because it was bloody frightening how the Takapuna shop took off.

'I was working in the shop on opening day, and there was meat passing over the counter like you wouldn't believe. I'd come from a shop that I thought was pretty gung-ho, where there were four of us and everything was ordered and organised, but this was like a hurricane of meat coming in the shop and going out just as fast.

'Just to complicate matters, there were traffic pointsmen on Esmonde Road and up on Hauraki Corner, and it was like a madhouse in there — it was frightening. But the thing about Peter is that numbers like that never worry him. In fact, the more hectic it got, he just went to another level, out there performing with the customers. That was what opened my eyes to what was possible if you have no boundaries in your head.'

The near-hysteria of the Takapuna opening was matched at Mt Roskill. Peter had arranged for David Hartnell, then a television gossip columnist, to open the shop, dressed to the nines in a pink bowtie, and Rod Slater's father recorded the chaos on an old movie camera. 'We opened it at 9 o'clock on a Wednesday, and it was unbelievable,' Slater laughs. 'My father stood up on a ladder in the shop to film it. The place was going crazy. God knows what we lost to shoplifting, because it was totally out of control. In those days the only way we knew what people were buying was by adding it up on a bit of paper, or using an old-fashioned calculator. There was no scanning, nothing like that. Who would know how many mistakes were made that day, but it put the place on the map, and from there on, there was no turning back.

The promotional urge was in full swing when the store at Mt Roskill reached its fifth anniversary.

Peter, of course, suggested a celebration, and, with blanket radio and newspaper advertising, the store was packed when he arrived for a personal appearance.

He was rigged out in full Indian chief regalia, including a massive feathered headdress. Round his waist rode a leather gunbelt with two replica Colt 45s in the holsters.

Chief Mad Butcher was soon whooping it up, dancing around the store, firing ear-splitting blanks from the six-guns. A cheery-looking middle-aged man caught his eye, and they were soon bantering.

'You're a shady-looking bloke, mate,' roared Peter. 'You could be a bank robber.' With a flourish he whipped out both guns and fired into the man's side. Cue laughter all round, shaking of hands, and the promotion marching on.

Next day Rod Slater, still basking in the satisfaction of another successful show by Peter, answered his office phone.

It was the man Peter had shot. Rod thanked him for the call, for being a good sport, and said what great fun it had all been.

'Well, not really,' came the reply. 'I have some serious burns to my body; I think you need to come and see me.'

Thumping back to earth he rang Peter, who urged him to make it up to the man as quickly as he could. 'He lived not far from the shop so I shot straight around,' says Rod. 'There was indeed quite a burn on his stomach.'

An agreement was soon reached. For the next year all the man's meat was free, and firing guns anywhere other than in the air wasn't part of any more promotions.

While the customers loved the idea of a Mad Butcher's store in Takapuna, there were immediate attempts to make things difficult from a quarter that remains the toughest opposition. 'When we opened at Takapuna,' Slater says, 'there was a New World supermarket next door, and we went to see the owner to introduce ourselves, trying to do the right thing.

'The day we opened, by a strange coincidence, two of their huge articulated trucks were parked outside our shop so they blocked people from coming in to get parking. They were saying that the shop would last six months. Well, work it out — 36 years later, the shop's still trading well there, but the supermarket's had owners who have come and gone.'

The attitude of some of his competitors towards the feisty butcher from Mangere irritated Peter, and he rarely missed a chance to strike back in whatever way he could. Don Graham, national sales manager at Tegel at the time, recalls a new product presentation he held at the Regent Hotel in Auckland, now the Stamford Plaza. 'In those days,' says Graham, 'the Regent was a very swanky new hotel. We had over 200 people at the function — food writers, supermarket buyers, and so on. Peter was at a table with a supermarket butchery buyer. During the evening, the buyer told Peter he was a very important person, in charge of 60 supermarket butcheries.

'Peter took an instant dislike to his attitude and during the evening he managed to slip the salt and pepper shakers into this bloke's jacket pocket. At the end of the night, Peter told a waiter he'd seen a bloke nicking the stuff off the table and putting it into his pockets. The waiter went to the supermarket butchery buyer and, to the guy's embarrassment, asked for the Regent's property back. Peter said later, "I fixed that smart arse."'

It was largely the threat posed by supermarkets that led Peter into his partnership with Rod Slater. A partnership would make it possible to advertise more, and to compete with the big media spending of the supermarket chains, they reasoned. 'But the supermarkets didn't put butchers out of business,' says Peter, 'butchers put themselves out of business. We gave the supermarkets a helping hand, because the old-time butchers were arrogant, and refused to have good specials.

'I used to go to butchers' meetings and say we needed to have specials, and they'd laugh at me. These guys had made a lot of money — they were very rich. We gave it to the supermarkets on a platter. What I've done is fight back. To be fair, I'm sure if you spoke to any supermarket owner, they'd tell you I'm a pain in their bloody arse.'

Rod Slater agrees. 'A lot of butchers didn't have any marketing nous, but then they didn't need it. I'll give you an example, how things were at my father's shop. There was just him and a boy, but before the supermarkets started selling meat, he was making more than the Prime Minister. When you're on a gravy train like that, you can't see an end to it. The margins then were massive. The old-time butchers would turn in their graves at how thin the margins are now.

'There were a lot of things the supermarkets did which the old-style butchers didn't respond to — one was discounting, the other was flexible hours. Specials were rarely seen in the old days, and shop hours were strictly Monday to Friday, nine to five. When Friday-night trading came in, I can remember my father saying, "It'll never work. Who the hell wants to buy meat at night?" That was typical of their attitude.'

Peter led the charge in terms of opening hours — he was the first independent butcher to open on a Sunday, when he saw that supermarkets were starting to do the same. At the time, it was a significant commercial risk, and was not an immediate success. 'I think the first Sunday we opened we sold about $500 worth of meat,' says Slater. 'Now it's probably the second biggest day after Saturday for sales.'

One of the many things Rod learnt from Peter was the ability to work relationships. At ZB he very quickly got to know Barry Holland, who was fronting the ads with Peter, and he made sure he fostered that relationship. 'He was very, very good at being straight up in business,' Peter says. 'He always made sure our suppliers got paid on time.'

At an early stage, in a situation that is common with small businesses that expand rapidly, they were flat out with a massive turnover, but weren't making a huge profit, and fell behind in their payments to Affco, their main supplier. 'We owed Affco about $30,000, which was a lot of money in those days, and we didn't have the money to pay them,' Slater says. 'I remember Peter saying to me, "Right mate, we'll go and see them." We sat down with them, explained what was going on, and worked out a plan to repay what was owed. I'm not saying I wouldn't have done that, but he was on the front foot straight away.'

In Rod's mind, Peter was badly misunderstood by the rest of the industry for a long while, and it is only in recent years that the industry has begrudgingly acknowledged his achievements. 'For a long while he was seen as a clown, bordering on being a bit shonky. In fact he was quite the opposite. Jealousy came into it big time, as it does in any industry. Some of the gossip out there was that Rod Slater was the brains behind the outfit, which was absolute bullshit. I'm not saying I didn't contribute, but he would have done it without me. In fact, look what happened when I got out in 1994, apart from still owning one of the shops. So that was a perception that certainly wasn't true.'

Rod also acknowledges the importance integrity played

in the business, where Peter firmly believed that his word was his bond, and whether it turned out to be a good deal or not, a deal was a deal. In those days, that was how the meat industry ran, and in most cases people played the game. Back then you did thousand-dollar deals on trust. 'Peter had a total integrity in his business dealings. Oddly enough, when he negotiated with suppliers I wouldn't describe him as hard-nosed. At times he was almost too fair. Suppliers loved dealing with him because he would pay a reasonable price, but he also used to get offered unbelievable sweetheart deals a less popular person wouldn't even get offered.

'If a supplier had a line of lambs he wanted to get rid of, he'd phone Peter and would usually get a deal. He was never afraid to buy in numbers. If someone rang and offered us 500 lambs that they wanted to be quit of, I'd want to take a hundred, but Peter would say, "No mate, let's get the bloody lot in."'

On one memorable occasion they were offered around 500 bodies of young bull beef, and when Rod arrived at 5 a.m. to start work at the Papakura shop, which was not a small shop, the delivery driver couldn't get the door shut around the huge bodies of beef. 'You couldn't walk around in the shop!' Slater hoots. 'Somehow we had to try to break them down and sell them. The funny thing is that we sold them all.'

The pair had a buyer called Max Freedman, 'a Jewish guy who escaped the Holocaust and came out here,' Rod says. 'He loved Peter. He would go to the sales — those were the days when you were buying live every week at Westfield, and later at Papakura. Max would ring and say, "Vhat do you vant today?" I'd say that Peter wanted 20 lambs, and I'd want the same, and if we could get them at a good price that'd be great.

'Later that day Max would ring again and say, "Is Peter there? Ah Rod, I got you a werry good deal. Five hundred lambs, and I got them at a werry good price."

'I'd wonder what the hell we were going to do with all those lambs. But we sold them — you had to.'

Peter's philosophy was always huge turnover, low margins. 'There are all these rules for business about what you should spend on advertising, but that didn't mean a thing to him,' Rod Slater says.

Peter would spend almost all the profit from one week on advertising the next week, without worrying about it. There was no science behind it, no complicated business theory. It was gut feel, but it was gut feel that worked, based on a gift for giving the customer what they wanted.

'Within supermarkets today, at their weekly meetings, people have told us that one of the first things discussed is what The Mad Butcher specials are for the week. That's how much impact he's had on the meat industry.

'Back in the early days, say 20 years ago, it became obvious he was something special. I'd go somewhere, and be asked what I did. When I said I was a butcher, they'd say, "Do you know the Mad Butcher?" He was a household name even then, and now, you can go anywhere in New Zealand and he's the first name that comes to mind when you talk about meat.

'He's got the personality that loves the attention — he loves being out the front. He enjoys himself the most when he is in the limelight. As a person, it's very difficult to win an argument with him. You can talk about his lack of education, but he always has an answer to come back at you. Having said that, our business relationship only stopped recently, when we sold the Mt Roskill shop, and in all that time we never had an argument that was in real anger.

'That says something for the guy. He went into partnership with me almost against his better judgement, because he does like to be the kingpin, but we stayed very good friends, and we still are.'

Peter agrees. 'Rod was going to be like the silent partner, doing all the office and administration work, and I'd be the front man. In all the time we were partners we never had an argument, and we're still friends, which I'm very proud of. There was never any nastiness. We eventually decided that really we needed to go our own way a bit. So in 1994 he took Takapuna, I took Papakura, and we kept Mt Roskill jointly.'

In all that time, Rod and Peter never worked together in the same shop. 'We are both "alpha male" personalities, and we had to have our space,' Rod says. 'At the beginning he was very clear that the Mad Butcher was him, and don't try to steal that away. I never did. The fact was that I was second fiddle, not in terms of the money we made — that was 50-50 — but in the perception.'

With success, inevitably, came jealousy. As Peter himself admits, a lot of people used to say the Mad Butcher was cheaper because he sold rubbish. 'It's one of the biggest myths about the Mad Butcher, and it's wrong.

'I remember a butcher in Remuera telling a lady our meat wasn't as good a quality as his, when in actual fact our meat was better quality than what he was selling. He was in a little shop getting two bodies of beef a week, and I was getting 200 a week. There was no question who the suppliers were going to look after with quality.

'You don't grow from one shop to 35 by selling rubbish. What I did was take a smaller cut of the profits, but I sold more, and I made more money. There were guys who laughed at me in the early days. They're not around now, and I'm proud of that fact. Our claim to fame now is that we keep the supermarkets honest with their prices.'

Rod Slater agrees. 'The supermarkets all over New Zealand are well aware of Peter now. It's almost a monopoly in supermarkets here, because there are only two groups: the Progressive chain, owned by overseas interests, which is your Woolworths, Foodtown and Countdown, and on the other side you've got the Foodstuffs group — Pak'nSave and New World — where each store is privately owned by a Kiwi.

'That's it. The competition between those two and The Mad Butcher is so strong that the consumer is winning. He's become the benchmark for prices. When he opened up in Christchurch, he was underestimated by the bigwigs down there. They tried to ignore the first store, but the turnover was amazing.'

Price, in Peter's view, is what drives real success. 'Quality and service are important, but price is the most important. We've had not exactly loss leaders, but stuff where our margins were very, very fine. So if we don't sell volume, we don't make money. We're the people who brought cheaper meat prices to most of New Zealand.'

If cheap prices get people into the stores, Peter believes there should be trigger points inside. 'I've never been trained, but I found I had a God-given gift in the store. Signage and packaging are important. You might put balloons or flashing lights around the meat, and it's also how you word the sign. "Rump steak, price slashed today, only $6.99 a kilo." Price slashed, where *slashed* is the word that counts. So the person reading it thinks, "Shit, that's a bargain, I'll buy it."

'We had an example in one of our shops recently, where we had chicken on special. The shop was next to Countdown at Mt Wellington, and they had chicken specials too, but our manager increased the sales from his previous special by signage, and how he marketed it in the store. It can be done.

'When we first went to Christchurch, you couldn't get good deals on meat. Since we went there the whole scene has changed, and that's purely because of The Mad Butcher. The biggest shock I got when we opened in Shirley in Christchurch was how people queued up to get into our shop. They waited 20 minutes to half an hour to get served. The retailers down there didn't bother to match me, but after a few weeks they did — they had to. We did virtually double what we'd bargained for in Shirley.'

There have also been tough times. In 1995, despite big turnover, costs were not being attended to, and the company started to lose money. For the first time staff had to be made redundant. Among those who lost their jobs was Peter and Jan's daughter Angela, who had been working in marketing for the company.

'Murray Deaker rang me, and I broke down crying,' Peter says. 'It was a measure of the man that he cancelled a big meeting he was about to go into and came out to see me instead. Likewise, Leighton Smith offered to do my ads for free. The way his contract was structured he was able to do that. I was very grateful for support like that when I needed it.

'It was a harsh reality. I had to step back into the

business and crank it up again. We probably over-reacted a little bit, because we did have the reserves to deal with it, but because I'd never been in that downward spiral, losing money, I panicked. It's a terrible feeling when you're losing money. Janice has been a rock to me in many ways, but in this particular case I didn't confide in her. She finds the business side stressful, and I didn't want to stress her even more.

'Until the problems with the business came along I could never understand how people could commit suicide. But one night I went out to the factory, and I was going through the spiral of losing money. When you've never been in a situation when you've gone from making good money to losing so much that you feel like it's spiralling out of control, it's very hard to deal with.

'For a split second in the office I did think, maybe it would be better if I committed suicide. Then I said to myself, no, bugger that, I've got to sort this out. I actually said to myself, "I'll eat some of those vegetarian sausages, that'll kill me." I know it sounds weird, but that was what I thought, and the humour helped me snap out of it. Then I just got stuck in and started getting up to go to work at 2 a.m. until we got it sorted out.

'To me, life has been my education. I learnt respect when

I was digging graves. Now I understand how people could commit suicide. The slide in the business really taught me something. How did it happen? To be honest, I'd got my head up my arse a bit, and I'd taken my eye off the ball. It was mainly the factory that was losing money. I'd let guys who were good at the talk take over too much, and when I got the bank statement, I was bloody stunned. The bank balance doesn't lie. The one thing you can rely on for the truth in business is the statement from the bank.

'I was embarrassed that we were losing money, so I rolled my sleeves up and got stuck back in. I've never been a brilliant businessman, but I'm a bloody hard worker, who can work enormous hours.'

The distress wasn't over. For the first time, Peter found he had to let members of his staff go. 'I could put my hand on my mother and father's graves and say that was one of the most traumatic times I've ever had in my life. I had good staff — loyal staff — that I had to make redundant. It came down to the fact that I had to do that, or close the factory altogether. Janice and I were both devastated. I did it to the best of my ability, and I don't mind admitting that I broke down in tears a few times. It was terrible. But some of those people are still friends today.

'With the franchise stores, the reality is that I didn't get to know all the people who worked in them. But with the Mangere shop, and the factory, I knew the people, and I believe I got on well with them.'

If Peter worked for more than 40 years to get customers to flock to his shops, there was at least as much effort needed to get people to work in them. 'You don't have people queuing up to work in a butcher's shop,' he says. 'You do your best, but it's hard.

'I wouldn't say it's got harder in recent years, because it's always been hard. Working in a butcher's shop can be cold, wet work. If you looked at what it's like in an office, where would you rather be? I've had people come and work for me, and say, "Look, I could go on the dole and get more." But you can't start people on top money. They have to earn that.

'There were nowhere near as many women working in butchery when I began. Butchery today is completely different in that respect. There are more women today — not a lot, because it's still a heavy job — but you see a lot more female counter staff today. One thing I learned as an employer is that you have to be more careful about what you say to a woman. I remember talking to a woman once, telling her she had screwed up, and she burst into tears.

'The staff numbers in general turn over a bit and it's a battle to get good staff. They're hard to come by these days, but having said that, we've had some great people. We've got people here who have worked for me for over 20 years. Some become, in a sense, part of the family. With the good people you make an extra effort. I've taken staff to the Fight for Life at $600 a ticket, I've taken staff to NRL finals, and I've sent people to golf courses like Kauri Cliffs. What I've tried to do with my staff is be fair.'

One of the team-building exercises that Peter launched in the 1980s was entering a team he called the Rosella Choppers in a social competition at the Panmure Youth Centre.

In charge of the Panmure basketball programme was New Zealand coach Steve McKean, the first man to coach the Tall Blacks to a win over Australia.

An endlessly enthusiastic American, McKean was quickly entertained by Peter, who he describes as 'one of those guys who could start a fight in an empty house'.

The Choppers were long on feisty, short on real talent, but eventually they won a game.

'In one of the best-quality games in the history of basketball,' says McKean, 'the game was won 5–2. The Butcher got a basket, and you'd have thought after the game they'd won a world title.

'That night the celebrations were unbelievable, and Butch talked me into taking them for a Sunday practice. He said to me, "I can't pay you because then you'd be a professional." But he did bring me about 15 different kinds of meat.

'In the years since, we've become really close friends. He's a special guy, and in those early days, he was flat-out nuts. But you just can't help but love him for his passion.'

One of the most loyal workers Peter ever had was Richard Ferguson, who managed the Mt Roskill shop for a period and then left to run his own pest-control business. Peter had advertised for a manager at Mangere when he was phoned by Richard, applying for the job. Peter told him he was really looking for someone younger, someone with more supermarket experience, but was then struck dumb by a sob in the other man's voice. 'Peter, I really need this job,' Richard managed to say.

Loyalty won the day. Richard was given the job, and from the start until he tragically died of illness several years later, no task was ever a problem for him. If another shop was battling, he would go there in his own time to offer support and ideas. To this day The Mad Butcher shop of the year is awarded the Richard Ferguson Memorial Trophy. Peter still finds it impossible to talk at length about Richard without tears filling his eyes.

Talking of loyalty, Peter has had the same accountancy firm and the same law firm almost from the time he started his own business. 'When I first started out, I had a guy for six or seven months who I thought, in my ignorance, was a qualified accountant. In fact, he just worked in a company — he wasn't qualified. It was a nightmare. If I could give anyone any advice, it would be that you must get a good accountant.

'As a prime example of what a trusted accountant can do, Inland Revenue was going to audit a whole year of GST documents, which would have been time-consuming beyond belief. When I went to them, and they saw who my accountant was, I got the impression they knew we were reputable, so we only had to do a month's worth of documents, which was bad enough, but not as bad as a year.

'It's really important to have a good lawyer, who these days can refer you on to specialists if need be, and a good accountant. My accountants are Milne Maingay, and my law firm is Wadsworth Ray. I first dealt with George Wadsworth there, and then later with John Ray. At Milne Maingay, my first accountant was Peter Ferrif, then I went to David Milne, and now I'm with Brent Maingay.'

Grant Waring, the foreman at The Mad Butcher's Holmes Road sausage factory in Manurewa, has been working for Peter for 23 years. A fanatical stockcar enthusiast, Grant laughs when asked what sort of a boss Peter has been. 'He's straight up and down. We've had our moments. I've even chucked the job in a few times. But if he nuts off, then ten minutes later it's, "Aw, I didn't mean that. See you later, I'm off."

'I'd say he was a very generous boss, by the standards of people that I know who work for other companies. My brother worked for 18 years for the same company, and when it was sold it was a case of, "We don't care how long you've been here. You can like it or lump it."

The likely lads. Paul Turner and Peter, on the town in Wellington in 1961.

Peter lives the outdoor life, on a farmer's property west of Wanganui. The farmer was happy to see Peter and his mates, and the only rule was 'you shoot one of my bulls, and I'll shoot you'.

In 1965 when a Kiwi male turned 21 his parents presented him with the key to the door, and there was a party to celebrate.

Love is in the air. Peter and Janice Granich, who almost turned down a blind date because 'she wasn't into gravediggers' which Peter was when they met in 1964.

Wedding day, 1965. Would Jan look so happy if she knew they'd have company on their honeymoon?

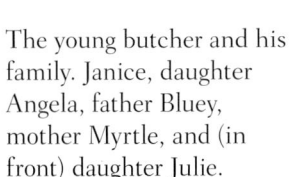

The young butcher and his family. Janice, daughter Angela, father Bluey, mother Myrtle, and (in front) daughter Julie.

Starting to put the Mad into Mad Butcher. Peter in the Radio Pacific studio, at home in earphones, and (bottom photo) talking up the mighty Mangere Hawks.

Expansion was soon needed at the Massey Road Mad Butcher store, and Peter hams it up with his builder, who has apparently missed the 'No smoking' signs.

Gossip maestro David Hartnell cuts the ribbon for the opening of the Mt Roskill shop, a day that has been described as being 'totally out of control'.

The heart of the Mad Butcher empire first really beat here, at what was originally Rosella Meats in Massey Road, Mangere East. At the shop before dawn, and there after it closed, Peter gave customers the full benefit of his unique style. 'I can honestly say I always tried to treat people the way I'd like to be treated myself.'

Behind the scenes at Massey Road Janice helps Peter and the team pack. At the back on the left-hand side is a veteran Mad Butcher worker, Tom Kuklinski, while at the rear right is Chris Cummings, and in the foreground (back to camera) is another long-serving butcher, George Melrose.

Pleased to meet you. At Massey Road from left to right are Keith Mitchell, Graham Cartwright, Peter, Tom Kuklinski, and Jim Wade.

'We had a happy time,' says daughter Angela (left) of the childhood her and sister Julie enjoyed.

Happiness is the mighty Mangere Hawks winning the 1989 Auckland rugby league Roope Rooster title.

Forget a loaf of bread and a jug of wine; what you need are the prime ox ribbons from the 1985 Easter Show.

Sports stars of many codes helped endorse the Mad Butcher brand, and 1987 World Cup-winning All Black Grant Fox was one.

'Some people can put their heart and soul into a job and get no reward, or recognition for it. It's not like that with Peter. He called me in one day, started ranting and raving, and I wondered what I'd done. But he knew my car was on its last legs, and he just said, "Here's $10,000 — go and buy yourself another car."

'He's sent me on a trip to Vanuatu, and I've been to the rugby and the league as a bonus. It's something you don't expect, but it's nice to go along and be part of it. I'm proud to work for him.'

For Dan Adams, who came to work for The Mad Butcher as operations manager from a stint with a major supermarket chain, a major incentive was the chance to work in a firm where you can be urgent, be nimble on your feet, and you can effect change. 'If you work for the big corporates, you have to go through marketing, accounting, the whole lot. Here, and I think it's one of the things Peter enjoys, if you want to do it, you do it. Perhaps that's how he won the race — he could get things done quicker than the guy down the road.

'He has a saying: "Let's not wait, let's do it today." People ask me, "Well, how do you do it?" And I say, "If it has to be done, you just do it." That's what we do here. Peter is a hard taskmaster, and he drives a hard bargain, but you always know where you stand with him. For me personally, what I look for is consistency. You know what you're getting into is head down, bum up.

'But this company also has the ability to enjoy itself. When there's time to let your hair down, no expense is spared. If people are motivated by money, the only way you can keep them enthused is to keep giving them more money. Everyone reaches a level where you can't get any more. There has to be something in addition to that.'

Adams is impressed by the thoughtfulness of the unexpected gifts that can arrive. 'Peter gave me golf clubs one time, because he knows that I love golf. Every time I play now, I think, "Gee, Peter's good to me." He does go out of his way to give you things you're going to enjoy.'

Best of all was a moment that took Adams back to the days when he was a young league player, taking the field in a Fox Memorial final, the premier award in Auckland league. 'I came here one day, and Peter said I had to go in and present the Fox trophy on a Sunday. I never thought in my wildest dreams I'd do that.'

Peter freely concedes that he's not corporate high flyer. 'I'm not Michael Fay, but you've got to take every race for what it is. I doubt that any of the big businessmen have had the fun building their business that I've had. I've enjoyed my sporting contacts, plus I've done a lot in the community. I think it's pretty rare for a businessman to do what I've done, which is to get into the other things. Most people are so focused on getting their business up and running that they don't have the time for anything else.'

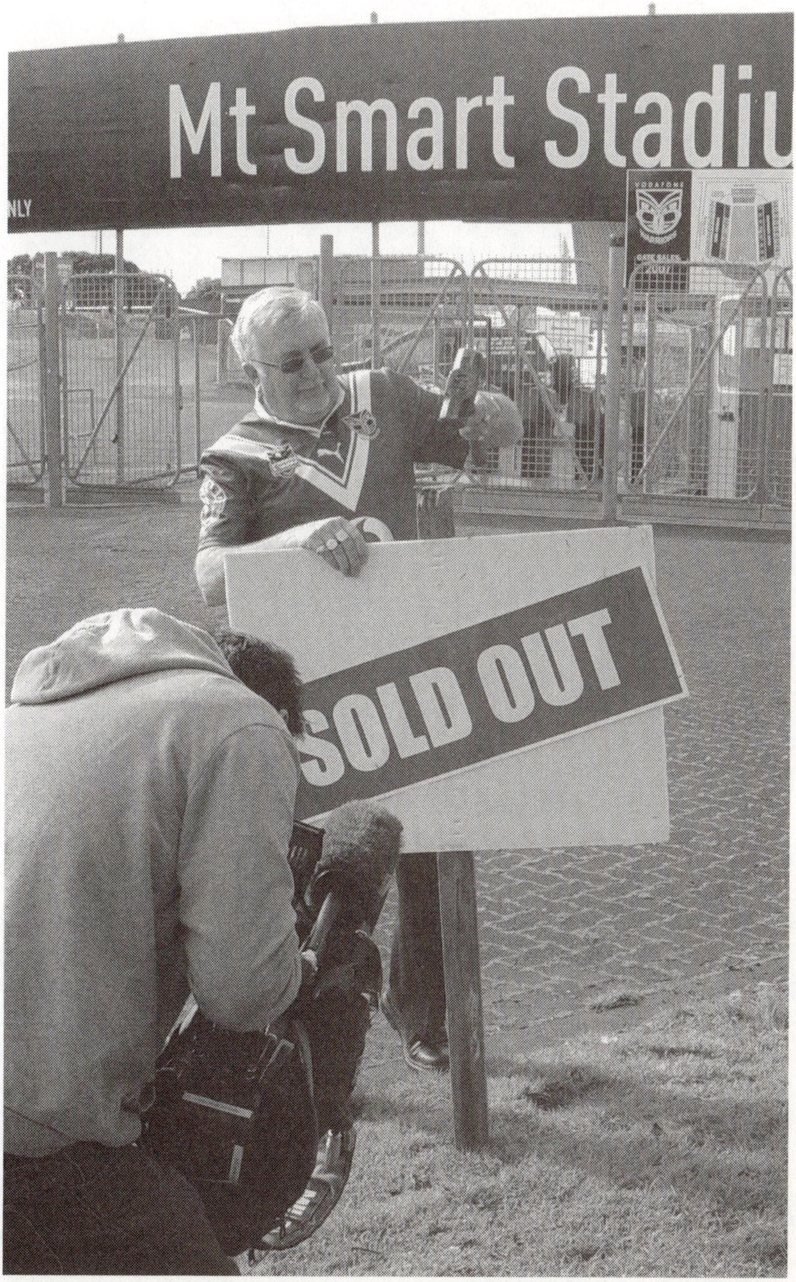
Mt Smart Stadiu
SOLD OUT

6

Mangere

Nobody can remember who he was, but many, many sports should be grateful to a committee man from the Mangere East Rugby League Club. The unknown official was the man who started Peter Leitch on a sponsorship trail that would run from club league to boxing, to soccer, to rugby, to world softball championships.

In the late 1960s the committee man hit up a young, manically hard-working Peter at his Rosella Road shop for some sponsorship. 'I had no real idea then what sponsorship was,' says Peter. 'He explained that if I gave him a bit of meat, he'd give me a plug at the club. I said, "Great, I'll be into that." I've always believed that the community is like your garden. If you put a bit in, you'll get rewards back.'

The club he was helping, the Mangere East Hawks, had fielded its first teams in 1964 out in that hard southern suburb, the sort of blue-collar area that Peter was entirely at home within. Jack Neal, the foundation president of the club, was a newspaper advertising executive who had spent over 20 years as an administrator and coach in the game, and one of many who were astounded by the way the club took off. 'It was beyond our wildest dreams,' says Neal. 'We'd hoped for six or seven teams, and in the first year we fielded fourteen.'

By 1971 Mangere East was building a 600-square-metre clubhouse, largely funded by bottle drives, raffles at the Star and Criterion hotels in Otahuhu, cake stalls, and selling second-hand clothes at the newly opened Mangere Town Centre. Every penny counted. The club secretary, Joyce Robinson, used to darn the senior players' socks when they got holes. 'I probably darned hundreds of pairs,' she once said. 'We couldn't afford just to throw them out.'

As a sponsor, Peter started to go to the club — 'for the odd beer,' as he says — and quickly found out they were his kind of people. A great love affair with the game had started. 'The people in rugby league are working class,' says Peter. 'To this day most of my friends are working class. Even in the professional era of league, the guys aren't from silver-spoon families. To say the game took over my life would be an understatement. And that was where it all started — at Mangere.

'My passion is a combination of the game itself and the people who are involved in it. No question that it was the Mangere East guys who I first became friends with. I was soon going to all the games, and eventually I became the major sponsor. At one stage I was even managing the top team. There have been some funny, good times at the club — giving a bit of cheek, having a laugh. I've even danced on the tables!'

The biggest star at the Mangere East Hawks was Olsen Filipaina, and the bond he would form with Peter was extraordinary. Olsen started as a seven-year-old with the Hawks, lured by the promise of a free hamburger and Fanta after every game. He was quickly a sensation as a teenager, using his massive thighs and powerful hips to swat away tacklers. At the time one of the most popular TV programmes in the world was *All in the Family,* an American comedy about a dysfunctional family headed by a grumpy, right-wing father called Archie Bunker. Olsen, to his footy mates, was Archie Bumper.

In the *Auckland Star* newspaper, he was described as 'the star attraction of Auckland rugby league. Opposing teams could never figure out how to stop him in full flight. In the end it seemed the only safe way would be to throw a net around him.'

In 1978 and 1979 the Hawks made two Roope Rooster grand finals (a prestigious pre-season competition for Auckland's premier league clubs), and Filipaina is in no doubt over who was one of the major contributors. 'Peter did a hell of a lot for the club. As you know, he doesn't do things in a quiet way, and it was great for Mangere. I'm sure that the reason the Hawks were so successful was because Peter was so involved. He had a real love for the people in the area, and they loved him.'

In 1977 Olsen became the first Mangere East player to be selected for the Kiwis. Not long afterwards, Peter was at the club when Filipaina, who was never one to leap at the chance to speak in public, did something unusual — he took the microphone. Peter, like all the other club members, listened intently.

'He starts talking about this bloke who helped him out, this great guy who had done so much for him,' says Peter.

'He says he wanted to repay this man who was at the club that night by giving him his first Kiwi jersey. Everyone was looking around, wondering who this great person could be. Well, you could have bowled me over with a feather when he calls out my name. When he gave that jersey to me, there were tears in my eyes.'

Today, Filipaina makes it clear his decision was no spur-of-the-moment whim. 'Peter was always there in my corner. He'd turn up for all my games, to the stage where he became like a second father to me. I just kept on making the rep side and, as well as my parents, Peter would always be there at the games.'

They got on really well together. 'If I was having a bad game and I heard that voice, I'd feel better, and would call for the ball to run with it. Week after week he helped lift me. You could be playing a game anywhere, and you'd hear his voice in the crowd every time — you couldn't miss him.

'He calls a spade a spade. He was always honest about how a game went, and when you got a rap from Peter it was a buzz. For me, if he praised me, it would lift me for the game the next week, and the relationship got stronger all the time.'

Filipaina was so good he became one of the first young Polynesian players from New Zealand to be head-hunted in 1980 for the Sydney competition. It wasn't a happy time, although he stuck it out for eight years, strictly for the money. In a 2006 interview for Sydney's *Rugby League Week* magazine, Filipaina said, 'When I was training at Balmain, blokes would deliberately try to put me out of action during opposed sessions. They were pissed off with me taking their spot and were deliberately trying to injure me. I spent a month playing with a cracked sternum that was delivered by an elbow at training.'

Racial sledging was the norm. 'I was called a black bastard, a nigger — I even had cans thrown at me.' Test-match football for the Kiwis was the only way he could strike back, and the legendary Wally Lewis, who made the bad mistake of refusing to shake hands with Filipaina the first time they opposed each other in a test, was one who especially suffered. As Filipaina says, 'When he didn't shake my hand, I thought, "Right mate, I'm going to become your worst nightmare." And I did.'

The Mad Butcher also had a role to play at test level. 'He still had the same effect on me,' Filipaina says. 'Even though they said I had up-and-down form in Sydney, when I came home I'd use his inspiration for the test, and then try to carry that within me when I went back to club football. I was in and out of the top grade, but when I spoke to Peter he always fired me up. When I came back to New Zealand for a test, I always looked forward to catching up with him. If I went for a jog past the shop and he was there, that was a bonus for me. But if I missed him, I made sure that at least I phoned and caught up with him.'

The friendship has stayed strong to this day. 'When Peter came over with the Warriors the first time, he rang me and I went down to see him. He introduced me to the players, and told them, "Here he is, boys, the best rugby league player to ever come out of New Zealand." I said, "Aw gee, I don't know about that."'

Before Peter forged his relationship with the members at Mangere East, he didn't make a habit of going to games at Carlaw Park. That soon changed, and by the end of the 1980s he was promoting the Mad Butcher's pre-season tournament. He would blitz radio stations and newspapers with information about upcoming games, and the crowds steadily grew.

If there was ever proof that he would put his body on the line for the game he'd come to love, then it was proved during a late round of the 1988 pre-season tournament.

I saw the drama unfold at first hand. To his horror, Peter found two rival gang members, massive hulks who had both played in the curtain-raiser, shaping up on the concourse where fans were walking past to the old wooden main stand at Carlaw Park.

'They were tough, bad dudes,' he says. 'I'd spent a week promoting a family day, and I just didn't need a fight. They were ready to get it on, and because I was the promoter I had to go between them, and separate them. You heard the term "put your balls in the vice"? Well, I was certainly in that category, and the vice was shutting very quickly. I was lucky that there was, deep down, an element of respect for me from them for what was happening in rugby league. So they went outside and had their scrap in the car park.'

They say the bravest man is someone who is scared but does the right thing anyway. Peter was ashen when the two giants lumbered away, but it was obvious to me as a spectator that they would only come to grips over his potentially unconscious body.

'There was another time at Mangere East, when we used to rope the ground off,' Peter recalls. 'We had a couple of gang members who refused to pay their two dollars. The guy on the gate was too scared to do anything. So I went over to speak to them, and they treated me like a Neville Nobody.

I had a friend who had done some work with the gangs, so I rang him up, and next thing a car pulls up and drags the guys away. When I look back on it, I'd have to say they were two times when I was shitting bricks. But sometimes you just have to do that. Love me or hate me, I genuinely love the game, and I want to do the right thing by it.'

The most obvious example of Peter putting a large chunk of his money where his mouth is came in 1988, when, sick of people constantly complaining about the quality of the weekly league programme, he took it over.

Eight months and $100,000 later he was a wiser, if poorer, man.

There's a legend that a magazine publisher once won Lotto, and, when asked what he planned to do, said he'd just keep publishing until all the money was gone.

Peter knows the feeling. 'It hurt big time,' he says now. 'It was a nightmare, and what I lost then was a bundle, believe me. It was a learning curve, and, looking back, I did it for the wrong reasons. I did it with my heart, not my head.'

What he quickly discovered was that league fans were reluctant to buy the magazine, a lesson that came like a slap in the face when he visited one of the clubs where the magazine was available for sale.

He had gone to the trouble of having a cardboard box made for the magazine to sit on the club bar. To his initial delight the box was empty.

'That's great, mate,' Peter said to the barman, 'you've sold all the magazines.'

Without any apparent embarrassment the barman said, 'No, they're all out while guys are reading them. They put them back when they've finished.'

Working with a print broker, Peter worked to get the magazine's content to what he felt was needed.

Today he believes he was looking to the wrong area when he tapped some of the country's top league journalists for help. Barry Clark was one, while Tony Gordon, then the coach of the Kiwis, contributed a column.

But the money in the bank with magazines, Peter now realises, comes from selling advertising, and that was something he was trying to do himself. The time he could spare for selling the ads was nowhere near enough.

'The fact is you can make money if you put out a magazine that doesn't have good stories, but has a lot of ads. No matter how good the writing is, if you don't have ads you'll lose money.

'If I was to start a magazine tomorrow I'd go and get the best salesman in town to head it up.'

The world is full of magazines that have closed down early in the face of mounting losses. With the league programme Peter stuck it out to the end of his season's contract.

'I like to be a man of my word. I wouldn't let them down, so I kept it going, no matter how much it hurt. I'd thought the league public would support it, but they didn't.'

In 1990 it wasn't his body but his business brains and energy that were needed to stave off the potential demise of Peter's beloved Hawks. The club's finances had become a disaster area. Outstanding debts had mounted to $160,000, and several creditors were in a situation where, if they'd called in what they were owed, they could have closed the Hawks down. Peter, for the first and only time in his life, became an administrator, chairing a four-man rescue committee.

'To be fair, that committee may not have been within the regulations of the club. But we couldn't wait around for the red tape. Sometimes you just have to do that. I've had three great loves in my life: my family, my business, and rugby league, and I think I've done some good things for rugby league.'

A plan was thrashed out for Mangere. The debtors agreed to give the club breathing space, a bar manager was appointed for the first time, and personality nights, featuring superstars Peter had come to know, like Wally Lewis and Mal Meninga, drew league fans from all over Auckland, enthusing even disillusioned club members.

The masterstroke was a raffle for club sponsorship. Instead of facing the almost impossible task of a suburban sports club hitting up one business for $30,000 worth of sponsorship, 150 raffle tickets were sold at $200 each, the winner getting the naming rights, $1000 worth of free radio advertising, and season tickets to Carlaw Park.

Within two years, Mangere East was debt free, and won the Auckland Rugby League's Autex award for being the best-managed club in Auckland. 'They'd got in the crap and they wanted me to help them get out of it,' says Peter. 'So we did that. We got them out of it in two years.'

But human nature, being the strange beast it is, caused the successful rescue mission to unleash the green-eyed monster. 'They had an AGM and some guy questioned my tactics, said we hadn't kept members well enough informed, that sort of thing,' Peter says. 'I was upset that my credibility was called into question, and I parted with the club for a little bit. I had a year with Northcote as the major sponsor.'

Neil Carpenter was the chairman of the Hawks at the time, and worked with Peter on the emergency committee. 'The club was basically in the cart,' Carpenter says. 'We were a long way into the ditch — it was pretty bloody awful. We slogged like crazy and more or less got it back on track, but we did upset a few people along the way, because I suppose you could say we more or less took over. That upset a few people, but we just had to do it — the place was a real shambles.

'Anyway, when the AGM came around, a couple of people got stuck in, and Peter was the one who copped it. You know what he's like — he wasn't about to stand for that — and he had no hesitation in telling people what they could do. In the end, he got so hot under the collar that he walked out. To be honest I didn't know what to do because I'd just been elected chairman, and of course I'm trying to calm things down and I knew we had to get Peter back into the fold.

'I mean, here was the guy who had made all these things happen for the club. We'd had Mal Meninga out there, and Wally Lewis was another one. Of course, people had had to pay to come to hear them speak, but these were probably the two biggest names in the game at the time. Did they give up their time to help out the Mangere East Hawks? I don't think so. They were there to help Peter out.

'But what can you do? When people get their noses in a knot, there's not much to be done, especially when this one is raking up that one. But you know what? Peter was great. Despite what had happened and being accused of being a dictator and that sort of thing, he never held any of it against me. He knew it wasn't me, but I was bloody sad about it actually, because you could see he was really hurt. I think it broke his heart a wee bit.

'We got him back full-time eventually. He did come round, but it took nearly 18 months or so, and even then he was a bit reluctant. To be honest, I don't think he ever really fully recovered. He held those responsible in contempt, even when he was back helping. I think for a guy like Peter to be accused of doing something out of self-interest, for selfish reasons, that's probably about as big an insult as you could chuck at a bloke like him.'

It was reported at the time that Peter had washed his hands of Mangere altogether, but that wasn't true. 'I kept watching them, and I still do,' Peter says. 'I continued sponsoring them, and still do — I gave them $7000 this year. To this day, I'll still go out in the weekend and watch them play.'

Rugby league, like many sports in New Zealand, has suffered from political infighting. As a man who has often been the public face of the game, there have been many opportunities for Peter to attack people in the sport. 'But I never have,' he says. 'There have been plenty of times when I could have bagged the game, but I wouldn't do it, because I don't want publicity that's bad for the game. I have a genuine loyalty to rugby league, and I've never had agendas. All I've ever wanted is what's good for the game.

'A thing that really annoys me is when people say that rugby league has been good to me. I've had great memories, had some good times, been lucky enough to manage the Kiwis — which was an outstanding time in my life — and made some great friends in the game, but I reckon that I've been good for rugby league too. Some people think I've prospered from rugby league, but I haven't.'

The reality is that every time Peter talked about rugby league on the radio when he was doing an ad, he was paying for the time. How much paid time he's given to league struck home when new company owner Mike Morton asked Peter to spend less time on league on air, and more time on the meat specials.

Morton had done the maths. Some of the phone-outs cost as much as $400, and there would be times when what amounted to $300 worth of the call would be devoted to league. Every time he put something about rugby league in an ad in the paper, he was paying, and there was less space for promoting the meat. Do the sums even roughly, and the final figure Peter's spent to promote the game he loves staggers the mind.

He's never been tempted to take up a controlling position in the game. 'I've tried to stay neutral at all times in league, and I've never gone on a board because I couldn't handle the political side of it. There have been some great administrators in rugby league. I thought [former New Zealand Rugby League chairman] Ron McGregor was a gentleman, a fantastic man. I had great respect for [former NZRL chairman] George Rainey too. In fact, I think George was the best leader the game has come under. He was a dictator, but he wanted nothing but the best for the sport.'

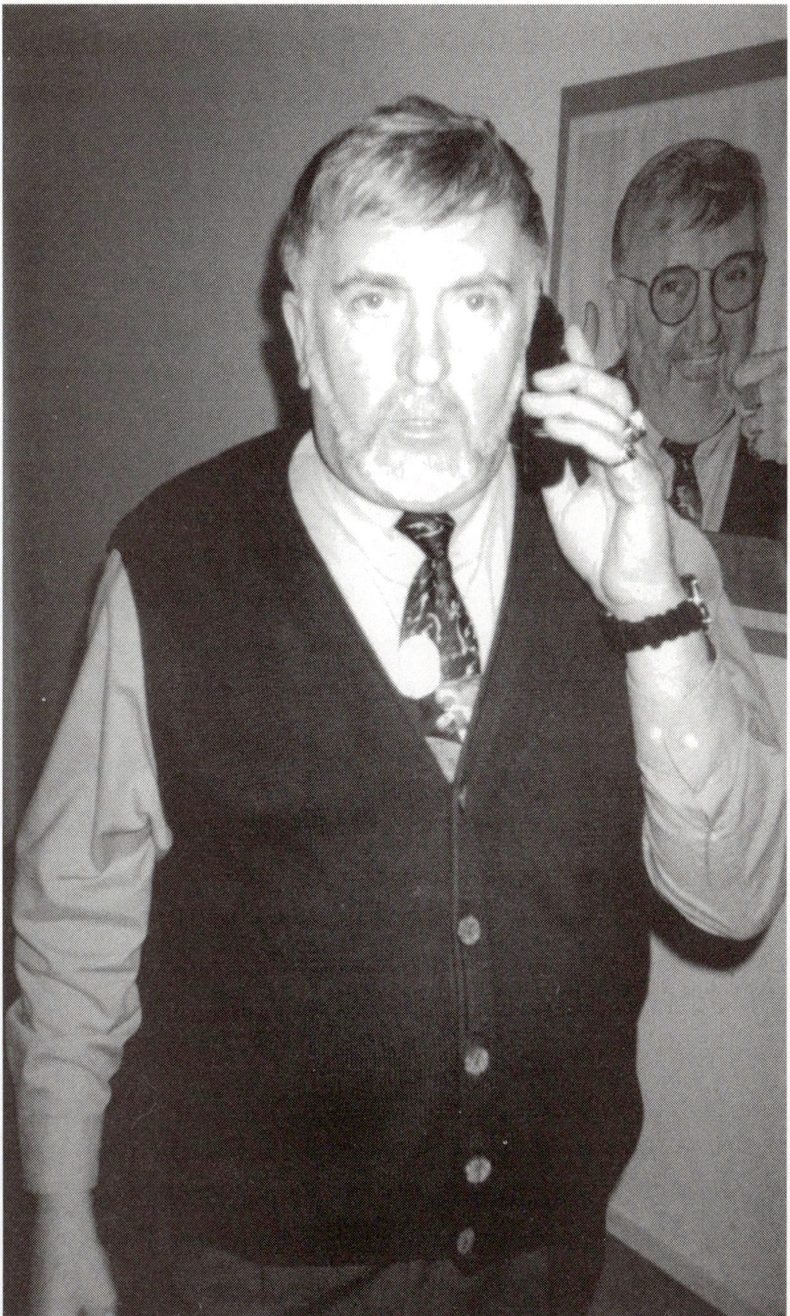

7

Television

A LASTING IMAGE of Peter Leitch on television was one the camera crew didn't want to shoot. In the middle of shooting *The Money Game,* he was staying overnight in a hotel in central Auckland. After a day frantically working the telephones to get a fund-raising luncheon off the ground, he retired to soak in a hot bath. 'Take a shot of this,' he said to the cameraman.

'They'll never use it,' was the reply. But arguing with the Butcher when he's sure of his ground is a pointless exercise. 'Take the shot,' Peter insisted, 'and let the producers decide whether to use it or not.'

Sure enough, they did use it, and a naked, soaped-up

butcher, if not the stuff of dreams, was such a memorable image that for years afterwards it was the first thing strangers would mention whenever the programme was discussed. It was the topic of choice for talkback radio callers the day after the show aired.

'I said to the cameraman at the time, "Mate, this is what'll make me stick out on the show." And sure enough, it was what everyone was talking about when that episode went to air,' Peter laughs. It was yet another example of the Mad Butcher's uncanny ability to seize an opportunity out of thin air and make the most of it.

The Money Game was a reality game show in which millionaire entrepreneurs were given $10,000 each and three days to turn it into as much money as they could. It was produced by Julie Christie, New Zealand's queen of reality television, for Touchdown Productions, and Peter found it a nerve-racking experience.

'Jan and I were on holiday in Fiji, and the producer rang there around four times trying to get me on the show,' he says. 'Apparently Julie Christie had someone else in mind, but they pulled out. The story I heard, right or wrong, was that someone at TVNZ said, "What about the Mad Butcher?" Darryl McEwen, who was working as a producer at Touchdown, rang and pestered me. At first I didn't want to do it, but in the end I agreed, and one of the reasons I did was actually just to get him off my back!'

The details of what would be involved were vague, to say the least. 'You really were left to your own devices. You could go where you liked, do what you liked. There was seed money from the television people, and you kept what you made. But I gave all of my money to charity.

'On the first day we went to Auckland airport. I didn't meet the other contestants until then. One of the others was a young guy who managed Red Bull, a young, very confident guy, and the other was a woman who was even more confident. I thought I was going to get creamed. I've never worked so hard in my life to win something. I didn't want to come out last.

'We flew to Christchurch and hopped in a van. They drove us up through Arthur's Pass and dropped us off in the middle of nowhere on the West Coast. I decided to hitch-hike, and a young girl stopped. She'd never heard of the Mad Butcher until, believe it or not, the week before. It turned out she worked for a timber company, and they were looking for someone to come down and do a speech. One of the guys at her work had said, "What about that Mad Butcher guy from Auckland?" and they'd got talking about it.

'She said to me, "You're not the Mad Butcher, are you?" I said I was and gave her a cap that one of the Warriors had given me. Part of the deal we struck was that her firm paid me to give a speech, which went into the pot for the charity.

'The young guy from Red Bull tried to pick up whitebait on the Coast — he was going to sell it in Auckland. The woman who did promotional work wanted to get a celebrity interview and sell it to a women's magazine. I thought, "Well, Auckland's my town, so that's where I'll head to." I had a bit of time to get things organised. I did everything from selling apples to auctioning a Stacey Jones jersey at the Albion Hotel.'

One of the show's cameramen was almost reduced to tears when Peter was selling apples at the Manukau City Centre. An elderly Samoan man approached Peter and said, 'You're the Mad Butcher, and I know that you'll be giving this money to someone who needs it. I'm going to give you all I've got.' The man turned his pockets out, and handed Peter $1.85. Peter admits to being a little choked up himself.

If selling apples tugged at the heartstrings, it was a luncheon put on for the New Zealand team when it arrived back from the Commonwealth Games in Manchester that hit the money jackpot. 'I got a good deal on the catering,' Peter says. 'When you've got a TV camera recording everything, it works well for you.'

At the end of the show the cash was counted, and the deal was that each entrepreneur could keep the profit. The celebrity-interviewing woman had made $4561, the Red Bull manager had made $9302, but when the result for the Butcher was announced he leapt in the air. He'd made $35,071, and immediately announced he would be giving the lot to charity, which he did.

Good Morning on Television One, fronted by Mary Lambie, was the first time Peter appeared on television on a regular basis. His four-minute segments were paid advertisements — advertorials, in the jargon of television — but you might not have thought that as a viewer.

Strictly speaking, the only person Peter should have been talking to was Alison Leonard, later to win a wider profile as one of the judges on *Dancing with the Stars*, whose role it was to speak with the advertisers.

Mary Lambie recalls: 'Peter was the only one we crossed the line with during the advertorial parts of the show. That speaks volumes for him, really — he was just such an entertainment package. On many occasions, given what he was forking out for the time, he'd spend the time not talking about meat. He'd promote the campaign to help with glue ear, and untold other charities he supported.

'Of course the Warriors were a great topic for him. I didn't know the difference between league, union, or Aussie Rules until Peter came along. He got me along to the games, and got me absorbed in league. I think he's a treat of a man, one of those truly captivating individuals. With Pete it takes a while to strike up a rapport, but once it's there, it's there for good.

'He'd ring me on Christmas Day, when I'd have my phone turned off, and leave a message just saying, "Hope you're having a great day." I thought it was so remarkable that he was doing that with loads of people, when most of us are battening down the hatches and switching off from the rest of the world.

'One occasion I'll always remember came at a time when we'd established a very good friendship. I was wearing some gorgeous creation I was going to have to give back, of course, and he said, "You look nice today, Mary."

'I said, "You know the business, Pete — it's all about fluffery and looking good. The content doesn't matter — it's just about looks." We were basically just taking the piss out of TV.

'Peter said, "It *is* about looks, Mary."

'I said, "You're right, Peter. It's how you look — you have to have the flash clothes. It doesn't matter what's coming out of your mouth."

'He said, "How good do you think I look, talking about things coming out of your mouth?" And he proceeded to take his false teeth out of his mouth on national television! I didn't even know he *had* false teeth. They were gone — there were just gums — and there was this really tight shot of his mouth with no teeth, talking about the glamour of television! There was just a deadly silence, and then everyone started screaming with laughter.

'I blurted out, "God, Pete, put your teeth back in!"

'He'd caught me completely by surprise. I thought it was just the funniest thing that ever happened on the show. It wasn't one of those behind-the-scenes things, where the audience is left behind, and it's an in-joke, which is the worst thing that can happen. We were all in on the joke.

'I believe Peter's the classic example of a true "man of the people". He's done so well in business because he's made it all about the people. He'd be the first to say he's not the Business Brain of Britain, but he's got something that all the courses in the world can't teach, making it about the people.

'And God, is that man generous to a fault. Nothing was a problem if he thought it was for a good cause. My parents came in one day to sit in on the show. Peter had no idea who they were. He came up and introduced himself, greeted them like long-lost friends, and made them feel completely at home. Then he found out they were from Wellington. He insisted they should come out to the sausage factory, and pick up some sausages to take home. He was doing that all the time — the man has enviable energy. I just think he's a remarkable man, and a great study of what enthusiasm can achieve in business.'

Alison Leonard, a woman with what could fairly be called a wicked sense of humour, had a running gag with Peter. She was, she claimed, his unacknowledged love child. At a charity roast, she purported to be appalled by what she claimed was a coldness he displayed towards her, compared with the friendliness he showed other panel members. 'They said terrible things about you,' she sniffed. 'They've called you terrible names. One person called you an attention-seeking media slut, and all I ever called you was "Daddy".'

In fact, she says, she had a lot to be grateful to Peter for. Without him, for example, she might never have discovered an urgent need for some dental work. 'One day he decided that I was saying far too much, and to shut me up he picked up an ice block, and said, "Oi, be quiet!" and jammed it in my mouth. He was horrified when I screamed with pain. I'd discovered, long before the dentist did, that I had the start of a nasty hole in one of my teeth.'

Leonard recalls that changing on set was never an embarrassment for the Butcher. 'He'd turn up every week for his advertorial, and I guess you would have expected that all he'd talk about would be his wonderful shops and the meat he had for sale,' she says. 'But on any given day, he might decide to chat about backing New Zealand, or the Warriors, or goodness knows what.

'He'd turn up, lug all the meat into the studio, and then realise he wanted to wear a Warriors jersey for the item. He wouldn't bother with a dressing room. The shirt would come off, and we'd all have the delight of the sight of Mr Mad in his singlet, with his lovely chest hair, arm hair, and back hair waving in the breeze. Then he'd taunt everybody by undoing his trousers to tuck his shirt in. He was always looking for ways to wind people up.

'His teeth played a big part in the jokes. One day we ended up in the kitchen on the set, and it was near his birthday. I baked him a cake, and turned it into a field for the Warriors — I used a scorched almond for the ball, that sort of thing. I made the grass by colouring coconut, and on top of this lovely green icing I used pictures I'd cut out from a Warriors brochure, and placed them strategically all over the field.

'I think he was actually a wee bit touched by the cake and, because he felt a little embarrassed by the fact, he decided to be a bit silly about it. He pulled out his top teeth, yelled "Give us a kiss!" and lunged at me. I grabbed the teeth out of his hand, shouted "Mary, catch these!" and threw them to her. There was a frantic dash by Mr Mad to get them back. He's a terrible tease, and he likes to shock you, so early on I decided to make attack the best means of defence.'

One of the most chaotic shows involving the Butcher, however, couldn't be blamed on him. Animal behaviourist Mark Vette was a regular guest on the show. Vette is the man who trains many animals for television commercials, whose most famous protégé was Hercules, the dog used in the Toyota 'bugger' advertisements. In a near-perfect example of Sod's Law, someone booked Vette and Hercules to appear just before Peter's chat with Alison Leonard.

'Nobody had really thought about the fact that the Mad Butcher would be in the studio, with a tabletop covered in raw meat at the same time as a dog, whose primal instincts would be to eat the raw meat,' says Leonard. 'So there we were, with the country's best-ever trained dog sitting with Mark on a couch talking with Mary, and this poor dog's nose is twitching like a flag waving in the breeze. Mark is trying to show the nation how well behaved, how wonderfully trained Hercules is, and he was a fantastic dog.

'But then his natural instincts kicked in, and Hercules just zoomed off Mary's set, and straight to the Mad Butcher and me, much to the Mad Butcher's delight. He started screaming, "That dog's bright all right! He knows great meat when he sees it. I told ya the meat was great!"'

Like Mary Lambie, Alison Leonard became a fervent Warriors fan. 'Mr Mad persuaded me they needed me, and I came to agree with him.'

For five years the Mad Mad Butcher has been a regular feature on *Pulp Sport*, the award-winning television show fronted by Bill and Ben (Jamie Lineham and Ben Boyce).

The Mad Mad Butcher (Lineham with 'horrible creped hair taped to my face'), as hard as it might be to imagine it, is an even more hyped version of Peter, with the twist that he always does things that are, literally, mad.

In the cause of comedy the Mad Mad Butcher has been used as a punching bag by boxer Shane Cameron, rucked to bits by a Waikato rugby forward pack, and peppered at close range with cricket balls by Black Cap Nathan Astle.

The character first emerged as a 30-second ad lib on Radio Sport, where *Pulp Sport* began. Ben was the frontman then, with Lineham providing sketches.

'With the Mad Mad Butcher I started raving about something,' says Lineham, 'and then at the end of the sketch my head exploded. We played it a couple of times on the show.'

There had been no contact with Peter before the show, but there was soon afterwards.

Ben's girlfriend, Amanda, now his fiancée, was a sales secretary at 91ZM, where Peter advertised. When Peter was talking to a sales rep, Amanda told him how funny the sketch had been on *Pulp Sport*.

'We were sitting at our desks when the Mad Butcher

suddenly appears, saying, "Are you the fuckin' bastards that have been takin' the piss out of me?" We were sitting there, shaking a bit, thinking he was upset.'

They played the tape, Peter loved it, and he asked for a copy to be sent to sausage heaven, the company's head office, which, Bill and Ben decided, was the seal of approval.

When the duo moved to television, they made a pilot which included the Mad Mad Butcher proving how mad he was by jumping off a building.

'We did a really hokey version by throwing a dummy off a building,' says Lineham, 'then exchanging it for me jumping up and screaming how mad I was.'

There would be another pilot before the first *Pulp Sport* appeared on Sky television, and just one item survived through two pilots to the actual show — the Mad Mad Butcher.

'I thought it was fantastic,' says Peter. 'How much do I love it? That much that when I bought a brand new car, which was worth over $200,000, I agreed to go driving down the motorway eating what was supposed to be pet food, spraying it all over the new upholstery.'

For five years the character stayed in *Pulp Sport*, an eternity in television. An end is only likely because dreaming up something else to do to prove he's mad has, according to

Lineham, not only become harder and harder mentally, but also more physically painful.

'You can do it with trick photography, or you can do it for real,' says Lineham, 'but the real ones do seem to be the most funny, at least for everyone else.'

There's no end in sight, however, for the Bad Mutcher, who appears twice a week on Radio Hauraki's breakfast radio show, courtesy of Morning Pirate Willie De Witt.

'There are quite a few people round the building who like to do a Mad Butcher imitation,' says Hauraki's manager, Mike Regal, 'but Willie's is the one that we all agree is actually funny.'

The Bad Mutcher basically talks sport, and in the time he's been on air has always signed off with news of a new shop opening. If the Mad Butcher has opened shops throughout New Zealand, his radio alter ego, Mr Bad, has several million shops, most of them in hot spots like Somalia.

The latest foray into television for Peter came with *A Mad Business*, a show for TVNZ that was the brainchild of the Top Shelf Production Company. Producer Sheila McLeod says, 'We wanted someone who was prominent in business to be a troubleshooter for people in their own businesses.

'In the past some of the business shows had been a little bit boring. We wanted a point of difference — someone who would bring real life to the show, and make the information easily understood by everybody.'

Peter was happy to oblige. 'I get people who ring and ask me for advice, so I thought, "If we're going to give advice, let's do it on TV." We did it for the right reasons though — we didn't do it for the publicity. We've made our name now. The Mad Butcher is a credible name. I get sick of people who reckon I do everything for publicity. I've turned down TV shows in the past — I was offered one of those *Intrepid Journeys*, but I turned it down.'

There was one condition for *A Mad Business* that Peter insisted on. 'It was a prime case of knowing your capabilities. I said, "Look, I can't do it by myself. Michael Morton [now the owner, but at the time the CEO of The Mad Butcher] is the one with the business mind."'

Sheila McLeod says: 'As soon as we went out to meet them, we knew that was how it had to be. Peter had the balls to say the things that most people wouldn't say, while Mike was the calm voice of business logic. They were really easy to work with. Mike did all the homework on the business before they went out. He went through all the figures. Peter went out and shot from the hip. He would never pussyfoot around; there are no airs and graces with him. But it's accepted better than it would be from some people, because there's never any malice.

'They didn't need any direction, beyond: "Could you do that again, please?" Everything was very much of the moment. We didn't tell them what to do. We just filmed what they did. You can't control Peter Leitch.

'We'd been a little concerned that they might meet some people they didn't really like, and might write them off from the start. But they were very fair. When I looked at the first lot of tapes, it just looked like gold to me. Peter was funny, saying at a home store he might get some plates for his wife — that sort of thing — but he also talked absolute common sense.'

For Peter, the aim of the programme, which he and Mike did for no fee, was simple. 'We genuinely wanted to help people,' he says. 'Television is very time consuming. To be honest there were some who just didn't want to listen, so that made it hard at times. But there were some people who we were happy to spend time with, and even put money into, which wasn't originally part of the deal.'

Sheila McLeod confirms that the offer of seed money

was a pleasant shock. 'We got a real surprise when they offered to put money into a firm. They'd never been asked to put their own money up.'

Mike Morton says he and Peter found that ninety per cent of the people had an idea more than they had a business. 'Once again, Peter genuinely wanted to help some of these people. We invested in one of the companies. In a lot of cases Peter wanted to help them because they were nice people.

'It's so easy to start up a company in New Zealand now. It only costs a few hundred dollars, and you can even go on the Internet and get the details of how to do it, and you're off trading. I heard a report that lawyers were advising builders to start a new company for every house they build.

'Hopefully the key message from the show will be that people should think hard about what they're doing when they start a company. You need to talk to the right people, not just to your friends, because all your friends will likely piss in your pocket, tell you it's a great idea, and tell you it'll work.

'We had a guy who wanted to start a comic company, because he loved them as a kid. He was a bit like Peter, very enthusiastic about it. We asked him, "Where did you do your research on the market?"

'He replied, "We showed them to our kids, and they liked them."

'We said, "How old are your kids?"

'He replied, "Six."

'We said, "How old are the buyers in the comic market?"

'He looked a bit sheepish. "Not that age."

'We hope the right points come out. Do your research. Find a niche in the market. Is it really a niche? There was a fair bit of harsh reality. I think that at some stage Peter told everyone they had their head up their arse. As he says, the problem with that is with your head up your arse you can't hear, and you can't see where you're going.

'When you could see that you'd helped people, it was really enjoyable. A lot of the things we did included comedy, because they said if we did a straight business show nobody would watch it. We did some pretty wacky stuff: Peter in the bath with his Warriors hat on, me sitting on the khazi with my laptop on my knees.

'Peter gets approached quite a bit to get help, but his message is simple: work hard and be honest. Have you got something people want? Can you make money from it? He says to our franchisees, "Look in the mirror and you might find the problem. You're buying at the same price, you're selling at the same price, but if you're making as much money as the next guy, look in the mirror. Are you working seven days a week? My wife used to kick me out of bed in the morning after I'd been up cleaning a pub's toilets after I finished work at the shop. I had to go to work, because I didn't want to fail."

'That idea of not wanting to fail is a motivator for a lot of business people.'

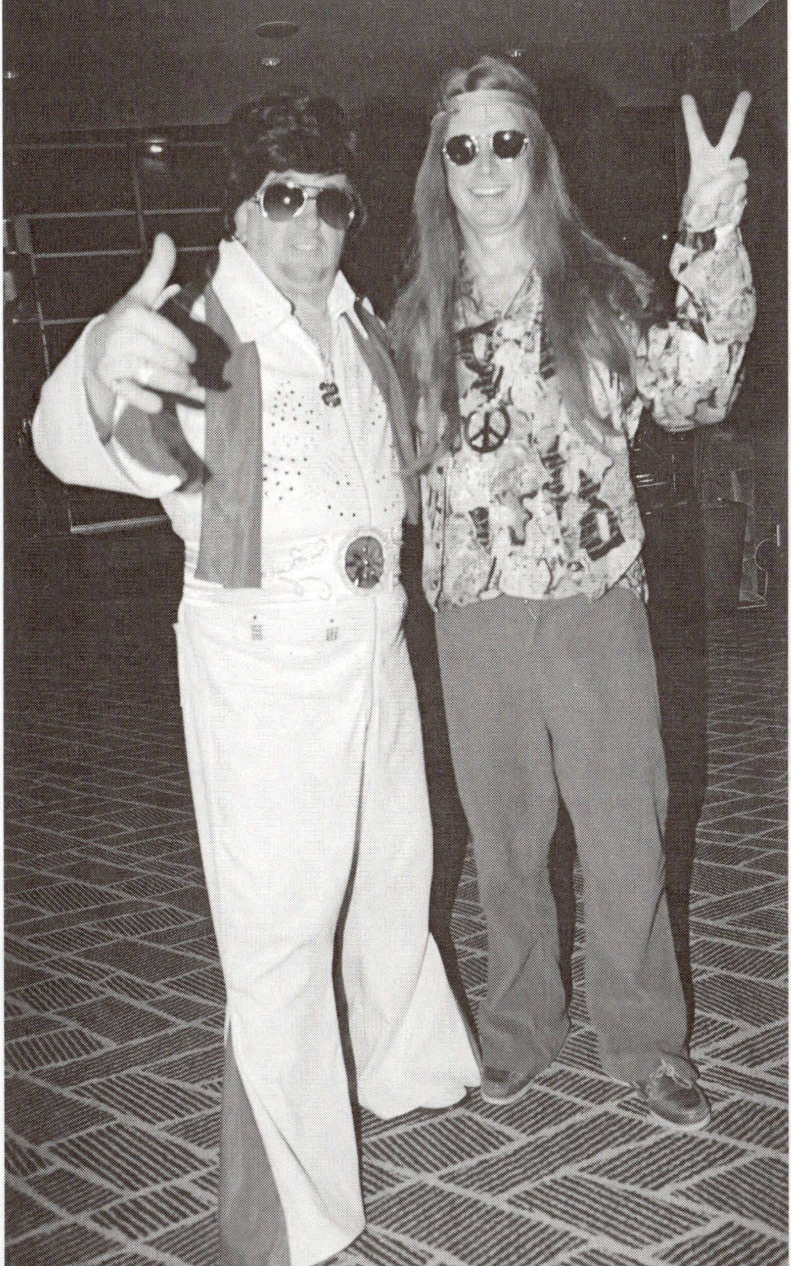

8

Charity

Dusk is falling across the car park of the Manukau SuperClinic on a Sunday afternoon in 1999. Two men are sweeping away what looks like the debris of a party. A few paper towels are swirling in the wind, and if you look closely at the tarmac there are stains that could be blood, but are actually tomato sauce.

One of the men, his hands heavy with gold rings, turns to the other and says, 'Mate, how bloody good is this?' The other man smiles, nods, and agrees. It does feel good.

Over the previous two days the clinic has seen 120 children operated on for glue ear, a condition that can devastate a child at school, especially boys, who are more reluctant to seek help. The men in the car park are Peter Leitch, the Mad Butcher, and Barry Leitch (no relation), the general manager of Suburban Newspapers in Auckland.

Just a year before, Peter and Barry had formed The Mad Butcher Suburban Newspapers Community Trust, and the weekend just completed, organised by them and the Trust members, has cleared, in one fell swoop, every single child on what had been a five-year waiting list for a glue-ear operation at South Auckland's Middlemore Hospital.

The Trust, both Peter and Barry freely concede, was initially driven by commercial imperatives. Michael Horton, a scion of the powerful Horton family who, for more than 100 years, had been major shareholders and executives with the *New Zealand Herald*, had left the newspaper and, with his son Matthew, was setting up a daily paper in South Auckland, the *Manukau Daily News*. Peter wanted to know what the Suburban Newspapers group, in which he had advertised for some years, was going to do to meet the threat of the new paper.

Barry Leitch says: 'We looked at who was the most influential person in Manukau City, and it was Peter. The last thing we wanted was to lose him. He came in and told us he'd been offered this wonderful deal from the new paper, so we had to put our thinking hats on. We had to come up with a good, public concept — it wasn't just a case of giving him cheaper rates.'

And so was born what was originally called The Mad Butcher Manukau Courier Community Trust. 'We took that to Peter, and he thought it was great,' Barry says.

While many thought it was Peter's idea, he was in fact the front person who drove it, with the original idea coming from Barry. While Barry agrees that it's fair to say the concept came from Suburban Newspapers, he believes the success of the Trust is due to Peter's personality and his position in the community.

Almost from the start the Trust zeroed in on health care. There was never a serious suggestion that it would be immersed, for example, in sport. 'In the first instance the approach was very much that we didn't want to give money to something that happened once, and then disappeared,' says Barry. 'It was about on-going benefits, and the best area to get into was health. Not sport, or the issue of under-privileged people, which is something we're not big enough to make a real difference with.

'You have to select something with which you can make a difference, something that's important enough to interest people and get them involved. We had to be careful that there was no downside to anything we did, so we decided that health was the best thing to get into. It's now much wider than South Auckland, covering most of the city, and isn't restricted only to Auckland.'

Suburban Newspapers seeded the Trust with $20,000, and from there it has been self-sufficient. At the end of December 2007, fund-raising by the Trust broke the million-dollar mark, when Christmas luncheons featuring Warriors captain Steve Price turned a profit of $145,000, all of it going to four Auckland hospices.

At the start there were luncheons at the Manukau greyhound track in Te Irirangi Drive. Peter's contacts got the speakers he wanted, and within a year there was over $40,000 ready for a major project.

Kidz First, a project by South Auckland Health, was in its early stages at the time, and Peter had become friends with Pam Tregonning, now the executive director of the South Auckland Health Foundation. It wasn't a relationship that got off to a great start.

'When I first got involved at Middlemore,' says Pam, 'we didn't have anything, so one day we decided to have a party for the kids in the community. Of course, Peter's name inevitably was put down for the request for the sausages. I volunteered to give a hand and wrote all these letters to people, asking for this and that, but unfortunately, when I got to work the next day, one of the secretaries said she'd signed all the letters for me and posted them out.

'The phone eventually goes and it's Peter. He tore strips off me, telling me he got hundreds of requests for things, and if I couldn't even be bothered to sign a letter myself, why the hell should he be bothered to support us? Of course the language he used was a bit more robust than that, and I was shattered — I felt awful. But you know, he taught me a lesson, and he was right. We have a rule here at the South Auckland Health Foundation now, that no letter can go out unless it is personally signed.

'He used to take me aside after that and give me little tips about how to get the best out of people. That's always stuck with me. I'll tell you something: Peter is a fantastic man and he's unbelievably helpful, but I never want to get on the wrong side of him like that again. But it's the measure of the man that he never held that against me, and he was always there for us, right from day one.

'When I first met Peter, and I imagine a lot of people feel this, I was just blown away by his larger-than-life personality.

Then of course there were always the cellphones. I swear he'd have two or three of them, all ringing at the same time. He'd be talking to you, answering this phone, and excusing himself to get another one because it was going to be a radio ad. I remember he actually handed one to me one day and said: "Here, you do it, it's just the radio. Talk to them about chicken — give them a recipe or something." Of course I was horrified, but he just thought it was hilarious.

'He's like that — he just loves to have fun, and if he can have a joke at someone else's expense, then all the better. I remember a horrible day when Stacey Jones was playing a charity match for us to raise funds for Kidz First and he broke his arm. It was the only time I've seen Peter in a flutter. He was going: "For God's sake, Pam, get your husband — get Garnet," because my husband is an orthopaedic surgeon. He kept saying, "They're going to kill me for this!"

'Anyway, Garnet got Stacey all sorted and took him off to hospital, and Peter and I stayed on because we had a collection to do. But after the game, Peter grabs me and tells me there's just one thing left to do, and that's to thank all the players. So he basically drags me down into the changing room and shouts to all the boys, "Pam's here to say thank you." Well of course there were naked men everywhere, getting changed and showering, and I didn't know what to do, or where to look. When we got out of there, he just looked so pleased with himself.

'The Mad Butcher Suburban Newspapers Community Trust was one of the very first big sponsors to get involved with Kidz First when we started the project. Peter used to come to the site — there are pictures in the office of him and me with hard hats on, up ladders and the like. I can remember how I'd be going scarlet with the things Peter was saying to me from below while our pictures were being taken. It was such fun.'

———

The most dramatic stroke by The Mad Butcher Suburban Newspapers Community Trust was Clear Ear, a project to slash the number of children suffering with glue ear. Why glue ear? Neither Peter nor Barry can really remember, although Barry does recall reading an article suggesting that the majority of male prisoners in New Zealand suffer from hearing loss.

'We were looking for something to do to make a stand,' says Barry. 'At the time Kidz First was starting, South

Auckland Health — as it was called at the time — was looking to lift its profile, especially for the new SuperClinic, which Middlemore was running for outpatients. Pam Tregonning pointed out that girls at school will acknowledge a problem with glue ear and sit up the front of the class, but boys will sit at the back of the class and hide, become disruptive, and don't learn.

'It was going to take five years to clear the backlog of kids on the waiting list for glue-ear operations. It was just a case of when the funding was divvied up, a certain amount was allocated to glue ear, and that's how many operations you could do for that much money. It was really stupid.'

Peter and Barry decided they could do something about it. However, it wasn't a concept that everybody embraced. On the set of TVNZ's *Good Morning* show, presenter Alison Leonard heard one side of a telephone conversation between Peter and a print journalist who accused Peter of only doing charity work for brown people. 'Peter was furious,' says Alison. 'He was outraged. "You people make me spew!" he yelled. "Here I am trying to do something for the community, and you accuse me of being racist. I'm bloody not, you know!"

'If he's on your side, he'll always stick up for you, and he'll always be on the side of the underdog. Everything he does is for the right reasons. But if he thinks you're trying to do people in, he won't hold back. You'll soon know what he's thinking.'

If the journalist saw unintentional slights in the glue-ear campaign, the timing was perfect for Middlemore Hospital. 'At the same time as we were pushing for the glue-ear operations,' says Barry Leitch, 'the SuperClinic was being opened, just outside Manukau City, as an annexe to the hospital. We decided that glue-ear operations were what we could do. We agreed to pay for all of the bits and pieces that were needed.'

South Auckland Health doctors, nurses and anaesthetists all gave their time for free for the weekend, and The Mad Butcher Suburban Newspapers Community Trust put in $40,000 for the materials. 'We were able to eliminate a five-year waiting list in just two days,' Barry says. 'They supplied the facilities, and we paid for the consumables. We had the Lions supply people, and a car hire firm supplied vans, and we went and picked everybody up. We hired bouncy castles, and put on activities for the whole family. One parent looked after the child with the glue ear, while the other looked after the other children. There was a merry-go-round, a sausage sizzle, and everything was free. Every child got a cuddly toy, and got taken back home afterwards.'

Pam Tregonning remains in awe of what happened that weekend. 'I mean, can you imagine the force of will it must take to be told waiting lists mean kids are missing out and doing poorly at school, with all the consequent problems, and to just decide to fix the problem? You can't think of many people who would have the ability to pull off something like that. It was an amazing thing, truly incredible, and who knows just how much good that did. We may never know the full extent of the benefits.'

Barry Leitch says, 'It was extraordinary. We had just one person who didn't turn up that weekend because they had a cold. The hospital people were amazed, because they were used to having a sixty per cent no-show rate at the hospital. Originally the annexe was only going to be open Monday to Friday, but because of that weekend, they basically changed their whole system, and they now open Saturday and Sunday at the SuperClinic. People out there [in South Auckland] often don't have somebody at home during the week who can take a child to the clinic to get their ears fixed. The other exciting thing was that never in the world had so many people been operated on in one weekend.'

Five years later, the SuperClinic conducted a follow-up. 'We managed to get hold of about 80 of the original kids, and they all went back there and were tested again,' Barry says. 'Now, when staff are trying to find out whether the glue ear is in itself a problem, or whether there is something else that is an issue, there is a meaningful group to check out.

'It's been an emotional experience. To be honest, we set up the Trust for commercial reasons, but the commercial side has disappeared. The turning point was the glue-ear weekend. What it did was make us less embarrassed about peddling our barrow, because we'd achieved something not many people had done. It's totally on-going. The moment you have faith that what you're doing is right, you have no trouble driving it, and it affects to an enormous degree what you're doing.'

A couple of years after the operations, Peter was in the Manukau City shopping centre. 'A lady came up to me and said, "Mad Butcher, I think you're a lovely man. I just want you to know that my young boy was one of the kids that your Trust did the glue-ear thing for, and he's gone on in leaps and bounds since." Moments like that make you feel very humble. It wasn't just me though, it was a team of people, but for her to come up and say that was lovely.

'I was in Pakuranga town centre one day, and a bloke walks past. You get to know when blokes want to talk to you, so I said, "How are you, mate?" and he said, "You are the

Mad Butcher, aren't you?" I said I was. He said, "You do a lot for the community, mate. I want to give you this." And he gave me $50. He said to put it towards the next cause.

'I asked him to give me his name and address, and I'd get a receipt sent out to him, but he said, "There's no need for that. I know it'll go to a good cause. Good on ya." Then he walked away. I thought, "Hell, he trusts me that much." Things like that are very humbling. You feel good.

'We haven't given millions away, because we don't have millions, but we've done our bit.'

In a world full of fund-raising, the Trust's income — of between $180,000 and $200,000 a year — comes from three main areas. There are the luncheons: one at Christmas and one during the year, now held at the Ellerslie convention centre. The speakers all appear for free, with the list ranging from sports heroes like Colin Meads, Eric Rush, Ruben Wiki and Steve Price, to radio and television performers like Paul Holmes, Murray Deaker and John Hawkesby, and comedians like Mike King.

In addition to Suburban Newspapers, the Radio Network — now a partner in the Trust — provides free advertising, but despite glowing reports from those who go to the luncheons, selling tickets is never that easy.

'I never realised how hard it was to sell tickets,' says Peter. 'Every lunch that we have, we find there are people telling us how much they enjoyed it, and what good value it is. But every lunch we put on, we have to work our arse off selling the tickets. To be fair, if we didn't make our suppliers support us, they wouldn't be as successful. Unfortunately, we haven't been able to tap into the corporate world as well as we'd like to. Maybe that's because I'm not a corporate sort of person.

'I always remember a guy called Richard Finny at the Sheraton Hotel, who used to put on big luncheons, and they sold out all the time. We send a letter to people who have been there, but it's hard work. And it is a team effort. Michael Morton, my daughter Julie, and many more drive the Trust along.'

In addition to money from the luncheons, Barry Leitch says that cash from a number of Peter's speeches and personal appearances goes into the Trust. 'We do health reports through our papers, and a percentage of the money we raise through advertising from them goes to buying specific pieces of equipment. They raise maybe $20,000 to $25,000 a year.

'We have a health page every week, and every quarter we have a 16-page liftout that focuses on the diseases that are rampant at the time, what the symptoms are, what you can do to help yourself. Sometimes they're non-time specific. We'll do allergies, for example — what it means to live with an allergy sufferer, and what you can do to make yourself and others around you safe.

'We have no administration costs and, except for the food at Ellerslie, there are no other costs. Everything else is picked up by The Mad Butcher or Suburban Newspapers.'

There have been other success stories too. When the first national burns unit opened at Middlemore Hospital, a unit that now deals with around 30 adults and six children every year, the Trust outfitted one of the rooms. And then there was the drive to urge New Zealand men to have regular checks for prostate cancer. Barry Leitch recalls that 'the guy who was running prostate cancer awareness was basically funding it out of his own pocket. We had no trouble going to Paul Holmes and Leighton Smith, saying, "We want your help with this."

'We raised $90,000 one year, and then $30,000 the next year to raise awareness, and it was on every radio station. Peter's had 30-odd calls since then from people who've said, "Hey, I took you seriously, and I went and took the test, and found I had prostate cancer in the early stages. You saved my life."'

The Trust has never been big on endless formal meetings. 'When there's a project, it's time-consuming,' says Barry, 'but Peter and I run into each other two or three times a week. He's in here at the office, and I've got a bach about 50 metres from his at Waiheke, so we can talk about things over there too.'

And if there's one occasion that allows the Mad Butcher to express his inner child, it's the Family Fun Day at Ellerslie race course. 'Every November,' says Barry, 'Peter cooks sausages, we get Tip Top ice cream, we get free soft drinks, and we have bouncy castles and train rides. Last year we cooked 8000 sausages. Peter also runs the lolly scramble. He loves to be very much un-PC. We've been told we can't have lolly scrambles, but we have one every year anyway.'

In recent years a charity that struck close to home for Peter was Allergy New Zealand. His grandson Reuben, his daughter Angela's oldest boy, has suffered all his life from severe food allergies.

Allergy is often a misused term. If you feel bloated after

drinking a cup of milk, that's a food intolerance. A true food allergy is the body's immune system overreacting to a protein, which triggers an allergic reaction. Symptoms can include hives, itching, swelling, vomiting, diarrhoea and nausea. At worst it can trigger anaphylaxis, either by breathing difficulties, and/or a sudden drop in blood pressure, which can be fatal. There is no cure yet for food allergies, but researchers are getting close to developing a vaccine. Avoiding allergenic food is the only guaranteed treatment.

Peter has felt the pressures that come with caring for a child who is susceptible to dangers that most people need never consider. Penny Jorgenson, the chief executive of Allergy New Zealand, remembers Peter telling her 'about how he had taken Reuben out, as granddads do, and he'd realised he'd forgotten to bring Reuben's EpiPen [a device carried by allergy sufferers that they can use to inject themselves in the event of a severe reaction].

'I think he was really scared. He told me he almost panicked, that he was so worried about what he'd do if "the little fella" got ill. At the end of the day, our work is about keeping gorgeous little children gorgeous, and Peter understands that.'

Peter is now an ambassador for Allergy New Zealand,

and, says Penny, 'of course we're always sad that any family has to go through having a loved one suffer allergies, but Peter's understanding of the problem — because of Reuben's condition — has been a blessing for us.

'To say Peter is unique as a champion of a cause would be an understatement. He's a most remarkable man. He doesn't ring up and suggest things we could do to raise money. He's more likely to ring and say, "There's a cheque for such and such in the post that I've raised from this event, or that lunch." He'll just ring up and say, "I'm doing a lunch, and I reckon it'll raise $25,000." And it does.

'He's done work for us through The Mad Butcher Suburban Newspapers Community Trust too. His most recent one was when he called up and said he was having a hypnotist night with Guy Cater and the Warriors, and we were getting the money. It came totally out of the blue and it was a hilarious night. The thing is, the players knew what was going to happen, but they still volunteered to get up on stage, be hypnotised, and have people laugh.'

For the audience, it was hard to judge which was the funniest moment. Was it two of the strongest, toughest men in the Warriors, Ruben Wiki and Manu Vatuvei, crying and hugging each other for comfort, while they watched an imaginary sad movie? Or perhaps four of the Warriors —

Wiki, Vatuvei, George Gatis and Corey Lawrie — dancing as ballerinas? Or maybe Wiki, living a James Bond fantasy, mowing down invisible terrorists with a smoking finger?

'It's Peter,' says Penny, 'who makes that happen. As another example, he just called one day and said he was having a lunch at Sails restaurant. We had Graham Henry there, and people like Murray Deaker and Leighton Smith. Of course, they go away and then talk on air about allergies, and that leads to more understanding, perhaps more sponsors, and so it grows.

'When Peter was first involved, we were having a charity dinner and auction, and he bought a table and was very supportive, spending up at the auction. He started to get more involved in what we were doing, and when the next one came around he donated all sorts of things, several of which I suspect he then bought back again at the auction, and eventually he agreed to become an ambassador for us.

'You couldn't really even guess at what he's done and how much it has been worth. But I'd say he's probably put in more than $50,000 of his own money in the last year alone, and goodness knows how much from lunches and auctions. Even more importantly, from our point of view, the coverage and exposure he has gained for us has been priceless. In terms of influence, Peter is amazing. I don't know where we would be without him.'

A real milestone for the Trust came when the 2007 Christmas luncheon at Ellerslie, attended by over 800 people, raised $145,000 for four Auckland hospices, pushing the Trust past the million-dollar mark.

The event also marked the resignation from the Trust of Barry Leitch, who was also leaving his post as Suburban Newspapers general manager.

'The Trust and the partnership we share with the Mad Butcher has given extraordinary support to the community,' says Barry.

As always Peter and Barry paid for their own tickets, maintaining the proud record of every cent raised on the day going to charity. Warriors captain Steve Price, who can demand a large fee for a speech, donated his time, while help from Lion Breweries, Glengarry Wines and Edwards Sound made it much easier for the Trust to meet self-imposed targets.

There's no end in sight for the Trust. New Suburban Newspapers general manager David Penny and the Chief

Executive of Fairfax Media New Zealand (which owns Suburban Newspapers) Joan Withers have both told Peter they want to keep the Trust going.

Judy Barlow, a sweet-natured woman from the Arthritis Foundation, came to Peter's office after a phone call of introduction from a mutual friend, the great former Kiwi league player, Ron McGregor.

After their first meeting, to discuss how she might improve the foundation's fund-raising, Peter realised that his casual swearing may have shocked her a lot more than most people he meets. 'She was a lovely lady, who I have a feeling had never heard the "f" word before.'

But with time they became close friends, and she would often call on Peter for advice and practical help. When she died several years ago she left a letter which was read at her funeral. Her heartfelt tribute to Peter for his kindness and his assistance found him choking back tears.

Being well known for his charity work means that Peter

is often asked to pass judgement on other businesspeople and what they do for the community. 'People often say to me, "Do you think other people should do more?" But I just say, "People should do what they want to do." One charity fund-raiser I do hate is telethons. I remember some butcher ringing up and challenging me to do something. I felt like saying, "Hang on, I do my bit for charity." I don't need to do something just for the sake of getting on television.'

Camp Quality, an organisation that provides camps for children suffering from cancer, is a group dear to Peter's heart. 'What makes it special, in my opinion, is that all the volunteers work for free. Nobody gets paid. They take ill kids away, and give them a week free from hospitals and doctors. Every kid has a caregiver, and most of them are young kids, who have to take a week's holiday to go and do it.

'I was there once and they were thanking me. I said, "No, I should be thanking you, because the greatest gift you can give anyone is your time." I say that a lot, but I mean it. I've tried to give my time for charities.'

Westpac
PAY
HOSPI
THE SUM OF
One hund
five thous
THE MAD BUTCHER AND
SUBURBAN NEWSPAPERS
COMMUNITY TRUST

9

Sponsorship

It's a quirk of fate that it was a rugby fanatic, not a league person, who led the charge for the 1991 award of a Queen's Service Medal to Peter Leitch.

In the late 1980s, Bob Houston, now a media man in Nelson, was running an Auckland motel, as well as fund-raising — in whatever spare time he had — for the Ponsonby rugby club. One of the schemes to raise money, in 1990, was a raffle for a sponsor. Peter had a ticket in the draw, and to the mutual delight of the club and himself, he won the right to be the major sponsor for the year.

He quickly found himself at home with the Ponsonby club members. The senior coach that year, Grant McCurrach, a highly successful city accountant, has a sense of humour that meshes easily with, for example, that of a blue-collar butcher from Mangere. When the Mad Butcher's name was announced as the sponsor, McCurrach sprang to his feet. 'Bloody hell,' he roared, 'it's bad enough we've a league man doing the sponsorship, but does this mean we have to eat his shitty bloody sausages as well?'

Peter leapt to his feet in mock outrage, all measure of physical damage was promised, and what would be the first of a number of long-term friendships with Ponsonby players was formed. Peter quickly warmed to men like All Black Joe Stanley, Manu Samoa captain Peter Fatialofa, and McCurrach himself.

Ponsonby won the championship too, so Peter is almost certainly the only Kiwi league team manager who has sponsored an Auckland rugby champion. He put on a Sunday breakfast at the club to celebrate the Gallaher Shield victory.

What he hadn't counted on was how seriously Ponsonby took Mad Monday, a pub crawl that had become a tradition. Peter told Janice that he had to go to town for a meeting, thinking he'd slip in, have a few beers with the players, and get back to Mangere without arousing any suspicion. 'They were too smart for the Butcher. I couldn't get away.'

Peter Fatialofa remembers vividly how, after a few hours and just as many hotels, Peter started to tap dance on a table at a downtown bar. When he slipped and crashed to the floor, says Fatialofa, 'we all went pretty quiet. Here's our main sponsor, and he's flat on his back on the floor. Then he got up and we laughed till we cried.'

Peter Leitch just felt like crying. For about an hour he sat trying to move without pain until the players realised the life and soul of the party was barely able to draw breath to say a word. A taxi was called, and they took Peter to Auckland Hospital, where they'd found he'd cracked a rib.

'I guess you could say he suffered for the boys,' laughs Fatialofa now. 'Looking back maybe Peter hadn't realised then that rugby guys aren't as civilised as the league boys. Being serious he was just a great sponsor, because it wasn't just a cheque from someone you didn't really know. He became friends with everybody in the side.'

Over that winter, Bob Houston and the club's committee saw at close range how dynamic Peter was at promoting a cause he believed in. 'As I got to know Peter better, I became irritated with people who were cynical about his motives,' says Houston. 'He's one of the most genuinely big-hearted people you could ever meet, and I decided to try to push for some sort of public recognition for him.'

Former All Black Grahame Thorne, at the time the member of Parliament for Onehunga, steered Houston in the right direction.

Houston enlisted friends to help him gather references, and was delighted with the response. 'I think in virtually every case I'd ring someone, tell them what I wanted, and within 24 hours a letter was in the mail,' he says. A submission in 1990 just missed a deadline, but the following year Peter was at Government House in Wellington, where the Governor-General, Dame Cath Tizard, awarded him the QSM.

It was a setting that resonated with him. He used to walk to school past Government House, and his maternal grandmother's house had almost backed onto it. Peter made sure his suit was spotless, his shoes highly shone. The occasion met all his expectations. In the waiting room he chatted with a group of people he knew had worked for their communities and had made the sort of efforts he'd done to assist charities.

Called to receive his award from Dame Cath, Peter, as serious as he ever gets, walked up, bowed, and was delighted when the Governor-General leaned closer to him and asked, 'So where's the barbecue? I would have thought you'd have one going today.'

Friends joked that the initials stood for Queen's Sausage Maker, but the reality was that Peter was — and still is — humbled by the award. 'It's something I'm very proud of — something I would never have dreamed would ever come my way.'

There are many causes Peter supports as an individual that are never publicised. A perfect example occurred while his friends were pushing for Peter's Queen's Service Medal. An Auckland softball official, John Giacon, said that he would happily vouch for the time and money Peter had given to softball. But there was more.

'I'd like to acknowledge something else as well,' Giacon said at the time. 'I've been involved with a group who offer blind kids the chance to go fishing. We had anglers who were happy to do the instruction, and parents and teachers who thought it was a really good thing for the children. All we were missing was $1000 to buy rods for the kids.

'I got in touch with any number of possible sponsors. A manager at one of the breweries said he would love to help, but as a commercial organisation he couldn't see any benefit because there would be no promotional value from the gift.

'In desperation I rang Peter. He listened to me, and asked what we needed. I said $1000. Before I could say anything else he asked where to send the cheque to. If there was ever a donation that came from the heart, that was one.'

Ponsonby wasn't the only rugby club that loved having the Mad Butcher on board. Jim Ruka, from the Pakuranga club, says Peter has sponsored the club's supporters' area for 'too many years to remember' and is now a life member. 'In fact he's such a bloody good supporter that we had to tell him enough is enough. That must be a first for a sponsor — telling them we can't keep taking all their help like that. We just refused to take more stuff from him.

'Every home game we have this licensed area at one end of the paddock, and the supporters are there in huge numbers. It's brought back the camaraderie to the club. It had been missing for years, but now there's an area where they all gather and enjoy each other's company. Peter has had a huge hand in that.

'Whatever we wanted we'd get. There would be meat and sausages of course, but there would always be extras he'd reckon we might just need. It's still nothing for the phone to go on a Saturday night or a Sunday and it's Peter calling from Australia with the Warriors or something, just to see how the boys got on. That's pretty special. I can tell you, he's a well-liked and respected fella out here.

'We might have told him he doesn't have to keep giving all the time, but it hasn't stopped him. There's always a call to make sure we've got everything for the end-of-season do. He must be incredibly busy when you think about it, but he's as loyal as, and he just always makes time for us. It makes you feel pretty special when someone still takes the time to take an interest in what's going on for you.

'Amazingly, there are still some people who bag him, but I think they don't know the real man. I was up in Whangarei at a bowling club, and there he was in the photos on their walls — just somewhere else he managed to find time to visit and support. At the end of the day, you can't help but like him. I always used to be the MC at our end-of-year functions, but once Peter got the mike, he'd have the crowd in raptures. I have to say, they've never laughed like that for me.'

In the early 1980s the Auckland Trotting Club seized on a promotional idea for the sport, celebrity races, where sports stars and media figures would drive.

Peter was asked to be involved in the first race, in 1982. He was far from being at ease with horses.

His only riding adventure had been when he was a primary schoolboy, at New Brighton beach in Christchurch, on a rare family holiday away from Wellington. At the beach there were donkey rides, and Peter was determined to have one. As many times as his mother rejected the idea he pleaded his case. Finally he wore her down and was duly placed on the back of a donkey that, to his pre-pubescent eyes, was a long way from the sand below.

It soon got worse. 'There was a bunch of bloody dogs that started barking and running round the donkey. I started crying, and asking to be taken off.'

No, said his mother, in a voice he knew he couldn't argue with, he wanted to ride on a donkey, he was going to ride on this one until the bitter end. He was red faced and howling but that was exactly what happened to him. He says it was one of the most daunting memories of his childhood.

Thirty years or so later, when he was invited to drive at Alexandra Park, Peter decided he would get some instruction before he placed himself, without the benefit of a safety belt, in the canvas seat of a sulky being towed by a tonne of rippling horseflesh.

He went to a stables in South Auckland, but when he

arrived the owner was busy and he was left in the hands of a boy, who, Peter swears, was probably no more than eight or nine years old.

'I thought that if I didn't touch the reins the horse wouldn't do anything. What I hadn't thought of was that the horses are like finely trained athletes. Once they step on the track they go.

'So here we were, going round the track at what felt like a million miles an hour, and I'm trying to stop it, and the bloody thing goes faster. I was shitting bricks.'

The small boy had disappeared. For a moment Peter considered jumping off the sulky onto the gravel track.

But then memories flashed back of the time when as a teenager he had rolled a 1947 Austin 10 car on a gravel road. Peter and his friend Paul Turner escaped uninjured, but the big metal hinges that protruded from the car had been basically chewed off where they'd skidded on the gravel.

'I thought about what the gravel road had done to the hinges. So I didn't jump off.'

Eventually the horse tired, and slowed enough for Peter to clamber off. After another lesson it was race night.

'I've got to be honest, and I don't mind admitting it, I was absolutely shit scared. But once the race started, and adrenaline takes over, you think you're the champion.

There's nothing better than coming down the home straight, shouting at the other drivers, and they're shouting at you to get out of the bloody way. You get a little insight into what the real drivers feel.'

Softball is a sport that strikes much the same chord with the Butcher that rugby league does. There's also a family connection — his nephew, Steve Leitch (his brother Jack's son), pitched for New Zealand. 'I love the game,' Peter says. 'I played it to no great level, and I coached it for one season at Howick. It was an absolute bloody disaster.

'There was a guy called George Henry at the club, who has since passed away. George was a tough man, a wild man, who had a couple of boys — they were right little bastards. On the second night of training, his boys were playing up. I thought, "I'll have to make a stand here." So I chased them with a bat, but I couldn't catch them.

'I went up to the clubhouse afterwards to have a few beers, knowing that George would have been watching. I was wondering if he was going to deck me. I was shit-scared actually. George came up to me, and said, "Good on ya, mate. Those little buggers needed that."'

So it was no surprise that when the women's world softball championships came to the Mangere ballpark in Auckland in 1986, Peter was on hand, providing thousands of free sausages that were cooked and sold at the park to help fund the event. Tournament organiser, Ross Williams, says that Peter was heavily involved in not only the women's championships, but also the youth men's championships a few years later.

Like John Giacon, the softball official whose fondest memories of Peter were for the support he also gave to helping blind children learn to fish, Williams recalls the assistance given to a truly low-profile group. 'What a good man Peter is,' he says. 'I've known him for many years, but the most remarkable thing I'd say about him is that it doesn't seem to matter who he helps — he gets an equal amount of enjoyment out of it.

'I'd known him earlier through my role at the New Zealand Rugby League, when Peter was mostly concerned with the Mangere East Hawks. But the one I really remember was the Mad Butcher midget cricket competition. We had this thing out at Suburbs–New Lynn cricket club where all the kids would come along — I think they were all six- to nine-year-olds — and Peter stumped up the cash to sponsor it. Peter's enthusiasm for those kids was amazing — he might as well have been sponsoring the Black Caps.'

When the men's softball world championships went to Christchurch in 2004, Peter was there to help the sport again. 'I took great pleasure in supporting the women's softball, and I got in behind the men's world champs in Christchurch, and before that in Auckland,' he says.

Haydn Smith, who became the chief executive of Softball New Zealand in 1999, five years before the men's world championships were to be held in Christchurch, says that from day one he had a loyal supporter in Peter. 'He was always there if you wanted a bit of publicity,' says Smith. 'He was very open to fitting it in with his paper and radio advertising — he saved us a huge amount of money. There was never a time, as the championships got closer, when he wasn't saying on air in his ads, "To be fair, it'd be wrong not to mention the world softball champs," and away he'd go.

'Peter was absolutely brilliant. We sent him a set of New Zealand softball gear, and the next thing, there he was in every community paper in New Zealand, dressed in the full gear, swinging a bat. Almost single-handedly he raised the profile of softball beyond anything we could have done.'

After the tournament, where the Black Sox won a remarkable third title in a row, putting themselves at the top of the world game for eight unbroken years, they were honoured with a reception at the Beehive, hosted by the Minister of Sport, Trevor Mallard. Two things from the night stick in Haydn Smith's mind.

'We'd had individually framed action photos made of every guy in the team — big framed photos, with a plaque saying the player was in the team that won the world title in 2004. We gave the players a choice of which photo, not knowing what it was for. Trevor Mallard was fascinated. I remember the ceremony was slightly delayed because he was so intrigued. We arrived at about 6 p.m., and at about 7.30 p.m. they closed the whole thing down.

'I remember Peter saying, "This is a disgrace. These are world champions here — we've got to celebrate, not close the thing down." So he took them all down to the Sports Café, put his credit card on the bar, and we stayed there until about three o'clock in the morning. He was determined that the guys celebrate properly.'

But a late night in Wellington wasn't enough to satisfy Peter. He organised a dinner at the Ellerslie function centre in Auckland, the profits going to the Fight for Life campaign. 'I know that he was delighted with the way the tickets for the Black Sox dinner sold out really quickly,' says Smith. 'He put it down to the fact that it was something different.

'We had a book written about the campaign, called

Relentless, and the photographer, Kevin Clark, came to the function. Peter asked who he was, and I told him. He said to Kevin, "Well, you're not here for a free feed, mate. Get over here and sell that book. If you don't sell one copy to every person that's here, you're useless." He was always thinking of what would help the cause. He was so good to the team, and really made them feel they were world champions.

'It was great to have someone like that driving the process, because with softball, no matter how much publicity we use to drive our profile, you just don't get the pick-up you do for main-tier sports. The guys were moved by how much he did. He put himself out. Whatever you asked for, he always gave the support.'

To Smith's mind, Peter is the epitome of a passionate New Zealand sports supporter. 'Rain or shine, hail or sleet, whatever; whether there's a reverse or not, they don't fold away the banners or hang up their caps. Peter's a high-profile version of the average man on the street who is absolutely passionate about his sport. The difference with Peter, of course, is that he's not the average man on the street, but a very clever bugger who knows what makes people click — he's a consummate salesman. When you add that passion for sport to that talent, it's a marvellous mixture.

'He's been so good to so many sports. It does amaze me sometimes, how many things he's behind. Of course, people see him supporting rugby league, but in so many areas he's there, kicking things along that need the help. Peter does focus on the underdog, and I think it wouldn't matter if it was a rugby club or an individual, he's a campaigner for the underdog.

'In this country, rugby league is an underdog . . . softball is an underdog. He feels a great rapport with that sort of environment, rather than sports that have enormous financial backing. There's no contradiction in him backing rugby, especially at club level. When you break it down in this country, rugby is still a blue-collar environment, unlike England, or even Australia, where it's a white-collar game.'

New Zealand's Fight for Life, organised by former Kiwi Dean Lonergan, became a huge event, drawing a massive television audience and a fervent live crowd. It grew, says Lonergan, out of The Mad Butcher's Big Banger night.

'A mate of mine had his house burn down and he had no insurance. We put on this event that raised $50,000. The first person I rang was the Mad Butcher, and at the drop of a hat he helped out. He gave us some money, he bought some tables, and he gave us a lot of meat for the meals on the night, which was fantastic. When you're starting off, to get encouragement like that is vital.

'When Fight for Life began, he then proceeded, through The Mad Butcher Suburban Newspapers Community Trust, to run an official luncheon for the weigh-in for our fight night. He'd go out and sell all the tables, run the auctions, and raise anywhere from $50,000 to $100,000. They'd set the Trust up to raise money for charities they'd sought out themselves, but they were open-hearted enough to help out other charities when I went along cap in hand. For that I'll always be grateful to Peter.'

Peter's friends in sport include the man selected as Oceania's leading soccer player of all time, Wynton Rufer. They met when Rufer played for the Kingz, and the fledgling professional football team shared facilities with the Warriors at Ericsson Stadium.

'We would be on the field training,' says Rufer, 'and the Warriors would come out, and every now and then we might actually do a bit of work together. The Warriors would maybe play a little soccer against us, and we would thankfully only play touch with them. There were some surprisingly good footballers in the Warriors too.

'Peter would often be at the ground, and I got to know him through that. Then when I moved on and I started working with the kids through my WYNRS [an acronym for Wynton Rufer Soccer] coaching programme, Peter was still there helping out, providing us with sausages for all the barbecues we had — and the barbecues themselves, come to that.

'I think a lot of people know about his involvement with league, but very few know he has given plenty of support to soccer — I know he was once the patron of the Manukau City Football Club. I've always thought that, basically, he isn't driven by the sport so much as the enthusiasm of the people involved in it.

'Of course, his involvement with charity is an example to us all. Here's a guy who keeps on giving and giving, and that involvement has led me to do a few things in support of him, and he's certainly done things for me too. I mean, you have to really, don't you? It's a matter of helping each other out, and fronting up. Peter is always at the coalface and I genuinely admire that.

'But perhaps the thing that really says everything to me

about Peter is when I saw him do an interview on television one time with Murray Deaker. It was a few years ago and they were talking about league. What I will never forget is that Peter actually shed a tear. I've seen that throughout my career in football — especially in Europe, where the fans have such passion for the game and their team that tears are often openly shed — but I'd never seen it in New Zealand until then. I thought it was wonderful that he was so obviously passionate about his sport, that he cared that much. To me it was totally great that he was prepared to show that, because too few of us would have. That's a very special level of commitment from a very special man.'

Boxing is a sport enjoyed by not only Peter but also by Jan, so in 1982 getting involved with Auckland promoter Mike Edwards, who Peter had known socially for several years, was a logical step.

Edwards, often in partnership with his father, Brian, had started his professional promotions when he matched Monty Betham, the Commonwealth professional middleweight champion, and father of Warriors league player, also Monty Betham, with Lance Revill.

That fight, won by Betham, was indoors, but in March 1982, when Peter weighed in as the major sponsor with, in Edwards' memory, $20,000, and a wealth of promotional support, the action moved outdoors, to Carlaw Park, for a programme involving three New Zealand title bouts.

In the main bout Alex Sua knocked out Lance Revill to win the light-heavyweight title; Young Sekona, a heavy-hitting Tongan, beat Rocky Salanoa on points to be heavyweight champion; and Fred Taufua beat Eric Briggs to be the light-middleweight champion.

'In the lead-up,' says Edwards, 'I'd arranged for Peter to go to George Cammick's gym in Otahuhu and get in the ring with Young Sekona for some publicity shots.

'As we were driving there, Peter said, in a really serious voice, "Mike, are you sure I'm going to be okay here?"'

Edwards made the right soothing noises, and when Peter eventually got in the ring he discovered, as Edwards knew, that while he was a thunderous puncher in the ring, with 14 knockouts in 26 bouts, Sekona was very gentle natured. They moved round the ring, posed for the photographs, and Peter emerged unscathed.

'Peter was always more than just a guy that wrote a cheque out — he was as enthusiastic as he is with everything he does.'

For the next 20 years there were numerous promotions that Peter and Mike worked on together. For Mike the arrangement always worked on a handshake. In a sport where the waters can be brimming with sharks, the delight for Edwards was that in every deal 'you always knew that Peter was one hundred per cent honest'.

Peter and stockcars were always a great fit. He liked the people, promoted the races, and sponsored some events. Although he's not actually a petrol head, and concedes himself he's a not a great driver, he does loves the idea of adventure.

And let's face it, there's something very wild and crazy about anyone who wants to strap himself into a hyper-charged two-tonne machine, cram it onto a quarter-mile dirt track with a dozen or more other cars, and drive at speeds that virtually guarantee metal-rendering collisions.

Then there's the demolition derby, an event that makes Mad Max movies look like sensitive costume dramas.

If stockcar racing sometimes involves crashes, then crashing is actually the aim of the demolition derby driver.

Twenty or more old cars, fitted with rudimentary roll cages, line the track side by side, facing the infield, where fire fighters, tow truck drivers and ambulance workers wait, trying to suppress the expectant looks on their faces.

In 1988, for reasons that will never be clear to me, I agreed to be a passenger while Peter drove a white 1950s Humber Super Snipe in a demolition derby at Waikaraka Park.

The Super Snipe, a British car designed for those who couldn't afford a Rolls-Royce, was basically a small building on wheels, and handled like one. We inspected the beast at Red Seal Motors in the city — it was five metres long and powered by a six-cylinder motor that you'd expect to see in a truck. A hefty mechanic assured us we had the winning of the derby in the car, which would, he claimed, 'knock a bloody tank out of its way.'

Come derby night in the pit area we were clothed in white overalls ('Easier for the doctor to spot the blood,' quipped a crew member), shoe-horned into helmets, and strapped into the car.

Technical advice ('Knock the crap out of them') was offered, and Peter drove us into the arena, backing up to the fence to prepare for the off.

As we sat with the motor churning over I noticed that

the young guy in the car parallel-parked next to us was waving to attract our attention.

It wasn't until I cheerily waved back we noticed the demonic look in his eyes. Then he screamed, 'I'm going to kill you bloody wankers, you're dead men.'

It got worse. He turned his car until it was aimed directly at the passenger's door, flipped a middle finger, and started to rev his motor.

I screamed at Peter to get going. The Super Snipe didn't move.

I screamed more. Peter screamed back. 'I can't let the bloody clutch out. My leg's shaking too much.' The flood of adrenaline had unleashed an Elvis Presley moment in his legs.

The maniac next door rammed into our car, which, true to the mechanic's word, didn't really buckle. But the shock wave passed through the car and bashed Peter's right leg into his door. Next day he was bruised from hip to knee, but the good news was that the impact loosened the tension in Peter, and we lurched forward, no longer a sitting target.

Once the car was moving it carved a metallic swathe through most of the field until a punctured radiator left us marooned, with just a couple of other battered cars left that limped to a finale.

We walked back to the pits. I was slightly dazed but Peter was still charged, and amused. 'Mate,' he said, 'you thought that joker was a fan, but he wanted to smash us. You've gotta learn to read people, mate.'

Auckland journalist David Kemeys got to know Peter after he came back from the United Kingdom and became the editor of the *Central Leader*, published by Suburban Newspapers in Auckland. 'Basically all the free papers had promised they'd have a Warriors club where people could write in and win tickets to the games,' Kemeys says, 'but it was one of those years where wins were hard to come by and the crowds weren't up to much. One or two of the other papers stopped doing the promotion.

'Peter asked me why I didn't, and I can remember telling him it was because I had made a commitment to do something and I didn't believe you should quit halfway through just because things weren't going well. It was a good line, but it wasn't really the whole truth. In all honesty I was a bit in awe of him, and probably a bit intimidated if I'm honest, but it struck a chord with Peter, who is big on loyalty and sticking to your word.

'Then we ran a special contest, and a young lad who came from the Kelston School for the Deaf won it. When I called them up to tell them he'd won, I found out they were a family with not a lot of cash to spare, and getting to the game was going to be a bit of a problem for them. There were brothers and sisters, and Mum wanted to come too, so I organised some more tickets and a taxi to collect them. But Peter — and I don't know how — found out about it and got the young fella into the changing rooms and into his Mad Butcher Lounge for a meal with his family before the game.

'I like to think he was impressed that I'd go that extra mile for people who maybe need a little bit of a hand. But I loved it. I can still do the sign language for league to this day.'

'I've done a lot of stuff with Peter as a member of The Mad Butcher Suburban Newspapers Community Trust, and I love it. I've been Santa, I've cooked sausages at the races . . . I've even run stalls at the Otara market. Look, hundreds of people will have told you what a great bloke he is and what a tireless worker he is for charity, and they're right, but he's also a tremendous friend to have.

'I'll tell you this story. Once my office phone went, and it's Peter. Of course he asks: "How are ya?" As it happens,

I let off a bit of steam about being pissed off, because I'd just had a bit of a run-in with someone in the office. About half an hour later, he walks into my office and drags me over the road for a cup of coffee. He says he wanted to make sure I'd get a chance to cool down, so I didn't do anything stupid that I might later regret.

'Okay, he rang me to get me to do something for him, but he dropped everything he was doing when he thought I might need him. That's the mark of a pretty good bloke to me.'

Another good friend of Peter's is Denis O'Reilly, someone mostly known to New Zealanders from his social work with gangs, dating back to the 1970s when he was a key figure that Prime Minister Rob Muldoon sought out to work with gang members.

Based for many years in the Hawke's Bay, what's not so well known is that O'Reilly is also a rugby league administrator. 'The first time I hooked up with Peter was in 1985,' O'Reilly recalls. 'I was the chairman of the Hawke's Bay Rugby League, and Ngavii Pekepo and I were working hard to support our under-19 team. If you were outside

Auckland or Wellington it was really hard to get a player noticed, so we decided to offer to host a national under-19 tournament to get our kids in on the mix. Our programme had some downtime in the evenings and we decided to fill that with rugby-league-oriented seminars. We had to find speakers, and we knew about this bloke in Auckland, the Mad Butcher, who was getting some air time promoting rugby league. In those days rugby league was very much the turf of the underclass and it received very little media sports comment.

'The Mad Butcher was also different in that he was a businessman and he was funny. I had never met him, but I rang him up and asked for his help. Sure, he agreed, "but, to be fair, mate," he said in that raspy voice that is recognised by the ears of the nation, "you'll have to fly me down and home again." No sweat, brother, I told him, not having a clue how we'd pay for it.

'Hawke's Bay retains many of the attributes of old-time provincial New Zealand and we have great networks. The word went out and help came to hand in the form of the Hawke's Bay Aero Club, who happened to have a training aircraft in Auckland and a club member who was prepared to fly the plane on the Friday at a time suitable to the Mad Butcher. We rang Pete with the flight time and instructions on where to present himself. He was duly flown to the Napier airport where we were waiting to greet him.

'I saw the plane come in to land and I mentally noted that it did seem to be rather small. I wondered how it would have handled the turbulence associated with coming in over the hills just above Napier. Even in the Friendship aircraft of the day it could be fairly hair-raising.

'Anyway Pete duly got out of this microcraft and looking around, spotted the most likely league-looking bunch at the airport, and headed towards us. Pete is known as a good white man, whereas in truth, like most Pakeha, he is normally more of a pinkish hue. But on this day, at that time anyway, he was white — pure white, Persil white, completely blanched — all the blood drained from his face by what we would learn later was a bumpy flight. He reached us, his eyes blazing. *"You fuckin' bastards,"* he roared, *"I'm getting my own flight home!!"* and with that started a very long friendship.

'Over the years when we'd have teams travelling through Auckland on our way to Whangarei for a second-division game, we'd stop off at the Mad Butcher's sausage factory. There's a little park up the road and the boys would have a run, and the Butcher would let them shower at the factory and then give them a barbie as a feed.

'It was fantastic. The boys would get such a buzz from meeting Pete and from the aroha of the man. Several times, if we had a Maori side in Auckland for the Maori tournament and we were short of bucks, the Butcher would come forward and supply enough meat to feed the entire team for three or so days. One time in Auckland we had so much kai that we had to invite the wahine team over, and we decided to put on a thank-you concert after the meal. Pete couldn't come so he delegated Pat Rippin.

'In 1991, I think, we worked in with Ken Laban and Andrew Chalmers to bring Manly to Hawke's Bay to play a Hawke's Bay invitation side. Graham Lowe was the Manly coach. It was the biggest rugby league game to be staged in the area since the New Zealand Maori versus Aussies test in the 1970s. Just to cover the costs was a challenge for us.

'We asked the Butcher to help. He told us to hire a swag of barbecues and to get volunteer teams for each barbecue; he'd look after the rest. Well, he drove this huge chiller truck full of sausies and steak down from Auckland and got all of these volunteers organised like an army. It turned out that we hit the jackpot — we had over 15,000 attend the game, the biggest crowd at Nelson Park for either rugby code. The Hawke's Bay Rugby League picked up over $15,000 for the Butcher's efforts.'

Like Hawke's Bay, Southland is another league outpost that Peter has thrown his energies behind. Southlander Greg Dawson first met Peter at an under-18 league tournament in Hopu Hopu. Greg was coaching the Southland team.

'Pete took a shine to the Southlanders right away. I think he was tickled by the fact the Southland Boys' High School rugby league team had made the national schools quarter-finals. Pete was a guest on a Southland radio sports talk show on a Saturday morning which was hosted by a good mate of Pete's, the late Ken Dickson, with Mike Hughes, and Peter Skelt, who also coached the First XV rugby team at the high school. When Peter Skelt starting grizzling about this league team that had been formed at his historically rugby-staunch school, the Butcher let him have it about how well we were doing, and started giving our games and players a huge plug on the air. So the relationship was formed between rugby league in the deep south and the country's biggest league fan.

'When he first approached us in Hopu Hopu, the boys were all over him. It was like Christmas when he opened the boot of his car: Warriors posters, drink bottles, hats, you name it. It meant a lot for us to have such a legend show us recognition as we battled with the stronghold of union.

'I remember he gave me a card after I'd met him and said, "Mate, give me a call and let me know how you're getting on and when your games are. I'll give you a plug on the radio and try to help you get some exposure for the game down here." After a couple of weeks the team had done well and there was a senior rep game coming up, so I built up the courage to ring Pete. When he answered, I said to him that I hoped I wasn't disturbing him and I'd try not to take up too much of his time. Well, he sorted me out very quickly. He said to me, "Greg, let me tell you something. If you were disturbing me, mate, I'd hang up, to be fair. Let me tell you something else. I've always got time to talk to my mates, and you are a mate, aren't you?"

'That was 11 years ago, and to me Pete is a legend. He's not only hugely generous financially to charities and sports clubs, but it's the time he puts in as a person as well which is incredible. The time and enjoyment he's given to others are priceless. Today's world doesn't have enough Mad Butchers in it.

'He's been able to grow an empire through hard work and commitment, but not at the expense of losing the person he truly is, a genuine working-class man that loves his family, is passionate about his footy, enjoys a beer and a laugh with his mates, and does whatever he can to help other people.'

Bob Lanigan, for several years the trainer at the Warriors, says he was always struck by Peter's commitment to sport at the local grass-roots level. 'He puts his money where his mouth is — he's always chipping in to fund this and that. I know he put a lot of money into the Fox Memorial, the Roope Rooster [Auckland club league competitions] and others like that. He always had his hand in his pocket, but it was never just a case of hopping on a bandwagon.

'Sponsoring the Warriors is one thing, because everybody always wants to be involved with the big names. But Pete was there for the long haul behind unfashionable clubs like Mangere East. He'd take me off to footy at Carlaw Park, and he'd be saying, "This is where you want to be, among the real people."

'He is still there with the smaller clubs. Sure he's enjoyed some success with the Warriors, but he's still at grass-roots footy and he's still interested in the juniors, and that sums him up really. He never loses sight of where he is going, but he never loses sight of where he has been, either.'

Greyhound racing in Auckland is now run at Manukau City, but before the track at Kumeu in west Auckland was closed down, Peter and Chris Carter conspired on Radio Pacific to bring in the biggest crowd ever seen at Kumeu.

They decided, after a raucous discussion on air, to race their own dogs against each other, and the voice of greyhound racing in the north, Peter Early, enthusiastically pushed the idea, and joined in.

Carter's dog was an eight-year-old Great Dane called Cole that he'd adopted after a pleading call from Bob Kerridge at the SPCA. 'I went out to have a look, and drove home with this ginormous dog in the back of my wife's little car. He was huge.'

Peter's dog was a German short-haired terrier called Clyde. Dogs take after their masters, and Peter says Clyde, like him, was hyperactive, with a habit of chewing every piece of furniture in the house. Despite that he grew to love him.

Early, who owned a string of greyhounds, including one, The Mad Butcher, with Peter and Geoff Sinclair, raced his family pet, a poodle called Can-Can.

The odd trio started at the 500-metre start boxes, chasing a traditional mechanical hare for 100 metres down the straight.

Cole was, for a Great Dane, very old, the canine equivalent of an 80-year-old man, but when the three dogs were let loose his giant strides saw him fly to the front and win. Can-Can, running ten strides to over one of Cole's, was second, while Clyde, strictly there for the fun, was third.

Later a real estate agent, ignoring a sign to beware of the dog, was bitten by Clyde, and Peter had to find a new home for him with a farmer south of Auckland. Peter remembers driving down the southern motorway, tears running down his face, apologising to the dog. The happy ending is that Clyde lived out his life a happy farm dog, the wide open spaces suiting his boundless energy.

One of the most extraordinary evenings ever organised by Peter was in 1987, to honour world squash champion Susan Devoy. She had just won her fourth British Open title, and when Peter discovered that no formal welcome-home function had been organised he was outraged.

He remembers that Susan's husband, John Oakley, was initially a little dubious, because he wasn't sure where Peter was coming from. I can vouch for the fact that it wasn't an ego trip for Peter. He asked me to compere, so nobody would feel he was hogging the limelight. Once John saw Peter's motives were pure, he gave the green light, and Peter was off like a rocket.

He booked a room at the Alexandra Park function centre, and immediately got a wonderful boost from the caterer, David Garrett, who offered a deal so good that he was providing the food ('as good as any I've ever been lucky enough to get,' says Peter) at a loss.

It was an on-air call to Leighton Smith that drove the ticket sales, which initially were very slow. At that time Susan was still near the start of her amazing career. Peter arranged for Leighton to quiz him on ticket sales, and with a catch in his voice Peter admitted they were poor. His phone started ringing almost straight away. A stockbroker, who rang for one table, was harassed into buying two, and before long a full house was booked.

Meanwhile Peter worked on lining up a list of well-known sportspeople to pay her tribute. The Kiwis were playing a test in Auckland, and the entire squad was organised to attend the dinner. Never daunted by aiming high, Peter also approached the All Blacks. That day they would be playing the first game in the 1987 Rugby World Cup.

He had a point of contact. Star winger John Kirwan was himself a butcher, working in his father Pat's shop. Pat and Peter were old friends, and in fact Pat used to smoke the bacon for Peter's Mangere shop. When John made the All Blacks while still working in his dad's shop, Peter never missed a chance to tease him, asking why he was such a 'soft prick' that he didn't play league.

Asked if there was any chance of a couple of All Blacks turning up at the Devoy event, Kirwan suggested he should shoot for the whole team. Peter approached the All Blacks manager, Richie Guy, who asked the social committee, headed by Kirwan and his close mate David Kirk, and it was agreed the whole squad would make a very brief visit to the function.

Halfway through the evening, with Susan in the midst of speaking, there were gasps from the audience. In stunned silence, which quickly turned to wild applause, all 26 men in the All Black squad, dressed in their famous black blazers, filed on stage. The atmosphere was so electric you felt that if anyone had struck a match the whole building would have exploded. Kirk, who had captained the All Blacks that day, spoke of how much he admired Susan.

Buck Shelford, who had also played in the opening game, says that the detour to Alexandra Park 'was worth it for the look of amazement on Susan's face when we walked in. She thanked us profusely, saying she thought we'd be celebrating our win. The reaction made us all the more pleased we made the effort.'

For Peter an indelible memory is how, far from moving in and then racing off, the All Blacks stayed on, most of them swapping notes with the Kiwis. 'That David Kirk was magnificent,' he says. 'He was one of the last people to leave.'

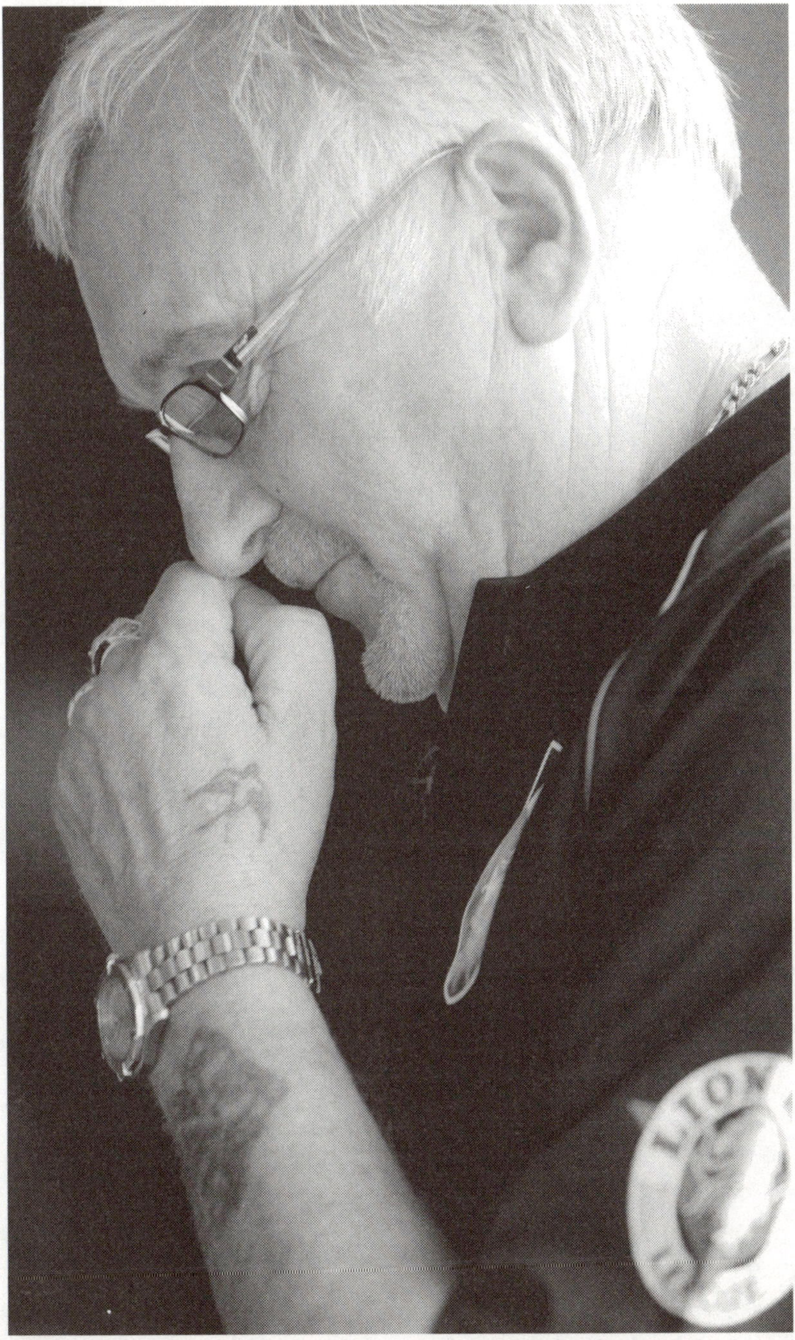

10

Speeches

It's rare to see the Mad Butcher silenced, but in 1991 in the Taranaki town of Waitara, he was unable to utter a word. A fund-raising night, sponsored by Lion Breweries, had drawn a good crowd to the local rugby club. Peter, former All Black Pat Walsh, and I had all spoken.

We then ran a quiz, and one of the first questions was to name the sport in which the Mad Butcher had represented Wellington. A genial young man in the front row of the audience asked if it was wanking. The butcher exploded in mock outrage. 'It was wrestling, ya bloody mongrel. Get up and I'll show ya!' So the young man stood up . . . and up . . . and up . . . By the time he was at his full height,

Peter had a good view of his impressively muscled chest.

By now the crowd was on fire. Peter danced around the local hero, hissing, shouting, and promising mayhem that would make the World Wrestling Federation look tame. The two came together. In one easy move Peter was spun around, and firmly secured in a headlock.

'Do you give up?' he was asked.

'Never,' he spluttered back.

The grip got a little firmer. 'Give up?'

'Nah!'

Now the squeeze was on. Pat Walsh and I noticed — with some alarm — that the Butcher was turning beet red.

'Give up?'

There was just enough air left in Peter's body to croak, 'I'll let ya off this time.'

Peter staggered towards me. 'Mate, tell them a joke. I need to sit down.'

It was a rare reversal for a man whose ability to read, then tease, cajole, and get close and intimate with an audience is a throwback to what we romantically think all old-style butchers were like in their shops. The difference is that Peter actually was a true character behind the counter.

On most of the Lion Red nights he was a sensation,

dancing into the audience, suggesting that the last time he saw a heckler was when the guy was coming out of a massage parlour, or offering a packet of his own sausages to a quiz winner with the remark, 'There you go, mate — my own dog won't bloody eat this kind.'

The Waitara night was a one-off, but didn't go near to the most embarrassing occasion for Peter, which occurred at the Ponsonby rugby club in 1988 in a debate that makes me feel guilty to this day.

As a fund-raiser for Ponsonby it was decided to have a rugby versus league debate. All Blacks Andy Haden and Stu Wilson would represent rugby, I would be the MC, and, to join former Kiwi coach Graham Lowe on the league side, the club wanted Peter. As we were already friends, my task was to ask him to take part.

At that stage he had done very little public speaking, so — reasonably enough — he was reluctant. After all, there would be an audience of several hundred at the club, and the debate was being shot by TVNZ for later use on a Saturday afternoon sports show. But over several weeks, I was able to cajole Peter into agreeing to appear.

Surveys have shown that speaking in public is the second most common fear after fear of heights, and on the night of the debate Peter was strung out like a rubber band. To ease the nerves he downed a few beers, then a few more, then a lot more. By the time the debate rolled around after dinner — which he'd passed on — he was just about incoherent, which was not altogether a bad thing, because what you could understand of what he was saying might have led to a brawl.

Eventually, he stumbled away from the microphone. As I was introducing the next speaker he rose from his chair, lunged forward, and tried to put me in a choke hold. We lurched backwards, in a desperately clumsy impersonation of Hulk Hogan, until he caught his foot on a cord from the microphone, and crashed to the stage. He was just able to get to a chair, where he soon nodded off and slept through the rest of the debate.

The wrestling match featured largely in the television coverage a few days later. Before it screened, I made numerous apologies to Peter for railroading him into a position in which he should never have been placed. But the truly weird thing was that for weeks afterwards we both kept running into people who had been there, who thought the Mad Butcher's act had been one of the funniest bits of slapstick they'd ever seen.

There were even invitations from other clubs, and Ponsonby considered arranging a rematch. Peter just

A big calming influence on a young Peter Leitch was an Auckland neighbour called Tom Cowley. One of Tom's ideas was a tramp in the Kaimanawas with Peter's daughter Julie (left) and Tom's grand-daughter Becky.

The favourite photograph of Peter's wife, Janice, is this one, shot for a radio station promotion.

How better to celebrate the announcement of being awarded the Queen's Service Medal (not, as many friends suggested, the Queen's Sausage Maker) in 1991 for a newspaper photographer than to pose in an Auckland rugby league jersey in the chiller at Massey Road.

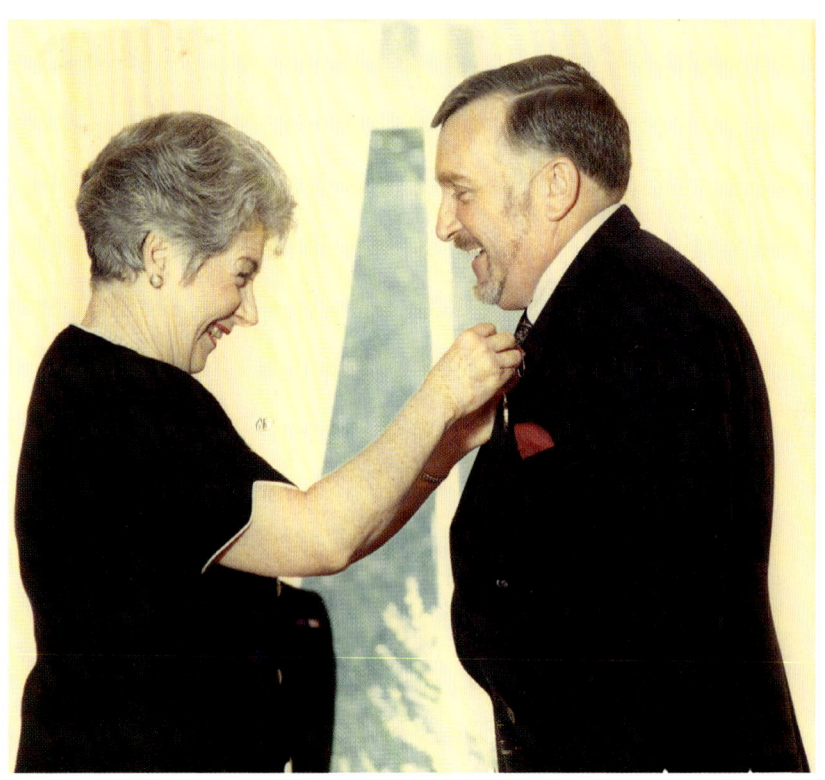

The Governor-General, Dame Cath Tizard, has a question for Peter as she presents his Queen's Service Medal: 'So where's the barbecue?'

A more casual celebration with new Mad Butcher owner Mike Morton, daughter Julie and wife Janice.

A special mate, Stacey Jones, joins Peter for a chat in the early days of the Mad Butcher's Lounge at Mt Smart Stadium.

Daughter Angela's wedding day, with Julie a bridesmaid, and her daughter Kristin a flower girl.

A spill for the founder of the Waiheke Kayaking Club can't stop a mobile phone call.

A little warrior, granddaughter Kristin shows what a pushover her Pop is for her.

Peter trained for the 2000 Sydney Olympic torch relay when it came to Auckland, but while he started happily the occasion was so big he felt 'absolutely buggered' by the time he lit the next torch.

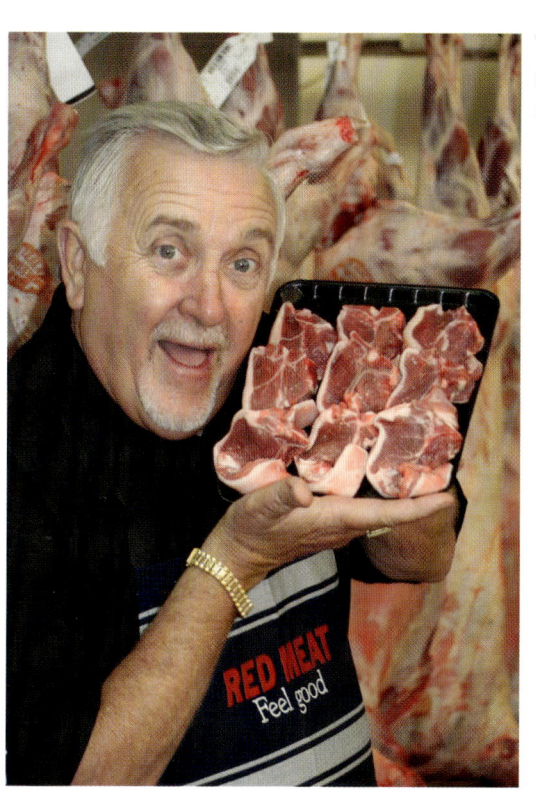

There's never a time when you'll see Peter unhappy about being next to meat.

Friends in high places. Peter is joined at a charity golf day by former All Black coach John Hart, now the Warriors executive director of football, and rugby legend Jonah Lomu.

At a Leitch family reunion, Julie, Janice, Peter, Angela and grand-daughter Kristin.

Peter, with his arm round brother Jack, sisters Edna and Dorothy, and brother Gary.

Grandsons Vincent (left) and Matthew.

Mad Butcher staff parties are rarely without a floor show.

Kristin with her grandparents.

Janice and Peter enjoy the luxuries of Emirates business class on their way to see Stacey Jones' first club game in France.

Grand-daughter Kristin, Peter, grandson Matthew and daughter Julie

The Family Fun Day at Ellerslie always brings out the inner child in Peter, seen (above) with grandson Reuben and (below) with Vincent and Reuben.

shuddered and turned them down. This time I didn't try to get him to change his mind.

❦

Since that dreadful night, while never losing a certain amount of stage fright, Peter has developed into a man that audiences love, from the rough-and-ready at a footy club, to the suit-and-tied at a business conference.

He's brutally honest in his assessment of his own abilities. 'What I can do, that others can't, is work the crowd. I'll pick on a bloke and say, "You're an accountant, aren't you, mate? I thought you looked bloody boring." A lot of the time I'm right, and the crowd loves it. I'll ask if he's brought his daughter with him, when his wife's actually the same age as him. I love that stuff, and feel at ease doing it.'

What he doesn't enjoy is the time before a formal speech. 'Two days out from doing a speech I can't sleep. I get nervous, and I lack confidence, even after all this time. I'm not a professional MC, or speaker — I'm an amateur.'

Peter tells the story of how, in the early days, he went to the West Coast to do a gig with Frank Endacott. 'Jim

Hopkins, one of the best-known public speakers in New Zealand, was there — he's a legend on the after-dinner circuit. It's how he's made a living for years. I go into the toilet and Jim's in there, dry retching.

'I said to him, "Mate, are you not too good?"'

'He said, "No, I always get nervous before I speak."'

'So here I am, as nervous as shit, and mate, his words sent the shudders right through me. The thing with me is that you never know how I'll go. It could be good, or it could be bad. It all depends on the audience. I can't go off prepared notes. I've tried that, and it inhibits me.'

On one occasion, Peter tried to rehearse his speech, rather than just ad-lib, because he wanted to tell a joke to begin his time on stage at a function in Rotorua. All afternoon he had rehearsed the gag, which should have run, 'Our finance minister wanted to be here with us tonight, but he can't make it. His wife insisted he stay at home and do to her what he's doing to the country.'

Peter started well. 'Our finance minister can't be here,' he said. Then it slipped away . . . 'He can't be here . . . he had to stay at home instead.' The internal tension mounted as he fought to find the punchline. 'No, he can't be here . . .' Panic took over. 'He had to shag his wife.'

What does work for him is his ability to connect with

so many different kinds of audiences, from those drinking draught beer out of jugs to the chardonnay sippers. The charm is in the reality. 'I don't even have a good idea of where a speech is going,' Peter says. 'I have the stories I want to tell, but the order will always change. There are some people who have written to me and told me that I am good at it, which warms the heart a bit. For me, doing a speech is like a footballer preparing for a test match. I get hyped up, I don't want to talk to people, I can't eat, and I'm champing at the bit to get on the stage, like a footballer is to get on the field.

'I did a speech in Invercargill once. I really didn't want to go — it was a bit far away, and I kept saying I was unavailable. But in the end they flew Jan down as well, and paid me a fee that was well in excess of what I usually get, which I donated to the Ronald McDonald House in Christchurch. The next day they brought me down a present.

'I said, "Look, you paid me a shitload, and flew my wife down as well."

'They said, "Yes, but you didn't get anything out of it, and we wanted you to get something." It was a really nice gesture. I was embarrassed, but it was very good of them.

'There's no question that you get treated better if you're

being paid. Eighty or ninety per cent of the time I give my fee to charity, but the reason I charge is that you get treated much better. It's an odd thing, isn't it, but perhaps people think that if you give your time for free, it can't be worth much.

'I could be public speaking every week, but I don't. I do enough to stay in the market, and I do them for different reasons. I went to Gisborne one time and did one for a fundraiser for guide dogs, which I thought was a good cause. If I was honest with myself, I did it at first because I like to be a little bit famous.'

If good deeds are, as they say, their own reward, sometimes kindness can lead to a sticky end.

Out of the blue a couple of years ago Peter was phoned by an officer from the Naval Base in Devonport, inviting him and Janice to a Friday-night barbecue.

On arrival he was immediately assured there was an ample supply of Lion Red beer awaiting his consumption. Lovely touch, said Peter, but he'd actually have to take it easy, because of the drive home to Bucklands Beach.

That wasn't even remotely a problem, was the reply. They

had ample accommodation for visitors, and rooms were available for him and Janice.

So the fun began. All was going well until the Navy personnel introduced a drink called a kamikaze, a multi-spirit blend that didn't so much sit in a glass as crouch waiting to spring.

'Me being a bit of a show pony,' says Peter, 'I took the Navy on. Well, the fact of the matter is, one of the blokes said to Jan, "Keep an eye on your husband, I think he might fade very quickly."

'I put on a gold-medal performance for a start, but then my legs just buckled. I went straight down. They had to carry me to bed.

'The next morning they wanted us to have breakfast, but to be fair I was in no state for breakfast. I had the mother of all hangovers. I was a dead man walking.

'I said, "Aw, we've got to go, I've got a function we've got to go to."'

Cheery goodbyes were waved, and Peter and Jan headed towards Takapuna and the harbour bridge.

They were barely out of sight of the base when the kamikaze struck. Peter screeched to the side of the road, and, without time to get out of the car, was violently ill through the open window.

'Well, I thought I had the window down,' he says. 'I didn't. I ended up having to go to the Takapuna Mad Butcher's store and wash myself down in the car park. I was as crook as a dog. It'd be fair to say it was a while before Jan was happy with me again.'

Speaking at business events is something Peter has found challenging, and he was especially nervous about one franchising conference held in Wellington.

'I was asked by the New Zealand Beef and Lamb Marketing Bureau to go down and talk to their conference on exports. I was very nervous, because they brought in highly paid speakers from the United States and England, while I spoke for free.'

Rod Slater, in business for many years with Peter and now chief executive of the bureau, recalls the event with great fondness. 'We held the conference, called the "William Davidson 125", in Wellington in April 2007. Davidson was the man who invented refrigerated shipping, and sent the first consignment of lamb to Britain on the sailing ship *Dunedin* 125 years ago. It was a really big deal, and we attracted world-class speakers. The conference looked at high-profile New Zealanders, like Geoff Ross, the founder of 42 Below.

'I thought, "Bugger this, there's only one guy in the meat industry in New Zealand who stands out above everyone, and that's Peter." So I asked him, and he was very reluctant. He said to me, "You know what I'm like. I'll be saying fuck this and fuck that." I said, "You'll be fine, mate."

'I can tell you that I had pressure on me from high-placed people to drop him, but Peter gave the most outstanding speech about his life. He talked about his beginnings, and there wasn't a swear word for 30 minutes. He was absolutely brilliant — it brought tears to my eyes. I knew it was really tough for him to do that, because it was so formal. That's not him.'

Veteran journalist David Burton wrote in the *Dominion Post* that 'the greatest entertainment was provided by the Mad Butcher, Peter Leitch, who appeared on stage and told his life story with as much candour and earthy colour as if he was leaning against the bar at his rugby league club. His story, from messenger boy to franchise king, offers cheer to high-school dropouts everywhere.'

Burton included Peter's account of how going on the radio with Tim Bickerstaff doubled his business in three to four months, and how one day he got a big lot of cheap ox liver from the abattoir, and offered it on the radio for 15 cents a kilo. A man came to the shop that evening and said aggressively to Peter that he didn't like him.

'I've never met you,' said Peter.

'Yeah, but I was just sitting down to my tea, and now my missus makes me come all the way over here from the North Shore to buy 10 kg of this bloody ox liver,' the man replied.

It was a review that Peter cherished, and one that gave him the confidence to accept more invitations, if with some reservations. 'I told one organiser, "I swear a bit, and I'm not the best around." But he said he'd heard me twice, and he wanted me anyway. I can't change for different audiences. That's me.

'I had a guy ask me to speak one day, and he said he didn't want any swearing. I said to him, "Look, mate, don't get me." They came back and got me in the end. That's the thing, you see — you get me warts and all.

'One of the things that is different about me is that I have the credibility of having built a business up, and supported charities over the years, so I think one of my secrets is that I get a serious message across, but I'm also entertaining. Recently there was a story about a guy who had been in New Zealand doing motivational speeches, but he was a bankrupt and a conman. You can get very good speakers who haven't actually achieved a great deal in business. I think some of the stuff you hear on the circuit is porky pie stuff.

'I say to people that I'll give them credibility.'

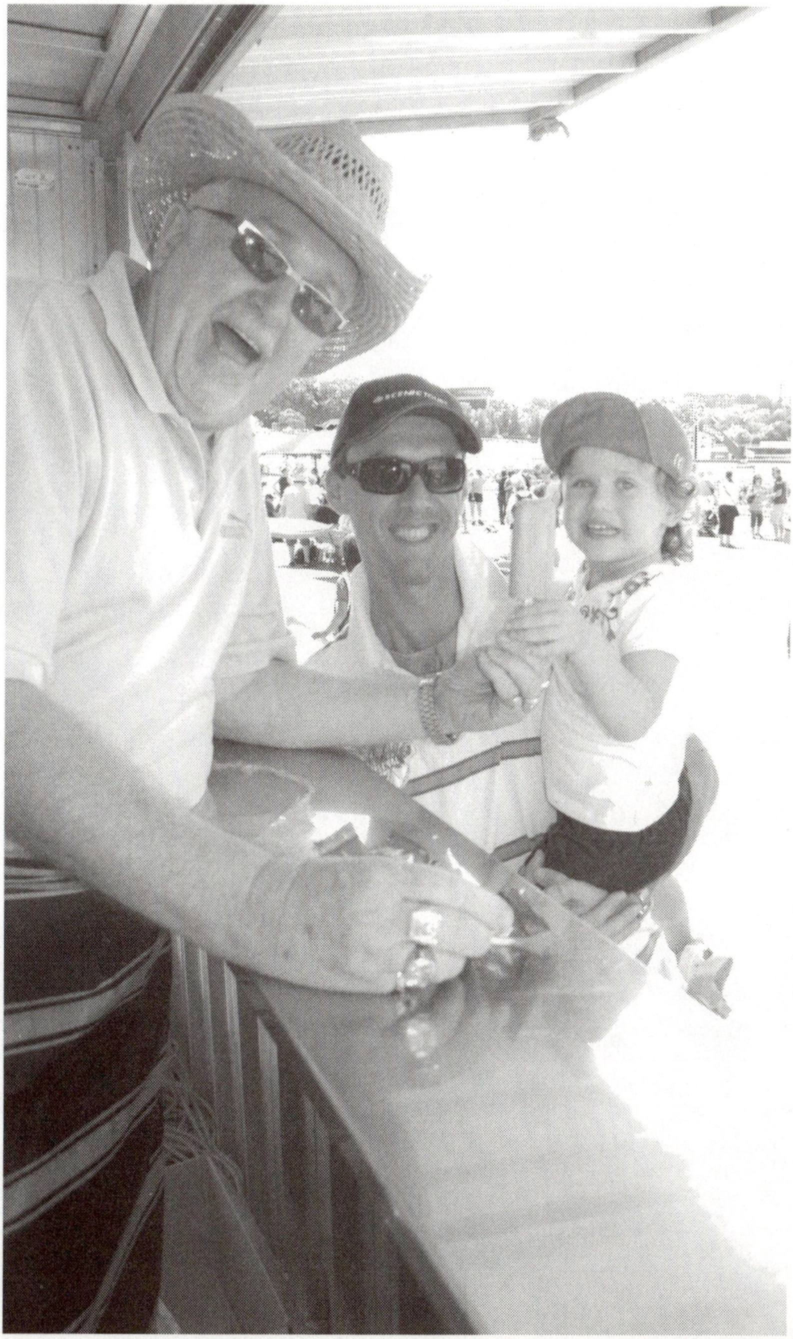

11

The Warriors

When Peter Leitch fell in love with rugby league, the home of the game in Auckland was Carlaw Park. At the foot of Parnell Rise, the old ground, first opened in 1921, had a wooden stand on the north side, and a covered concrete terrace to the south. In the middle sat a playing area which set rock-hard in the summer, and turned into a glutinous, muddy graveyard for many international sides in the winter.

But by 1995, when the Warriors were formed, the new team didn't go near Carlaw Park, deciding to play instead at Mt Smart, originally a track-and-field stadium where the 1990 Commonwealth Games athletic events were staged.

Peter didn't immediately embrace the idea of the Warriors, or dumping Carlaw Park.

'When Carlaw Park was going to go, I started a bumper-sticker sales campaign to save Carlaw Park, with the idea that if we sold 20,000 we'd take a couple of full-page ads in the *New Zealand Herald* to create some interest. We didn't get any support at all. We wouldn't have sold 200 stickers. I look at things in a businesslike way. I may not be the best businessman you'll ever meet, but I could see that Carlaw Park didn't have the facilities.

'The other reason why I wasn't worried in the end about Carlaw Park being lost was that nobody was going. I had blokes ringing me up and saying, "Hey, we can't have Carlaw Park being lost," and I'd say to them, "Wait a minute, the crowd's so small at Carlaw Park, you know who's there and who's not, and I know you haven't been coming."

'So it just couldn't be saved. It'd had it, mate — it was old and run down. So in the end I had no qualms. I'm more than happy with Mt Smart Stadium now. I don't cry about Carlaw Park. There's no question I had some wonderful, wonderful times at Carlaw Park, but you've just got to move on.'

The Warriors concept concerned him because of the effect he felt a fully professional team playing in the Australasian National Rugby League (NRL) would have on local club league. 'Originally I'd said that for New Zealand rugby league to do well in the future, we needed to get our own game in order. The fact is, our game locally has got weaker since the Warriors were here. But of course, when you see the battle is lost, you need to throw the towel in and get on with it. I was never against the Warriors as such — I was just worried about our local competitions.'

When the Warriors did start, against the Brisbane Broncos, a crowd of 30,000 packed Mt Smart Stadium, and Peter was very much involved. At no charge he promoted the Warriors heavily, putting game details in his ads on radio and in newspapers.

The Warriors were originally owned by the Auckland Rugby League, and there were some who thought the Mad Butcher's rough-and-ready style didn't fit the corporate image they saw for the Warriors. But Peter immediately got on well with Ian Robson, the club's first chief executive. Robson, a towering former Aussie Rules player who would go on to be the CEO of Sport Scotland, was someone loved by the media, but whose open-handed ways would see just a $63,900 profit from a $15-million turnover in the first season, and a $473,700 loss before he was sacked in 1997.

One of the reasons why both players and fans hold the Mad Butcher in such regard is that he's never got embroiled in the often cut-throat internal politics of the Warriors. There's hardly been any dirty linen that he hasn't been aware of, but despite a wide range of media outlets that would have been delighted to give him the time or space to vent his spleen, he never has.

The 2007 season was the easiest just to sit back and enjoy, Peter says. 'Without doubt it's been the best season I've had with the club. The chief executive, Wayne Scurrah, their director of football, John Hart, and the coach, Ivan Cleary, have been fantastic. I've never felt so much a part of the club. The communication I had from them in 2007 was special.'

It may not have always felt like it, but Peter has never been on the board of the Warriors. He's never had a paid position at the club, and when he was travelling to every game they played in Australia, he paid for his own ticket. 'I've never taken a penny from them,' he says. 'I've never had an official title, but that's not my go. I'm happy to be picking up the bags. And I've never taken sides when there have been upheavals in the Warriors. I don't like going to war all the time, and in rugby league you'd be going to war every week if you wanted to. There's no point, because it's not going to alter anything. Talkback radio guys can go on as much as they like, but they don't make the decisions.

'A bloke said to me the other day, "What did you think of that decision by the referee when he disallowed Wade McKinnon's try?" Now personally, I thought it was a try. But as I said to him, "It doesn't matter what I think, because the video ref made the decision." You can't change much by talking about it.'

But there have been times when Peter has stepped up for a mate who he felt was being poorly treated. Bob Lanigan, a firecracker Australian, came to Auckland as the Warriors' trainer in 1994. He and Peter warmed to each other immediately. Their mutual enthusiasm for league saw them socialising not just around the Warriors, but in their free time too.

According to Lanigan, 'the real measure of the man for me came when Tainui came into the Warriors and I was off on tour with the Kiwis. Before I left with the Kiwis, the new management team had said the players all wanted me to stay, and that there would be a place for me. But when I got back I was basically shown the door.

'The next thing, I was talking to Peter and I asked him if he'd go for a coffee with me, but he said: "Bugger that,

I'll call you back — the only place you're going is to see my lawyer."

'Well, we were there inside an hour and we talked about what to do. We set up a meeting with the club and, to cut a long story short, they decided to pay me out. Now you've got to respect a bloke who will do that for you. Here he was, tied up with the club, knowing all the people involved, and knowing he was going to have to keep working with them, but he thought what had happened wasn't right, and he wasn't going to stand by and say or do nothing.

'Pete's one of those people who seems to live off nervous energy. It's as if he's never satisfied and he's always on the lookout for whoever it is that next needs help. I have to say that one day it was nearly him who needed the help, because me and Phil Blake [one of the club's founding players] were cricket mad and we dragged the poor fella to Eden Park to see Australia play a test match. He endured it, but that's all. I think the poor bugger had nearly lost the will to live by the end of it.'

By never being on any gravy train — by giving, not taking — Peter has stayed friends with virtually everybody ever involved at the club. Today he still hears from original CEO Robson, and original coach John Monie, whose error in a game with Western Suburbs — when five interchange players were used instead of the allowed four — led to two competition points being deducted, and the Warriors missing the top eight; Monie infamously quoted: 'I slept like a baby after the game. I woke every two hours and cried.'

Peter says, 'I got on very well with John, who was a real league man, and a good bastard. I had a lot of laughs with him. To be fair, we've had no bad coaches at the Warriors, as individuals. They've all been good people.

'In the early days I didn't actually do a lot. But by the end of the 1990s I started to travel with the team on a regular basis, with a good friend, Terry Baker, who runs the Koru Club car care at the airport. At one stage I was more or less like the Warriors' away manager. I used to do whatever I could to look after the team.'

Peter stayed loyal through the next rocky phase of the club, when it was bought by former Kiwi coach Graham Lowe, public relations man and former league player, Malcolm Boyle, and the Tainui tribe. That period would end in boardroom tears, and Tainui left with a debt of $6 million.

Next to the plate, in 2000, were Cullen Investments, the

investment vehicle of Eric Watson, a New Zealand rich-lister, with an estimated personal worth at the time of $220 million. Watson appointed Mick Watson (no relation) as the CEO, an Australian who had been the general manager of sales and marketing for Kellogg's in Australia for three years following marketing and sports sponsorship roles with Pepsi and Coca-Cola.

Peter was invited to chat with Mick Watson, who told him he was keen to see his association with the club continue. 'Mate, I thought you might be going to tell me you wanted me out,' said Peter. A surprised Watson said that with the time and effort that Peter devoted to the Warriors, he would have to be crazy not to encourage the relationship. With time, Mick would even retire a Warriors jersey, number 19, in honour of Peter.

'Mick was different,' says Peter. 'He had two personalities: the good-natured guy, and the other one. When he wasn't happy, I travelled under the radar, so we always got on fine.'

In 2002 when the Warriors made it all the way to the NRL Grand Final in Sydney, it was Peter who was asked by Mick Watson to fly to Australia ahead of the team and whip up support. 'He said he wanted me to go over, and to be honest I was dumbfounded. But it left the players to concentrate on their footy, and Mick to concentrate on the administration. I went over and I felt like a rock star. There were TV cameras everywhere, and interviews every day; I got a taste of stardom in a way.

'We did the barbecue outside the stadium, and I remember going down there, thinking there would be a couple of hundred people, and over 4000 people turned up. We did a live cross to TVNZ's *Breakfast* show with Mike Hosking. I was going along the queue, interviewing people, and then a lady in a skin-coloured lycra outfit ran past — she looked like she was nude. I just went, "Hey, I'm after her!" They reckon Mike Hosking just about fell off his seat laughing. It was one of the funniest things I ever did on TV. Then on the way to the game we had a police escort, and I made the motorbike cop put a Warriors jersey on.'

Those who didn't know him well may have been surprised that when the Warriors were beaten by the Roosters 30–8 in the final, Peter wasn't inconsolable, nor a bad loser in any way. 'Rugby league is like my relief from business,' he explains. 'When we lose, a lot of people get all pissed off, and think I should be crying too. But I say to people, "It's only a game of footy." When I think of people who are very ill, then a game of footy's no big deal.'

The coach of the Warriors at that Grand Final was Daniel Anderson, a former schoolteacher, recruited by Mick Watson at the urging of Matthew Ridge. When he took the Warriors job at the end of 2000, Anderson was a 33-year-old assistant coach at the Parramatta Eels. He had never heard of the Mad Butcher.

That soon changed. Now coaching the St Helens club in Britain, and the first man from league to be named, in 2006, the BBC Coach of the Year, he says his most vivid memory of Peter is the endless bottles of Coke. 'My first recollection is of loads of rings, and him constantly sculling on a bottle of Coke. People like Peter are the sort you need to have in your organisation. They bring a lot of energy, and their motivation is very genuine.

'I warmed to him almost straight away,' Anderson says. 'He was very straight up. He was great to chat to about a lot of things. He was a businessman who had come from nothing, so he always knew where people had come from, and he always retained those qualities. From the start we utilised his generosity with the barbecues, which were a great source of team bonding.

'I remember in our first year when he started to travel with us. Our first ever win was at Gosford when we played the Northern Eagles. It was very funny that night. Peter said to me, "Look, can I shout the bar?"

'I said, "Sure, but the problem is there's already a fight up there between Eric Watson and Mark Hotchin about who's going to buy all the drinks."

'The Butcher went, "Mate, I had a good bet on the boys, and I've had a good day. Don't worry about it."

'To me he's the New Zealand equivalent of an Ocker — a good bloke. He loved to shout a beer, and he loved to drink it with the staff and the players. He never crossed the line, ever. His strength was that he put himself out. He just enjoyed being around the team, and he loved the camaraderie. His attitude was always, "What can I do for you?"

'When we talked football, he would never give his opinion. He never said, "That bloke had a good game." If I said someone had played well, he might say he thought so too, but he never pressed his opinion on you. I did speak to him a number of times about management skills, business models, dilemmas over decision making, conflict resolution, and so on. With all the business acumen he has, I tapped in to his general knowledge as much as possible.

'I wanted him involved in managing the Kiwis, because I thought he had so much to offer — basically, he just looked after the details so well. He was extremely attentive to all the little things, and that's not easy to find. For a bloke of his stature in business, he took to and enjoyed all the roles that were asked of him during my association with him.

'It's even more impressive because of his dyslexia, but he's a man with an incredible memory for details. Nothing escapes him. I don't know what the process is that he uses to retain what he needs to remember, but it's obvious from his success in business that there's plenty of intelligence there. As a person it's easy to see how successful he is because of the genuine warmth he has for people, and his strength of character.

'He was a decision-maker when decisions had to be made; he never danced around an issue. He's a man's man. He's a great friend of mine. We started out as acquaintances, became friends, and now I consider him a great mate of mine. I went through some adversity in New Zealand, and he was always there. He was positive, and made some of the harder things easier to swallow — as bitter as any pill was, he never sugar-coated it. I still talk to him every week or so. I consider myself a loyal friend of his, and regard him as a loyal mate of mine.

'The thing that got me was when he swore off the Coca-Cola. I think everyone was expecting a bit of a lull in the personality, but it just didn't happen. He revved up probably as much, or even a bit more than before.'

When Peter went cold turkey on his Coke habit it startled everyone who knew him. He was urged to do so by Mick Watson, who suggested that an expanding waistline stretching the fabric of a Warriors shirt wasn't exactly the image the club wanted. But to stop overnight was a massive change. Peter had been drinking Coca-Cola in vast quantities since he was a child, always cold and always straight from the bottle. He would put the first bottle of the day to his lips at 5 a.m., and have it drained in minutes. On an average day he'd put away at least a couple of litres.

When he stopped it actually proved to be far from easy. 'I got headaches and nausea,' he complains. 'I don't doubt that as much as I loved it, I think I was literally a Coke addict.'

Daniel Anderson says that 'in Australian league circles, Peter's extremely well known, and as for New Zealand, let me give you an example. One night in Auckland, we went to go to a nightclub with Eric Watson, and he couldn't get us in. But the Butcher could — he got us all in. It was amazing. I think he's so well known in New Zealand, from the very poshest circles to the very toughest, lowest socio-economic areas.'

To this day Peter is still in contact with Daniel Anderson every week. 'When I went on tour with the Kiwis and he was the coach,' says Peter, 'he made me look very good with my family, because, with three young children of his own, he was a very good shopper. He told me what to buy, and when I came back, my family thought I was God, because I'd bought all the trendy stuff — all the good gear. I've never told them, but it was Daniel who steered me in the right direction. He's a good bloke — a great guy. He got me the Kiwis' manager's job, for which I'll always be grateful.

'Where does he rate? Every coach I've worked with has had the skills, and some limitations. When you look at what Daniel Anderson has achieved in Britain, he's obviously got the X factor. I think Daniel was on a learning curve at the Warriors. I think he's a better coach now [at St Helens] than he was at the Warriors.

'For any coach to do well, they have to get the players working together. If you've got six guys in the team going one way and seven going the other, you won't get anywhere. When Daniel was at the Warriors I think he was learning to relate to players. It was a combination of his coaching and the players' ability that took us to the Grand Final.

'He had to learn how to work with Polynesian players. I think a big difference between us and the Aussies is that, in Australia, they don't mix with the Aborigines like we do here with the Polynesians. The Polynesians have different values — their family values are a lot higher than a lot of Europeans'. They care for their grandmothers, their extended families. You can't swear at and abuse a Polynesian player. You can't shame them.'

To get the best out of the talented Polynesians at the Warriors was where, in Peter's view, Frank Endacott was made to measure. 'He knew the culture. His nickname was Happy Frank — I've never seen him angry, to be fair, and I've never struck him in a grumpy mood. Frank was just a wonderful guy.'

To Frank Endacott, the face of the Warriors was Peter Leitch. 'With all the changes over the years, the one guy who was always there was the Butcher,' Endacott says. 'There was always a friendly face, someone to talk to, and someone to have a laugh with. His barbecues after training on a Saturday morning became legendary. We'd train, then have a barbecue with the public, which was terrific.

'I can remember Peter in rugby league when I first got into it. I can remember his ads around Carlaw Park, and I had an image of this real mad bugger with eyes popping out of his head. When I was coaching Canterbury in the 1990s he came down with the Auckland team as a supporter. We were talking and his phone rang. Peter handed the phone to me, and that was how I had my first interview with Murray Deaker.

'I was appointed Kiwi coach early in 1994, and in July 1994 I also went up to Auckland for the first season of the Warriors as assistant coach. I had a dual job — I was also coaching director at the NZRL.

'Peter did a hell of a lot of work over the years. He was someone you'd always see there, whether it was the good times or the bad times. That was the thing about Peter — he wasn't just there for the glory ride, like many of the people round a club. You don't forget loyalty like that.

'There's no secret that he's like part of the family to me. I trust him totally. You know that if you say something to Peter, it will always remain in confidence. As a coach you sometimes need someone to talk to, because things can get to you. He was one of those you could trust with your life. You could put a flame thrower on him and he wouldn't tell.'

Don Mann, now football manager for the Warriors, left the police force to take on a six-month project, helping to set up the Bartercard Cup, the national club championship. When he moved on to the Warriors in 2001 he got to know Peter well, although the Butcher was already familiar to Don, as his father and his Kiwi team brother, Duane, had been involved with the Mangere East club.

It took Don a while to acknowledge that he'd also met Peter when he was the sponsor of the Ponsonby rugby club, when Don was a member of their championship-winning team. 'He asked what the hell I was doing playing rugby, and which bloody Mann I actually was,' laughs Don.

'Basically I'd come straight out of the police, and ended up at the Warriors without really knowing much at all about what I was supposed to be doing. I couldn't have managed half of what I did without him. I know that sounds cheesy, but when you come out of a process-driven government organisation like the police and into a fluid environment like professional sport, you can bring some bad habits with you.

'I really had no idea, but I do know when I look back that

I'd have failed miserably without him. I remember thinking, "C'mon, Don, you're a reasonably smart guy. What are you going to do?" I thought: "I'll just get alongside the Butcher," and it was the smartest thing I ever did.

'He kept me grounded and helped me build relationships. He opened doors that I could never have opened on my own, introducing me to radio, television and other media people. He was always saying things like: "I'm only here to stop you getting your head stuck too far up your own arse, Don." In fact he still tells me that pretty regularly.

'Because Mick Watson and Daniel Anderson were both Aussies, there was no one I could go to when I started who understood the Kiwi networking thing, and just how vital it is to getting things done. Match-day and event-management stuff were bread and butter to Peter, and he never stinted from giving me the help I needed. It's not like there was ever really anything in it for him. Sure, he can be demanding from time to time, but it's always for the right reason, and he's always grounded.

'Coming out of the police, I perhaps didn't always value people's time like I should have, and I could be a bit dismissive with people. Pete showed me that that had to change. He loves telling people, "The greatest gift you can give to someone is your time," but it's not some cliché with him. He means it. He taught me the value of returning calls, stopping to speak to people, and listening to them.

'For Pete it's about giving people the time of day, and being the advocate for the little guy, the battler, maybe the person who hasn't got it all. He once said to me, "Don, when you move on, you only get to take two things with you — your name and your reputation." I've never forgotten that, and I'm just thankful to have had him as a mentor. That's a very lucky situation for someone like me. I mean, you'd be a fool not to take the opportunity to get alongside someone like him who is willing to help you.

'New Zealand is a small place though, and there are some narrow-minded people around, maybe some who are a bit jealous or envious, and we have that tall-poppy syndrome thing where we like to knock people down, especially people who we think are full of themselves.

'I've seen Pete broken-hearted because he felt like he'd failed. We had an event a few years ago before a Knights game and Pete had put up $10,000 for anyone who could beat the world sausage-eating record. We were on television, in the papers and on the radio, we were getting coverage around the world, but we only had a crowd of about 10,000 — not bad, but not brilliant either — and Peter was almost heartbroken. It was as if it was his fault that the crowds weren't turning up. He'd put his heart and soul into it. But of course he was back, as big and bold as ever, for the next game.

'You think of events like the testimonials for Stacey Jones and Awen Guttenbeil, and you'd have to doubt they'd have happened without him. He just gets things done.

'I was delighted when they retired the number 19 jersey for him. They do that sort of thing all the time in America, but it's not done here. It was unique, and that's kind of fitting, because Pete is one of a kind too. I was really pleased for him, because you could see what it meant to him.

'He still cracks me up to this day. My favourite is when he gets a player's name wrong — and let's face it, one or two of the Warriors have had names that have been a bit of a mouthful. But he always turns to me when he slips up, winks, and says, "That's my bloody dyslexia." I've never corrected him.'

Another constant for the Butcher and the Warriors is the Mad Butcher's Lounge, an upbeat lounge bar within Mt Smart Stadium which is always lively and raucous, whether the Warriors have won or lost. Invited guests have ranged from the Prime Minister, Helen Clark, who has drawn raffles there, to television and film stars and rock singers.

If you've been invited by the Butcher though, there can be a price to pay. In 2000 Simon Barnett and I, then working together on a Christchurch breakfast radio show, ventured inside as Peter's guests. He introduced us to a packed crowd. 'Here's Phil Gifford — he used to be an Aucklander, and now he bags the shit out of us.' Cue mostly good-natured booing. 'And here's Simon Barnett — he's not on television now because they found out he was a fuckin' poofter.' Cue uproarious laughter.

About an hour later we went to Peter to thank him and to tell him we were leaving, as we had to be up at 4.30 a.m. to broadcast back to Christchurch. 'That's fine, guys, just slip away quietly, and nobody will know you're leaving early,' he told us. Naively we started to drift towards the door. The music stopped and Peter's voice boomed across the room. 'Look at those two mongrels. The free piss has stopped and they're too bloody mean to buy their own. Go on, fuck off — we don't need you here anyway.' We slunk out to a massive chorus of jeers and raucous laughter, the loudest coming from Peter.

The lounge dates back to 1995, when one of the roles

for Hamish Miller, one of the original staff at the Warriors, was to find ways to increase revenue for the club. 'I figured that one way of achieving this would be to establish facilities where fans could go to enjoy a few drinks before and after the game,' Miller says. 'Given that we had limited space within what was then Ericsson Stadium to do this, I thought we could sell season tickets for members only.

'To make it more appealing, I thought they should be themed and offer members some special privileges such as meeting the players after the game. The club would generate revenue from sales of the membership passes, and would also get a share of the bar takings. Given the mana in which Peter was held in the club, I thought it logical to ask him if he'd consider having one of the facilities named after him. He was — and still is — loved by fans and players alike, and I was confident that attaching his name to the lounge would prove very successful.'

Miller was correct. He sent information regarding the new facilities out to season ticket holders, and season passes to the Mad Butcher's Lounge sold out within two weeks. 'What Peter has done with the lounge has been simply amazing. He's turned it into an institution. I'm proud of the fact that I came up with the idea and created the opportunity, but without his drive, enthusiasm, commitment and passion, it certainly wouldn't have reached the legendary status it now has.'

Auckland journalist David Kemeys will always remember his first visit to the lounge. 'Peter used to ask me to bring the kids to the lounge before the games at Ericsson. I didn't really want to, because the language can be fairly robust and the kids were little, but this particular day was family day and he said I had to bring them.

'I made the mistake of arriving as he was just getting on the stage with the microphone. It was all: "Look who's here. Hello, David, thanks for coming. Pity you couldn't get here on time," and stuff like that, but it was peppered with a more colourful spray here and there. "Have you got the kids a bloody ice cream yet, you miserable prick? Christ, it's free, and you still haven't got them one . . . You know who this bastard is? You don't need to know, but I can tell you he's the meanest man in Auckland — he won't even get the kids an ice cream when it's free. You know the only thing you can fit between this man's hand and his wallet? Glad Wrap, that's what, he's so mean." Of course the place was in fits, and my kids were falling about with laughter. They just thought he was the funniest man on earth. They still give me shit about it to this day.'

Peter admits to having some great times in there. 'We're

not PC. My humour is not everyone's humour, but it gets packed out most weeks. I don't mind getting up on the stage at the Mad Butcher's Lounge. I never get nervous, because it's my domain — I feel at ease. It's in-your-face stuff — good basic humour. Hamish came up with the idea that we'd have the Mad Butcher's Lounge, and the theory was that I'd shoot in for a minute or two, then take off. But I'm the sort of bloke that if I'm going to do it, I'm going to do it properly. So I run the raffles, have a yarn, get people up. I run it for the club, but I don't own it. I get no money from it. I pay for my drinks like anyone else. You have to be a member to get in, but if it's a poor crowd at the game I'll let any bugger in.

'A couple of times when the team's suffered a heavy loss, I've been very lucky in that I've had a disco come every week, run by Elvis, who some people might know as a truck driver who works for me. He would be possibly New Zealand's number one disco operator. We can get thrashed and he gets the room rockin', and the great thing for me is that I take the credit for it. I'm very lucky to have him as a support act.

'We've had some great entertainers. We've had Tom Sharplin, one of the country's best rock-and-roll singers, and a terrific comedian and hypnotist, Guy Cater.'

The lounge has also had the support from day one of Lion Nathan, a company Peter has promoted for decades, and done his best personally to help boost their Lion Red consumption figures.

His relationship with Lion is summed up by Lion Nathan managing director Peter Kean as 'bedrock loyalty', which Kean wryly notes is not always the case in the corporate world.

At a time when league often struggled for sponsorship, Kean says, Lion Red was a major backer, and he knows that fact has never been forgotten by Peter.

When Peter was awarded the QSM in 1991 Lion held a luncheon for him. 'A company like ours doesn't run a luncheon unless there's a real connection,' says Kean. He's been with Lion for 22 years, and in all that time says he could count the number of people they've honoured in that way on the fingers of one hand.

'We love the energy and the wit of the man. I go to most of the Warriors games at home, and I'll text Peter to say I'm there, and he makes a point of popping into the box to entertain guests we have there for as long as he feels it's right. When Peter arrives the box can go from being reasonably quiet to being absolutely on fire.

'He makes people feel so good by his personal efforts.

My in-laws visited from the South Island and he made such a fuss of them, and then, as he'd promised, sent a signed poster to them when they were back home. They were astounded at how good he was to them.'

Late last year Peter, not a man easily stumped for words, was amazed when what he thought was a quiet visit he and Jan had been invited to, was another tribute luncheon at Lion Nathan.

There were flowers, a voucher for a top-line spa treatment for Jan, and then the gift of a pallet of beer for Peter, a special limited edition brew of Mad Butcher beer, with a caricature in the centre of the label, the words 'Thanks for your support, Butch' running around the edge, and the number 19, the number the Warriors retired in his honour, under his image.

No bottles were ever sold. It was a gift strictly for Peter, says Kean, to share with friends and family. 'We keep in regular touch,' says Kean. 'Sometimes maintaining contacts is something you have to do with your business. With Peter it's a pleasure.'

One of the more unusual commercial connections between Lion and Peter will be the Madtastic figurines, a plastic replica of the Mad Butcher, about the size of a stubbie bottle of beer that has an extra tweak. It talks.

And it doesn't just talk when you trigger it. Sophisticated American time-release technology means the figurine will spring to life when a Warriors game is near, urging you to get to the game.

In Australia a David Boon figurine has become a much sought after collectors' item, and Lion are sure the same thing will happen here.

Visiting the Lion box before a match at Mt Smart is a fairly regular occurrence on game day for Peter, but then, until he goes to the lounge when the game's over, he has no special habits.

'I might walk around. Sometimes people ask me to go and talk to people. I've got a friend called Tony Herewini who has a box, and I might go and sit with him. I might go and stand on the sideline. I just do what I want to do now, because I'm not so actively involved. I know Eric Watson on a friendly basis. I know his business partner Mark Hotchin better, but then he's based here.'

At the core of why the Butcher has stuck with the Warriors through the good times as well as the many bad times is the genuine affection he feels for the players. The great

American humorist Will Rogers claimed he never met a man he didn't like, and Peter says the same of the Warriors players. 'There really haven't been any players I haven't liked. They've all been good blokes, really. I'd be hard-pressed to think of an arsehole.

'In his own way, even a guy like Matthew Ridge was good. You'll find people who will knock him, but I reckon you have to respect Matthew, because he was such a fantastic player. The thing I loved about him was that he liked winning, and he *hated* losing. Losing could never become second nature to him.

'Then there's a guy like Marc Ellis — just a wonderful person. P.J. Marsh still rings me. I kept in touch with Phil Blake for a long time. I was invited to Monty Betham's wedding, which I considered a real honour. And I got very close to Awen Guttenbeil. There was Jason Death, who lived at our place for about a year, and Kevin Campion, who lived with us for a couple of weeks — two great guys who I keep in contact with. I was close to Logan Swann, who I'd regard as a very professional guy, and also to Ruben Wiki, who's a terrific person. One of the reasons I went around with the Kiwis the second time as a manager was because of Ruben and [coach] Bluey McClennan — it was my love for them, I guess you'd say.'

Logan Swann, with the Warriors from 1995, says he's proud of the strong rapport that's developed between himself and Peter. 'He's a fantastic guy to chat to and to confide in. He's been a league supporter since way back when in his Mangere days when he started backing the Hawks, and he never loses sight of where he has come from. That's really important, because he doesn't hesitate to remind you of who you are either.

'He's so persuasive — it's infectious. It comes across in everything he does. I don't know how many times I've been to things to support him and come away thinking: "Why did I do that?" But you know, I never regretted any of it either. I've also always come away thinking: "I quite enjoyed that, actually." I've never begrudged doing something for Peter because whenever he asks it's never for him — it's always for a charity.'

Logan's fiancée, Jennifer, had a taste of the Mad Butcher's style the very first time she met him. 'I felt a bit sorry for her,' says Logan. 'Pete bowls up and goes for his favourite line: "Hello, dear, are you on TV? You should be — you're totally gorgeous, darling." Well, she's a shy little Welsh girl and Pete is Pete. He's standing there with his arms around her and she's looking at me with "rescue me" in her eyes.

'I couldn't do anything except laugh. I mean that's just

who he is. He's straight in, whether he knows you or not, and that's the beauty of it. No matter how hostile the crowd might be, or how nice, he just gets people to warm to him. Jennifer thinks he's great.'

If there's one player the public associates with Peter more than any other, it's Stacey Jones, the 'little general', whose brilliant play was a major factor in the Warriors making the 2002 final. The public perception is 100 per cent correct. 'The Butcher's a special guy to me,' Stacey Jones says. 'From the start of my career at the Warriors we've become really close friends. Our birthdays are a day apart [Stacey's is the 7th of May, Peter's is on the 8th] so we usually celebrate them together. He always takes me out or does something — we're really close. Certainly when we were away he was like a father figure to guys like me and Awen Guttenbeil. Over the years he's become one of my best mates. We still ring Awen, and I know Peter still rings Clinton Toopi and Brent Webb.'

Peter says, 'The best thing Stacey and I ever did was go out for our birthdays. One year we went for a meal at the Iguaçu restaurant in Parnell with Ian Robson and John

Monie, and gee, we had a big night. I gave Stacey a present for every year of his life, which at the time was around 20 presents.

'Since then we've been out quite a few times, but that was the big one. I had to crawl to the taxi. There's a big age gap between us, but we just got on with things, shared a few beers, and shared the same interests. Janice and I went to France to see Stacey play his first game over there for the Catalans Dragons in 2006. We travelled with a friend, Tony Herewini, and his wife, Dorothy. They'd won a raffle at the luncheon that we had for Stacey's testimonial. We travelled together through Dubai, then on to France.

'Stacey and his wife couldn't have done more for us. They stocked the fridge up, made sure everything was right. It was lovely. Every week now we send them all the New Zealand papers and the women's magazines. Stacey's a very modest sort of man, and a kind person too.'

When Awen Guttenbeil joined the Warriors in 1996 as a 20-year-old, he thought, as many of the younger players did, that Peter was an official of the club. 'It was only later that we learned he was doing it purely for the love of the game,' Awen says. 'He would do whatever the guys wanted, whatever was needed from the club's point of view, from drumming up publicity right down to going on pre-season tours where he'd organise barbecues for the public in the towns we were going to. He was always there — he was just fantastic.

'He was as excited as we were about playing in a professional rugby league team that the country could get behind. What he cared about was the team harmony, the team spirit — making sure that everything off the field was catered for. He was basically the go-to man for everything that you required outside of rugby league, off the pitch.

'And Peter was a great man to have on your side, because he'd bend over backwards to make sure you were comfortable in the environment. I'm pretty sure that he's put on a barbecue for every single player who's ever been in the Warriors.

'He'll come to your home with meat, or a whole pig, and put on a barbie for you. He did that for quite a few of our stag nights; he'd rock up and do it without any problems. He just wanted to make sure the players were happy.

'At times I think it would have been hard for him not to get involved in the politics around the club. But he was someone who always put the jersey and the team first. It didn't matter who was in charge, or who was playing. He's still got the same amount of passion he had at the start, and it's the team and the game of rugby league that he's pushing. You have to admire him for that.

'For myself, it was good to have one constant there, and that was Peter. It certainly helped us bond. You knew he was always going to be there on your side. He was always optimistic, and one of his strong points is that he can make you feel good, even when things aren't great. I think that's why players gravitate to him in the tough times, because no matter what, he's always on your side. He's a friend.

'He had time for everyone. One thing I learned early on was that if you gave him some time, it'd come back with a bit more besides. One of his sayings that has always stuck with me is that the best gift you can ever give someone is your time. He certainly lives by that motto, and I learned from him early on that it's a good thing to give up your time for people.'

Awen showed the same sort of consideration to Peter when the Kiwis were in Wellington in 2006 for a test match with Australia. 'My brother Gary was very ill with bowel cancer,' says Peter. 'Stacey and Awen came to me, and said they'd like to go and see my brother. That was very emotional for me. In my role as team manager I had to ask them to do a lot of things, but I tended not to ask for personal favours. But they offered, off their own bat, to visit my brother, which was fantastic. My brother got a big buzz out of it. That's just what they were like.'

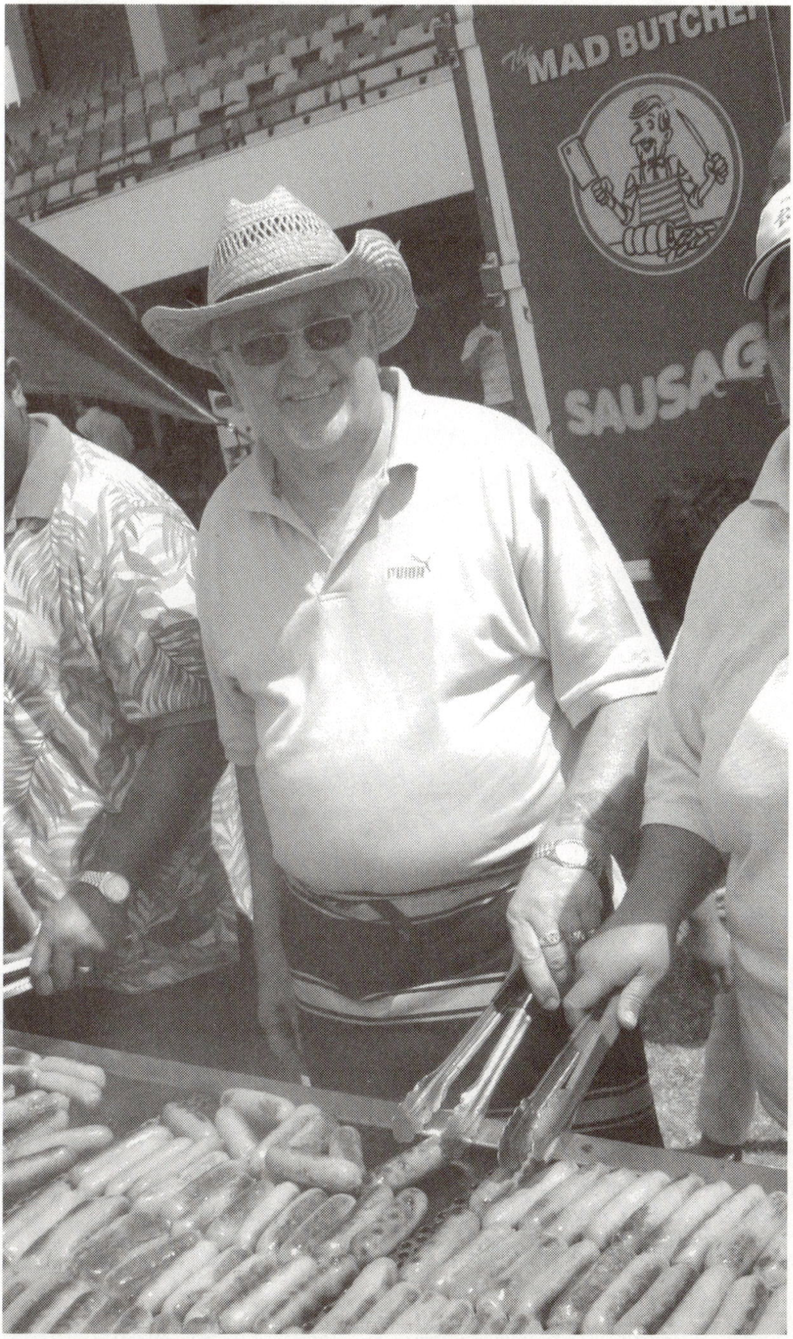
MAD BUTCHE
SAUSAG
PUMA

12

Touring

There are tours, they say, and then there's Papua New Guinea. Peter Leitch loved the place. 'There was something about it, just that sense of adventure because you are so far outside your comfort zone.'

In 1994 Peter and Sel Bennett, from the New Zealand Rugby League, made up the entire supporters' contingent for the Kiwis' tour of PNG. According to coach Frank Endacott, while the two men weren't in the official party, they might as well have been. It was also when Endacott really got to know the Butcher. 'We had a lot of respect for both men,' Frank says, 'and if we needed a hand, nothing was ever any trouble for either of them. They were on the team bus, they were at all of the functions — they were a part of us.'

The PNG tour lasted for three weeks, in a country where league is king but money is short, and playing conditions are intense and very different from the manicured, highly organised world of professional league in New Zealand and Australia.

Things had improved since 1986, when the Kiwis, under coach Graham Lowe, experienced the stuff of nightmares in Lae. First the bus driver, after drinking straight whisky at a stop on the way, started to veer towards the edge of the cliffs on what manager Tom McKeown would later describe as 'not a road, but a track'. The driver only gave up the wheel when threatened with his assistant being thrown out of the door. Kiwi Dean Lonergan drove the bus for the rest of the journey.

At Lae they found the field littered with stones. Lowe refused to let his side play. For the next 24 hours the Kiwis stayed in a locked hotel, while riot police and extra security guards kept an angry mob outside at bay.

Endacott was told in no uncertain terms by the New Zealand Rugby League not to cancel the game at Lae. 'As it turned out, I went down and checked the pitch beforehand with a couple of the local staff and it was very good. They'd done a lot of work.'

There was drama in '94 even before the Kiwis left New Zealand. The first game was due to be played in Rabaul, but a week before the team left, a volcanic eruption spewed lava across the local airport, so the match had to be cancelled and an extra game added in Port Moresby.

The first test was in Goroka in the steamy highlands, where local tribesmen walked out of the mountains for three days to see the match. Endacott says he grew concerned as the Kiwis' bus neared the test ground for a training run. 'We were about 200 metres from the ground, so we could see it, but there was just a sea of heads, literally thousands of Papua New Guineans between us and the gates, and the bus driver couldn't get through. These people were in bare feet, shorts and T-shirts, and they looked tough. I swear there was one guy with a bone through his nose, and there was some sort of a road block. I'll never forget it.'

As the Kiwis' bus shuddered to a halt, something in Peter erupted. 'I thought to myself, we're never going to get in,' he says, but the night before in the team room, Peter had picked up a Lion Red luggage tag that was lying on a table. It would prove to be an important prop. He leapt from the bus, waving the Lion Red tag like an FBI badge, and roared to the PNG cops, 'Head of security for the Kiwi league team. I want this bloody road block taken down, and the way cleared now.'

To this day, you hear the note of disbelief in Endacott's voice when he tells the story. 'The crowd parted like the Red Sea. Pete ended up walking in front of the bus with this red baggage tag, and we ended up with a clear pass to the stadium. Only he could have done that. The bus was travelling at about two kilometres an hour, and the local people were standing back to let us go.'

Peter remembers that 'there were coppers everywhere, and it's fair to say they weren't the friendliest blokes you've ever seen. But bugger me if we didn't get what we wanted.'

A visit to the renowned Asaro mud men, in the highlands northwest of Goroka, by the 1994 Kiwis will be remembered for ever. The legend goes that the mud men were defeated in a tribal battle, and whilst retreating took shelter at night in a muddy river. When they emerged, coated in white clay, their rivals thought they were ghosts, and ran in terror. Today the mud men still coat their bodies in clay, and wear clay masks decorated with human teeth and pigs' fangs.

'You can't get in to see the mud men unless you pay quite a large amount of money,' says Frank Endacott, 'otherwise you don't go there, because they're still walking round with bows and arrows, machetes, and so on. Our manager in '99, Ray Heffernan, negotiated a trip up there. He paid some money to this bloke in the street who was organising it. We went up there in two transit vans.

'We were driving down this mountain road, and we turned into a clearing cut out of the jungle. Then all of a sudden, this fellow, all painted in clay, was in front of us with a machete. The driver said he couldn't go any further, and a hell of an argument started between him and this guy with the machete. The next minute, I have no idea where they came from, but 20 of these guys just walked out of the jungle with masks on, all carrying machetes.

'With the way they looked, and knowing that perhaps we shouldn't be there, I was the most frightened I've ever been in my life. I know that everyone else was too. I looked at the Butcher, and his mouth was open, but he couldn't speak. It was the only time I've ever seen the Butcher lost for words — he couldn't say a thing. I looked at John Lomax and Hitro Okesene, and both of them had turned grey. I thought, "We're in trouble here." It was no joke. I could just see the mud men getting on the bus with their machetes swinging.' When Peter noticed how stricken Lomax was, he felt even worse. 'John's not a man who scares easily,' he says.

At first Peter suspected that the local tour guide had been trying to rip the tribe off, but that almost seemed immaterial. 'There were raised voices, a bit of finger-pointing, they were stood there waving their spears and clubs, and I was thinking, "Holy hell, there's going to be a real war on here in a minute." I thought we were going to get carved up and eaten. I nearly bloody shit myself!'

To the vast relief of the Kiwis, a car came screaming up behind the bus with the bloke they'd paid their money to, who handed over the cash, and immediately the whole tribe's demeanour changed. The head of the tribe smiled, happy now that he had his money.

'Everyone was a lot more relaxed after that,' says Peter. 'We went up to their camp, and they did dances for us, and made us very welcome. We all bought bows and arrows, and took them back as souvenirs to our hotel in Goroka.'

When the tour moved into the towns Peter regained his voice — with a vengeance. In the Kiwis' hotel in Port

Moresby, where guests walked from their rooms down a long, sweeping staircase, Peter would position himself at the bottom of the stairs. Players like Gary Freeman, John Lomax and Jarrod McCracken, standout performers in the Australian club scene, were superstars to Papua New Guinean fans, and as each came along, Peter would boom out the player's name with a voice that could wake the dead.

When the team first came down each morning, there would be two or three league fanatics hanging around the front door. By lunchtime, stirred by the Butcher's spruiking, that number would grow to two or three hundred, clapping and cheering when their heroes appeared. It took very little time for the Butcher to have his own following.

'After a couple of days he was a local hero,' says Frank Endacott. 'They took a while to figure him out, but eventually they realised that every time he started shouting and yelling, it meant the boys were appearing — they loved him.'

On a walk down the street, Peter and the players were never alone. A hundred or more fascinated local people would be at their heels, smiling, chatting, or just getting a close look. On one walkabout Peter and a few players glanced up a hillside and saw what he swears was 'a whole tribe' coming down the hill towards them, fully painted with tribal decorations and armed with spears. 'They were singing and chanting, and were soon all around us,' Peter recalls. 'They just wanted to see the boys up close. I noticed that one of them had a massive knife up his sleeve, and I asked him what it was for — he said in case there was any trouble. I told the boys it was time to get back to the hotel.'

Johnny Lomax in particular was hero-worshipped in Goroka, a fact that Peter used to his advantage. There were endless queues at meal times until Peter persuaded a waiter, by pointing to a skin graft on his arm, that he and Lomax were blood brothers. From that moment on, there were no more queues for brother Butcher.

Game days in Papua New Guinea were never boring. They got even livelier when the Butcher became the security man for the tests.

He and Sel Bennett had been invited to visit the head office of the PNG league to discuss concerns over security at the games. Peter offered to do whatever he could to help. An official said they needed someone on the gate, because some people were trying to sneak in for half-price, and the local security men were often too easily persuaded.

Before the tour was over, the local officials — who Peter says were among the most friendly he has ever encountered — were keen to let him act as a security adviser. With 20 or so policemen backing him up, he was at the gate in Goroka, deciding what was acceptable to bring into the ground, and what wasn't.

'It must have looked quite a sight,' says Peter, 'with this mad whitey at the gate, deciding who could come in and who couldn't. But although it's a wild place in some ways, I thought the local people were fantastic.'

Everybody on the tour knew that, historically, overcrowding at tests in Papua New Guinea often meant many fans were unable to get into the ground, leading to riots outside, which would be met with tear gas fired by the police. It was almost a rite of passage. Sure enough, come the last test, played in Port Moresby, with the game well under way, people without tickets tried to charge the gates. With their backs to the ground, police started to fire tear gas into the crowd.

So far, so scary, but then the wind shifted. Acrid clouds of gas started drifting back over the ground. Firstly, people in the ground starting choking and weeping, then Kiwi winger Sean Hoppe, making a thundering run down the touchline, was brought to a choking, wheezing halt as he sucked in a big lungful of gas.

A few nights before in the team hotel, Peter had been spinning tall tales to some of the players. Drawing on a fictitious stint in the SAS, he told the Kiwis how to deal with a possible gas attack. 'You hit the deck, grab a towel, and stay low. That's how we used to do it.' The day after the test match, the biggest photo in the local paper didn't show any action from the game, but a shot of all the New Zealanders, face down on the turf, with towels over their heads.

The Kiwis had blasted into the game at Port Moresby, up 16–0 by half-time, and despite a comeback by the locals in the second half, and a jittery referee, who had been showered with cans at half-time, they held on for a 30–16 victory.

The tests were won, but not without massive efforts. In the first test, played in oppressive humidity, the Kiwis were just 2–0 up at half-time. During the break, trying to get out of the blazing sun, the Kiwis huddled inside what appeared to be a big car case. The most talkative player in the side was always veteran half-back Gary Freeman. But on this occasion, recalls coach Endacott, he didn't have the energy to say one word, he was just trying to suck in air. 'I looked at him,' says Endacott, 'and I thought, "We're in trouble here."

But about five minutes later, big clouds came over, and we won by 16 points. It was hard fought. They had a very good team at that time.'

Colin McKenzie called the Kiwis' games on the radio for two decades from 1982, and he has extensive first-hand knowledge of how becoming friends with the Mad Butcher is to learn how big-hearted the man can be.

It was no surprise to Colin when another friend told him of a group of Auckland league fans who had derided Colin's commentaries in front of Peter. Bagging the caller, as Colin is the first to agree, comes with the territory, but bagging him and not realising you're doing it in front of a close friend can be acutely embarrassing.

The jeering was barely under way when the Butcher exploded. Now, an angry Peter Leitch defines the phrase 'force of nature'. Verbally pinning the group to the wall, he left them shell-shocked, but a little wiser about making comments when you don't know the background of those listening, and a whole lot wiser about how attacking one of his mates brings out the fighting side of the Mad Butcher.

'I think because we'd both come from what used to be

called working-class backgrounds made a difference to our friendship,' Colin McKenzie says. 'We had old-fashioned values, if you like — mateship, helping anyone who needed a hand, that sort of thing.

'He just never forgets you. I was sitting at home one Sunday morning in the early hours, watching the Kiwis play, and the phone goes at half-time. It was Peter calling from the ground at St Helens to tell me he was thinking about the last time we had been there together.'

Colin loves to tell the story of how Peter is the only person ever to almost get him beaten up during a commentary. The Kiwis were on a British tour in 1999, playing a night game in Hull in the northeast of England. Colin was broadcasting in the stand, alongside the Hull supporters, with an engineer from the BBC working on the sound, and Peter as his comments man. A local woman lit up a cigarette. The stand was officially non-smoking, and Peter, not being a man to let a sleeping dog lie for a nanosecond, was quick to remind her of the rules.

She snapped back at him, and a loud, lively debate erupted. The crowd mostly loved it, and when Hull took an early lead, Peter was copping it not just from the smoker, but from all corners of the stand. It turned a bit sour, in Colin's memory, when the Kiwis rallied and took the lead.

'Peter wasn't going to miss the chance to give them a bit back, and of course the mood maybe wasn't as good-natured as it had been. I looked up into the dark and all I could see was this huge shape looming towards us with the glow of a cigarette butt in the air. I thought, "This is it, bashed in Hull," and then I felt this sharp pressure on my head. But then whoever it was just turned and shot away.'

When he was packing up after the game, Colin found a huge gash in the top of his headphones. The lady smoker, or one of her friends, had stubbed out a cigarette on the top of his head.

On some earlier tours, Peter would arrive without being highly organised. Colin was one he knew he could rely on for a room to share. 'I think it was the same year as the headphones incident,' Colin recalls. 'Peter turned up for a few days and announced he was going to sleep on a stretcher in my room. Of course he used to turn up with barely a change of clothes, and my room — because I was a working journo — used to be set up like an office.

'Well, Pete had been there about three days, all unofficial of course, although the hotel obviously knew he was there, when he decides he's going to pad down the hall and have a chat with Tank Gordon, the coach. Anyway, I had to ring down for some milk, and this beautiful young Scandinavian lass brings it up. She bends down to put it in the fridge for me, and is just standing up when in walks Peter in his baggy undies and his string singlet. What a sight he was!

'Well, he's basically standing there while this young lady doesn't know where to look since they are almost nose to nose. Ever the gentleman, and despite having no teeth in, Pete just sticks out his hand and says: "Peter Bloody Leitch from New Zealand. What's your name, dear?"'

Gary Endacott is the son of former Warriors and Kiwis coach Frank, but while the Endacott family is famous for its close, affectionate and supportive nature, Gary is a man you feel would have made his mark regardless of his family background.

A sufferer of cerebral palsy, his grit has carried him through some astounding physical feats, from playing club rugby league, to running a marathon, to climbing Mt Kilimanjaro in Tanzania. His courage is matched by a keen sense of humour, and a zest for life that made him a perfect fit for a supporters' group led by Peter on a 1995 Kiwis tour of Great Britain, a team coached by Frank.

'Peter's just a top bloke, but everyone you talk to is going to tell you that,' says Gary. 'I reckon you'd do well to get next to Janice, then you'd understand that old saying about behind every good man is a good woman. Sure, Peter's been successful at business and that, but I know he'd tell you Janice played a huge part in that. The reason I chuck Janice into the mix is because probably everyone is going to tell you stories about what a good bloke he is, and he is that — he's a real top bloke.

'But the way to get to the real Peter is just to talk to him about his family. He can be full of bullshit and showmanship about anything, but when he talks about his family — Janice and the grandchildren in particular — there is no bullshit whatsoever. That's when you see the real person inside that big personality. Peter gives more than he takes, and the world would be a better place if there were a few more like him.

'On that '95 tour we used to spend a lot of time riding in the bus and, of course, Peter would get on the microphone and be the hard shot that he is. Pity you if you got in his eyeline, because you'd cop it big style. But one day I said, "I've had enough of this." I got up and took the microphone off him and turned the tables on him. I was giving him heaps and he just looked at me and said, "I'll get you for that."

'I just laughed and thought nothing of it. But he waited until it was something like 3 a.m. in New Zealand, and he rang my mum up. He told her he was putting me on the next plane home. When she asked why, he said it was because he wasn't going to put up with anyone who could talk more bullshit than him.'

Gary Endacott has become an inspirational speaker, and Peter has been one of his most enthusiastic supporters. However, what means the most to Gary is the knowledge that Peter's extensive work on his behalf has come from Peter's belief in him, rather than from loyalty and friendship. 'That's meant an awful lot to me, that he did it because he believed what I had done was genuinely inspirational. He admired me in my own right. When you have a disability, that doesn't always happen — people see the disability and not the person — so it's all the more special when it comes from someone you respect so highly.'

In 2003 the New Zealand Rugby League initiated a 'league supporter of the year' award, and at that year's awards dinner, Gary was announced as the first winner. 'There I was with all these big names, legends of the game really,' says Gary, 'and I think I was more excited to be receiving the award from Pete than he was in recognising me. It was bloody awesome.

'There are those out there who bag Peter, but they are people who either don't know him or are jealous. I believe there's confidence and there's ego and there's arrogance. Peter might have bundles of confidence, and he might even have a big ego, but anyone lucky enough to know him well knows there isn't any arrogance. He's just a top bloke doing the best he can. He gets heaps of respect in our home.'

Greg Dawson is a Southland league man whose relationship with Peter began when Greg was coaching an age group team at a national championships. In 1999 it was arranged that he would join Peter and a couple of Peter's friends from Auckland and travel to a State of Origin game in Brisbane.

At the last minute, for a variety of reasons, everyone else had to pull out of the trip. Greg rang Peter and said he'd already had his air fares to Auckland paid, so he would fly up, see some friends and family, and hopefully catch up with Peter at some stage. Letting people down is a terrible sin in the Mad Butcher's book, and he immediately assured Greg that he'd make sure he had a great weekend in Auckland.

Sure enough, there was a trip to the races at Ellerslie,

a dash to Carlaw Park to catch a secondary schools' championship semi-final, and then an invitation for Greg and his friend Mike to join Peter at his home to watch the State of Origin game on television.

Picked up and driven to Bucklands Beach by the Butcher, the pair were escorted into the bar at the back of Peter's house, and told to enjoy whatever they liked to drink while watching the game on the room's big television screen. 'So we settle down to watch the game, and it's absolutely pissing down in Queensland,' Greg says. 'The Butcher is saying, "We're lucky we're not there. We'd be absolutely soaked by now, to be fair."

'We all agree. Then he carries on, saying, "Actually, I'd rather watch it from my armchair in my own home. I can concentrate on the game more, mate." The game kicks off, Mike and I settle into another stubbie, and five minutes later we look over to get a comment from Pete and he's fast asleep.

'At the end of the game, Pete comes to during the after-match comments from the commentators, who are raving about how good the match was. Peter agrees, saying, "Mate, what a great game. But we'd have been soaked by now if we were there." Mike and I both agree with him, then after finishing off our beers we say to Pete we're going to call a taxi. He goes off at us and says, "Don't be stupid, I'll drop you guys off. I've had nothing to drink."

'So we're all in the car going down the Pakuranga highway, talking about the game, and Butch again says, "Mate, I'd really rather watch a game like that at home, so I can analyse it from my own armchair."

'My mate Mike, who's pretty cheeky himself, can't help himself, and says, "Butcher, the only thing you analysed tonight was the inside of your eyelids!"

'I swear to you, the Butcher almost exploded. We were lucky the car didn't take off and fly.'

A year later there was another near-transport-disaster, on the way to the final of the 2000 Rugby League World Cup at Old Trafford in Manchester. The home of Manchester United and test cricket in the summer, it seemed inconceivable that a local bus driver could get confused, but that was exactly what happened. The driver arrived late and, in Greg Dawson's memory, that added to the already highly charged emotional state that as usual had overtaken Peter on his way to support the Kiwis.

'Peter wasn't impressed, and there was a lecture for the driver on what was expected. Amazingly he missed the turnoff to Old Trafford, and when you're on an English motorway system, on a ring road around a big city, it's very hard to double back to where you want to be. The Butcher was beside himself. He threatened to take the wheel and drive the bus himself. We kept going faster and faster and eventually arrived, just making it into our seats as the Kiwis began the haka.

'I'm sure there's a bus driver in Manchester who'll remember the day of the final — and the Mad Butcher — at least as long as we will.'

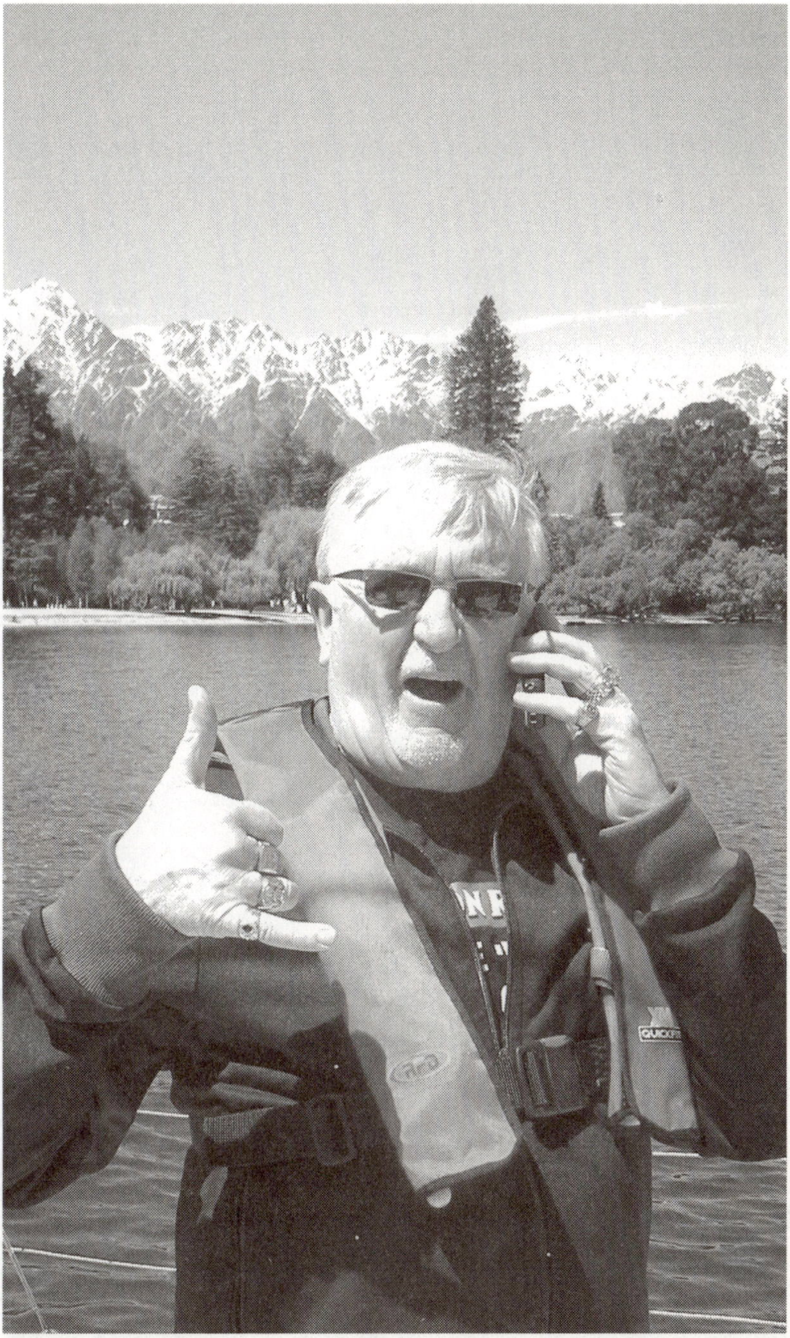

13

Kiwi manager

It will surprise some people, but Peter Leitch hasn't spent decades inside the Kiwi camp. It's true he's a massive supporter, and has been for many years, clocking up tens of thousands of air miles, cheering himself hoarse at grounds everywhere from Brisbane to Bradford, leading supporters' tours more often than Shane Warne has woken in a strange room, and toasting the boys with Lion Red in all parts of the league world.

Former Kiwi trainer Bob Lanigan speaks for many when he says he was blown away by Peter's passion for the team. 'He'd pay his own way to everything, and he was just as happy as a dog with two tails. I suppose when the curtain finally does come down he'll be able to say he enjoyed his life and has few regrets.'

But until the 2004 Tri-Nations, Peter had never been on a major trip as a Kiwi official. He clearly remembers his feelings on the day that changed — Saturday, 9 October 2004 — when he crossed over the Auckland harbour bridge to join the Kiwi squad at the Millennium Institute in Albany. 'I was bubbling with excitement as I drove over the bridge,' he says, 'because I'd never gone away on a long trip in an official position with the Kiwis. It was six weeks, which was going to be quite a challenge. I was listed as gear steward — sort of an assistant to the managers, Gordon Gibbons, who was the business manager, and Pat Carthy.'

He had been brought into the group at the urging of coach Daniel Anderson. 'At that point in time Peter seemed to be at a stage in his life where he was really fizzing along, and it radiated out to everyone around him,' says Anderson. 'I think his grandchildren were at an age where he could spoil them if he wanted to. He was so happy with his lot that every day he felt like he wanted to do something for someone else. Rarely did I see him want something for himself. I think that was the big thing I got from him as a person. He could never offer enough of himself for you.'

Right from the start, Peter was enthused about the

attitude he found in the camp as the Kiwis prepared for their first game against Australia at North Harbour Stadium. 'On the Monday night, all the players went off for massages, except for [the captain] Ruben Wiki, who went to Mt Wellington to Sky TV to go on Murray Deaker's programme,' Peter says. 'I drove Ruben out to Sky, so I had him to myself for 20 minutes, and I quizzed him about how close the guys really were. He said that they were genuinely very close.'

The memories from 2004 remain vivid for Peter. The man everyone was talking about was Sonny Bill Williams, already being cited by Aussie league legends as potentially one of the greatest players the game had ever seen. Boy genius or not, Sonny Bill shared the same sense of humour as the rest of the team, which quickly became evident. 'I had the time to watch them when they were relaxed and being themselves,' Peter says. 'They played a lot of jokes on each other.

'For example, Clinton Toopi was playing pool, and he was lining up a vital shot when Paul Rauhihi jostled the cue. There was some evil eye going on, and then they start laughing. When we came back from training on about the third day of camp, someone had put all these clippings out of the paper on Sonny Bill's door. There was no malice in it. Sonny Bill's a lovely young boy, very modest — even a little bit shy, to be fair.'

Others remember the time when the Butcher, whose dearest friends wouldn't rate him as the world's best driver, took control of a van for a trip to a North Shore restaurant. From that night on, Kiwi Matt Utai, without fear on a footy field, wouldn't go near a vehicle if Peter was anywhere near the wheel. Even 2005–06 coach Brian McClennan, who basically doesn't have a bad word to say about Peter, gives his driving the thumbs down. 'He's the worst driver I've ever been with in a car. Peter always has about five or six things going through his mind but, unfortunately, when he's driving, that's actually one of the last things he's thinking about.'

Peter will always remember the first time in 2004 when he had an official task involving a member of the public. 'We were having a closed session at North Harbour Stadium. There was a guy inside the stadium. I had to ask him to leave, which he wasn't too happy about.' So any chance of spying was averted? 'No, he just went outside and looked through the chain-mesh fence.'

Peter saw how Wairangi Koopu had been painstakingly teaching Brent Webb the haka. 'He was working at it with Wairangi, and then Ruben Wiki said it was time for the whole team to begin on the haka, and it turned out Wairangi had been teaching poor old Brent a different one from the one the team used.'

Peter was astounded at how laid back Francis Meli was before a game. He'd often leave it so late that he'd go onto the field with a cup of drink in his hand. Peter asked coach Daniel Anderson if he thought Meli could actually go to sleep in the changing shed. 'He has that potential,' laughed Anderson.

David Kidwell was one of the Kiwis, based in Australia, who didn't really get to know Peter until he became a Kiwi official. 'He was just a bloke I knew to say hello to from the early days of the Warriors,' Kidwell says. 'It really took off in 2004 with the Butch and the Kiwis. That's when I realised that he was one of those characters who wasn't just a league fanatic; he was a genuine mate too.

'That's not changed since then, and whenever I'm in town I always contact the Butch, and he does the same with me. I think he's a presence the New Zealand Rugby League is really going to miss. I know the players love him and I think the public does too, because he has that larger-than-life persona.

'I don't know how many times I've been walking along with him and you can see people looking at him, and thinking, "That's the Mad Butcher." Then he'll do his "Hello, dear" thing and you'll ask him afterwards who that was and he says he doesn't know, just someone who obviously knew who he was, and it costs nothing to be polite. That's old-fashioned advice, but it's right, isn't it? With his personality he can make anyone feel welcome in any situation, and I can't speak highly enough of any man who can do that.

'I know he regularly tells people about his soft spot for Souths, but you can bet he has a soft spot for Leeds, St Helens, Parramatta, the Storm, and any other team that's got one of his former Warriors or Kiwis in it. Once you've crossed his path, you are like one of his family. That was really important in the Kiwis' camp for the players and all the officials. When you put that black-and-white jersey on, you are representing something special. I mean, it's obviously about your country, but to us it became playing for your family. To Peter, it was as if we were all his sons.

'You know how "to be fair" is a bit of a Butcher saying? I reckon that's bang on, because it says more about him than he realises. He can be a hard man, but he's also a fair man. And I don't reckon that's a bad thing to say about any man. I know I'm proud to call him a friend.'

During that first test week in 2004 the Kiwis had trained at Hato Petera College in Takapuna. The occasion was marked with a powhiri from the boys at the school, which touched many of the Kiwis, but Peter was disappointed that very few fans turned up to watch an open training.

'It was an impressive occasion and I really felt it was worthy of more attention than it got,' he says. 'So I called everyone I knew in the media and whoever else would listen, and I asked them to give a plug to the last open day we had at training, at North Harbour Stadium. We got a reasonably good crowd. Monty Betham cooked a barbecue that I put on and it went well. On the night before the game with Australia, Gordon Gibbons [the football manager] arranged for us to go to the Northcote league club. They decorated the club rooms in black and white for the occasion. We were back at the grass roots, not in a flash hotel.

'Daniel Anderson had arranged for [Olympic triathlon gold medal winner] Hamish Carter to speak to the team. The guys seemed quite taken by it. Hamish Carter commented that he wasn't going to tell the boys how to get motivated. If you weren't motivated by the black jersey, you'd never be motivated.'

Inside the team for the first time, Peter's job on game day was to make sure everyone got on the bus at 2.45 p.m. to go to North Harbour Stadium, and that the players had their number-one outfits with them for the after-match function; they travelled to the game in tracksuits. Earlier Gordon Gibbons had gone to the ground with Willie Halligan, the Auckland Rugby League's development officer — someone Peter rates as a great guy for league — and the physio, Jonathon Moyle, to set up the room and the jerseys.

'We set up a table at the hotel with what the guys needed to make their own sandwiches,' Peter says. 'Some of the players were there, and some were in their rooms asleep. It amazes me how much some of the boys sleep on game day. There had been some negative talk about the promotion of the test, but I thought the league had promoted it quite well. The million-dollar question was whether it would have drawn a bigger crowd if it had been played at Mt Smart. You could get a family pass for $50 though, which looked reasonable to me. I do wonder sometimes if the theory about rugby league's heart and soul is sometimes overplayed.'

Speculation before the game was that the Kiwis were in for a hiding. Aussie league hard man Mark Geyer had suggested the Kiwis needn't turn up, because all they would get was embarrassment. Injuries in the Kiwis had reached such a point, he claimed, that the Aussies were playing a reserve grade side.

But after 80 brutal minutes, the game was drawn 16-all. Tony Puletua, the Kiwi and Penrith second rower, said, 'I'll have to give Mark a call when I get back to Australia.' The Kiwis paid a toll for their gutsy effort. Willie Halligan says that the team 'gave it death. From the number of ice packs that were being used after the game, there were some real battered and bruised guys in the shed.'

The Australians were supposed to have a meal afterwards with the Kiwis, but they went straight back to their hotel. 'Their excuse was that it was pre-arranged,' says Peter. 'It worked out good for us, because the players could have a meal with their families. After the game I was interviewed on television, and I looked straight down the barrel and said, "Mark Geyer, if this is our reserve grade, watch out Australia when we put our top side out."'

The next day the Kiwis flew out to London, via Kuala Lumpur. 'We needed two buses for the trip to the airport in Auckland,' says Peter, 'one for the players, one for the luggage. We had two-and-a-half tonnes of luggage — 160 pieces.' In a karaoke bar in Kuala Lumpur on their one-night stopover, Daniel Anderson stunned the players when he sang *All Shook Up*, the Elvis classic. 'To be fair, you wouldn't pay to see him,' says Peter, 'but then two of the locals got up, and they made him look sensational.'

On the first night in London, in a warm British bar, a combination of Speight's and jetlag nearly wrote off the Butcher's phone, an item that is to him what oxygen is to the rest of us. 'I went with Dayne Norton, the team's head trainer, to a hotel to see Manchester United play Prague Sparta on television. I was able to get a Speight's. The jetlag kicked in and I fell in my beer, dropping my phone. The battery went flying one way and the phone the other. It's not good for the Butcher to lose his phone, mate.'

London, and England, had its surprises in store for the group. A visit to the House of Lords had been arranged by Neil Turner, the MP for Wigan. Turner told them he reckoned the Kiwis would win their next game against Australia, at Loftus Road, because they were so much bigger than the Aussies. Guests or not, a lunch in a meeting room at the House of Lords still cost £15 a head, for a very English spread of salmon and cottage cheese sandwiches, washed down with lemonade and orangeade.

Taking the players who wanted a meal away from the hotel to a restaurant was an eye-opener. 'I got Kirk Pittman, who used to work with the NZRL and now lives in London, to guide us,' says Peter. 'So we got a bus and went to an Angus Steak House. The guys had a good feed, but the bill was £336 ($900) for 16 guys, with no alcohol, and most of the guys didn't have an entrée. A rib-eye steak was £14.50 ($39), and each extra vegetable was £2 ($5.40). It's not cheap in London. I got a haircut at the hotel, and it was £24!'

The two assistant coaches in 2004, Brian McClellan and James Leuluai, shared a room. McClellan found getting a night's sleep hard work when he discovered Leuluai was a world-champion snorer. 'Brian's got two hearing aids that go inside his ears,' says Peter. 'The first night, he got out of bed and took the batteries out of the hearing aids, but it still didn't help him. In the end he had to buy some ear plugs.'

The jerseys for the Loftus Road test were presented by Sean Fitzpatrick, the former All Black captain who now lives in England and works as a commentator for British television. 'Sean was inspirational,' says Peter. 'He did it for free, and he'd just flown back from a sports conference in India. He then drove for 50 km through London traffic to get there, which is quite some feat.'

The game would hurt the Kiwis, as the Australians kicked away to a 32–12 victory. 'After the game we went upstairs and had a bit of a feed,' says Peter. 'It was a bit chaotic to be honest, and it's never pleasant when you lose. The boys suffered this loss.' The next day, the team departed for the long slog up the motorway to Leeds, where a 6 November date awaited for the test against Great Britain at Galpharm Stadium in Huddersfield.

Prior to the test were two other events, one of which — a day trip from Leeds to Blackpool — is now world famous in New Zealand league. There were ten in the mini-bus that headed off to that famous northern England seaside resort, all expecting a good time. As Peter describes it: 'We got up there, and everything was turned off. There were no bars open, all the fun rides were closed, and there was this cold wind blowing through — and I mean cold. At least the shops were open, and I can tell you that the players do not mind going shopping.'

The other event was an odd fixture that was played in Workington, an eight-hour round trip from Leeds. A combined Anzac side, with players from the Kiwis and the Kangaroos, played an England A side. 'Originally some of the players weren't going to go up,' says Peter, 'but a few of them got together, and went to the coach and said, "Hey, we all want to go up and support the boys." So it was eight hours on the bus, and back at about 3 a.m.'

The day before the Anzac game — a free day for the rest of the Kiwi squad — Peter was supposed to take Brent Webb to the dentist because he'd had a toothache the night before. 'But this tough Vodafone Warrior and Kiwi didn't like the thought of being in the chair, so he pulled out,' Peter laughs.

A crowd of about 4500 turned up for the Anzac game in Workington. 'They had a speedway track around the outside with the field in the middle,' Peter recalls. 'You'd compare it with the likes of Carlaw Park — it was a pretty old stadium.' The test was won 64–12 by the Anzacs, and that was pretty much the end of the good news for 2004.

First came the game with Great Britain, which the Kiwis lost 22–12. With it went their chances of success in the tournament. Clinton Toopi summed up the feelings of most of the team: 'It was hard to be there with the British guys after the game. I don't want to sound like a sore loser, but I just wanted to get out of there. I didn't want to mix and mingle. That's just the way it is. It is good to get to know the guys, but I was hurting a bit. So my first thought really was to get out of there ASAP, and on the bus.'

The dismay was everywhere in the side. After the game

Murray Deaker rang Peter and asked if he could speak with Ruben. 'At first Ruben turned me down when I asked him,' Peter says. 'But a minute or two later he came to me and said, "I should do it. I'll do it, Butch." He was just so gutted by the loss.'

Worse was to come. In the next pool game, the Australians, to the astonishment of everyone, lost 24–12 to Great Britain. If the Australians had won, the Kiwis could have made the final if they beat Great Britain in the last pool game. Peter was at the JJB stadium in Wigan for the Great Britain victory. 'I've never been so devastated with a loss. I was gutted, just gutted — I really felt it. I'd left home thinking we were going to do well in this tournament.

'The Poms in the crowd were incredible that night in Wigan. They were on their feet, shouting "Britain, Britain" right through the whole game. It was devastating for me to be watching it. I was lucky enough to be in the director's box with people like Mal Meninga and Alex Murphy — I get on very well with Alex. But it was a sad night despite the good company.'

The final test against Great Britain in Hull was close, but the Kiwis lost 26–22, which left assistant coach James Leuluai bitterly disappointed. 'Knowing that you had a chance to be there is what hurt the most. We were leading at half-time on both occasions, but then had two ten-minute periods where we lost the games, costing us a chance to be in the final.'

Peter was disappointed too, but looked, and found, positives. 'We'd got seven or eight new caps. We'd got four teenagers who had a real taste of test footy. It was going to get better.'

A key man in the revival of the Kiwis in the 2005 Tri-Nations was Brian 'Bluey' McClennan, who with his Mt Albert team in the Bartercard Cup had become the most successful local coach in New Zealand. McClennan became the Kiwis coach when Daniel Anderson went to St Helens in Great Britain at the end of 2004. Before Daniel Anderson left, Peter was appointed to the football manager's job, and also became the media liaison man.

'To be the Kiwi manager was a dream come true for me,' Peter says. 'I was asked to go into the office by Sel Pearson, who at that time was the head of the New Zealand Rugby League. He and Daniel were there. They put it on me to be the football manager. At first I rejected it, because, as I pointed out to them, I'm not too good with the bookwork.

They explained to me why they wanted me to be the football manager, and that Pat Carthy, the business manager, would look after the paperwork. So I accepted the position, and then, of course, Daniel took the job in England.'

Peter confesses to having a little worm of unease in his mind when the Kiwis assembled for the 2005 Tri-Nations campaign. It was over how much experience McClennan had. 'It'd be fair to say when he got the job that I had some doubts. I wasn't sure he was ready for the big time. It's a big jump to international league from being a Bartercard Cup coach.'

Within days Peter knew he had no need to worry. 'Any doubts [about the coach] were soon dispelled. I came away from the tour a very, very big Brian McClennan fan. He has great wisdom. When he first got the job, I remember him saying he might get his father, Mike, to come into the coaching box with him. Mike's always been a great mentor to him. But I thought to myself, "That's no good, mate. People will say it's your father that's doing the coaching." But I didn't have to say anything to him. After a couple of days he said to me, "I've changed my mind about that. I think I'll go on my own."

'One of the key things was that Bluey had a way of turning a loss into a positive. He was never negative. He had a saying that he joked about with me. He'd say, "I love finals, Butch, and I love winning finals." It wasn't head-up-your-arse stuff — he genuinely loved what goes with a final.'

Peter's respect for McClennan, as a person and a coach, would continue to grow massively during the next two years that they worked together as manager and coach. 'Brian is very humble, very calm and collected, very balanced in what he does,' Peter says. 'Even in the changing room he's not a screamer or a shouter. He'll talk very quietly, and say something like, "Fellas, this is from the bottom of my heart. If you keep going forward, we will win the game." It was a pleasure to work for Brian. He's so down to earth, and, obviously, he's a very good coach. He communicates very well with the players.

'With coaching in New Zealand, he's won the Bartercard Cup so often that some people say they should rename it after him. Locally he's got a great track record. Part of Brian's success was that he got to work under Daniel Anderson, and Daniel was a very good mentor to him. Brian got to see how Daniel went about things.

'I've got on with all the coaches, going back to Graham Lowe and Bob Bailey, and I think most of them knew that I had a true passion for the game — that there was no motive, no hidden agendas. The only coaches I didn't really have a lot to do with were Gary Freeman and Howie Tamati. That's no disrespect to either of them — it just didn't eventuate. I've known Gary a long time, and Howie's a good friend.

'We've had some very good coaches. Look at Daniel Anderson, who has won everything in front of him since he's coached in England, or Frank Endacott, or Graham Lowe. No disrespect to any other coach I've ever worked with, because I respect them all, and I've been lucky enough never to work with an arsehole, but in my opinion Brian McClennan has the X factor. He has a God-given gift to communicate with people. I'm a big fan, I believe in him. I like his principles. I rate him.'

McClennan first became aware of the Mad Butcher when Peter was running pre-season tournaments in the 1980s in Auckland. 'He was one of those guys who was always doing something for league. I'd met him many times even before we went on tour together. He's so outgoing — you feel like you know him anyway. I would have called myself a friend of his, but I would have been one of thousands.

'In 2005, when I was the coach and Peter was managing the tour party, we worked together really closely — you have to — and that was when we got to know each other as good mates. On tour for about six weeks, day in, day out, with 24 young men full of testosterone, there's plenty to do, and you've really got to have your wits about you, and stick together.

'I think the main reason we got on so well together is that we're both positive people. I know the players just love the Butcher. He's a very upfront sort of person, out in the public view, where I'm a bit more withdrawn — not when I'm with the team, but in public I'm happy to lie a bit low.

'I do think we have a lot in common. I think we're both kind people, we like the company of others, and have the same sort of values. With the Butcher, he's not only really positive, but there's energy with a capital E. There's that old saying, "Show me, don't tell me." Well, he's definitely a "show me" guy, and it rubs off on you.

'I learnt a lot off the Butch. One lesson was about getting things done. When you're involved with him on a daily basis, you see why he's so successful. He's so relentless. When something has to be done, he gets it done right then, right now. He never puts it off. He just keeps going and going until it's done.

'What made him the best manager was that it's a pretty thankless job at times, and the number of little things you have to do for people is endless. He suits that. He wants to do that. In that touring environment there's a lot of giving that you have to do. He was tireless. He is so successful because he makes sure that everything is right. He'll double-check, then double-check again, that everything is how it should be.

'We always had more than what we needed. If we needed Powerade drinks, there would be Powerade drinks to last us a year. He just made sure we had all the extras he could find. He almost spoils you to death. He's so generous with his time, and I think he demonstrates that in his general life, with the things he's done for charity and the things he's done for players; the sheer volume of what he's done for people is just phenomenal. To me he's just a great New Zealander.'

Louie Anderson, the young Kiwi forward now playing in England, echoes McClennan's views on the energy Peter threw into his job. 'I don't know what the Butcher takes, or what he does, but every day from early in the morning — and he's a man who gets up at 6 o'clock — he's noisy, and full of energy. Then he'll be awake all day, with no rest, and he'll still be going at 10 o'clock at night, still full of energy.

'He's the funniest man I've met. To be honest, I don't

know how he does it. I'm about 40 years younger, and some days I wake up and I just want to be quiet, and be by myself for a while.'

A key member of the 2005 Kiwis was inspirational half-back Stacey Jones, who earlier in the year had left the Warriors to play for the Catalans Dragons in France. His intention then was to play only club league. Peter and Bluey McClennan were pivotal in getting Jones to change his mind and make himself available for the Kiwis.

'The one thing about Butch is that he never puts pressure on me,' says Jones, 'but when he talked about me maybe coming back, he said, in his words, "it'd be bloody fantastic" if I did. He does make you, in his own certain way, want to be involved. He has the knack of doing that.'

Discussions between Jones and coach McClennan had been going on for a couple of months leading into the 2005 tournament, before Jones agreed to play. 'Bluey would ring me, and we'd talk, and as soon as I hung up the phone I'd think, "Yeah, I'm going to play — I'd love to play for this bloke." Then I'd get home and think about it, and talk to my wife Rachelle, and I'd have second thoughts.

'Eventually I reached a stage where I thought, "I've *got* to do it." And it's been good. In 2005 when I was asked to play, I initially agreed just to play two games, but then Lance [Hohaia] got injured, and things just went from there.'

Jones sees the combination of Bluey and the Butcher as one that always had genuine concern for the players' well-being. 'Butch was always going around asking the boys what they wanted to do. He was always on his toes, and making sure everyone was happy. They were always talking to the senior players about what we thought we should be doing, whether it was too much, or not enough.'

McClennan places great emphasis on team harmony, and that's where the Butcher was a godsend. 'If you're ever striving for success, the first thing you have to do is create the right environment,' says McClennan. 'If you've got a manager like the Butch who makes sure everything is spot-on, then you're halfway there. He'd be the last to bed and the first up. He'd do things like making sure the team room was all stocked up with drinks, that it was clean — the sort of things people wouldn't expect someone like him would need to do.

'When all the details are looked after, it gives you the time to concentrate on football, and it also gives you the confidence that the emotional feeling in the team is going to be strong. Other than being very professional at his job, he's a very funny man. When you have meetings, obviously he chairs it, and our meetings would have a lot of laughter. In fact, wherever he walked around the hotel, you could follow where he'd been by the laughter. He kept everyone happy.

'I remember that he'd do the whiteboard in the team room and fill it with details of what we were going to be doing the next day. He had to work hard on that. I was well aware of his dyslexia, but it's a condition that doesn't have anything to do with the intelligence and wisdom of the man.

'The word "love" was the one that we used the most. We loved what we were doing. We loved the opportunity to do what we were doing. We loved each other's company. Our saying was that we love winning more than we hate losing. That was the philosophy.

'You can't deny that the Butcher loves every day that he's living, because he fills up every minute of a day. Whilst we were in camp, he was living proof of that love of life, every hour of every day. He had fun, and he made sure everything was right. I was never ashamed to talk about love in front of the team, or to talk about it in public, because that's how it was.

'It was a huge strength, because whether we like it or accept it, the fact is that when you play the Australians at rugby league they're usually better than us. But team spirit is the one thing we knew we could beat them at. So it was very important to us that we got that right. Of course, you've got the tactics and so on that go with it, but you've got to love what you're doing, and what you're fighting for before you can carry out any tactic with purpose.

'The culture you create is critical to how you're going to perform as a team, because you want everybody working together as hard as they can, with all the arrows going the same way, to reach the best of your potential. I'm proud to say that with the Butcher, and myself, and all of us working together in 2005, I believe we were somewhere close to our potential.

'There were so many times when there would be a word from the Butcher at just the right time that helped you. He's so kind, but he's also so mentally tough. He's never worried about confrontation if it's needed. If someone was doing something that was going to affect the well-being of the team, he was straight onto it. Fortunately we were lucky enough to have a team that had a lot of pride in what we were representing.

'They really bought into the fact that you have to be great

off the field if you're going to be great on the field. Butch was a father figure to the players — he made it so that they didn't want to let him down. You have so much respect for him. On the odd occasion when a player did let him down a bit, they felt pretty bad about it afterwards.

'The way he is in a team environment is contagious. If you're enthusiastic, that's contagious. So being the style of man he is, and being in a senior position as a manager, what happens on the field is reflective of him, as it is of the captain, or the coach, or the other staff. His job was to keep it all together.

'We came up with the idea where we wanted to build for the World Cup [to be held in 2008], so we made up a DVD we called *Kiwiana*, about all the great athletes from New Zealand. It was headed by Sir Edmund Hillary climbing Everest, the greatest feat by someone from our country, and was set to the music of people like Dave Dobbyn and Neil Finn. On our 2006 tour of New Zealand, I said to the Butcher, "Gee, it'd be great to have some of those people come in to see the team." No sooner said than, bang, he was on to it.

'In Auckland we had Olympic gold-medal kayakers Ian Ferguson and Paul MacDonald come in, which was superb, then Sir Richard Hadlee in Christchurch, and Olympic gold-medal swimmer Danyon Loader in Wellington. When those guys were just standing there, these great icons, it was just a hugely powerful thing for our young men — they'd grown up with these guys as their heroes. Then they said they loved what the Kiwis were doing, and our guys could ask them questions about what they did to be so successful.

'It was the Butcher's networking that made that happen. He would do anything to make things better for the Kiwis. He's a genuine guy, and he's got empathy for people, which is what makes him such a great person. He's been successful, but he's richer in character than he is in money.'

In 2005 the campaign began with a test in Sydney, a graveyard for Kiwi hopes since 1959, when a test was last won there by New Zealand. Coach McClennan and his assistant Graeme Norton fixed on a theme, as they would before most games in the Tri-Nations. For the game at Telstra Stadium on 15 October, it was 'Bully the Bully'.

Determined not to yield to the power and ability of a side that could start Andrew Johns and Darren Lockyer in the halves, the Kiwis began like maniacs, and were up 18–0 after 20 minutes. The Aussies fought back, but at the

You don't often see political statements at a league game, but this fan at Mt Smart is very clear where his vote will go.

Warrior Jerry Seuseu, a huge crowd favourite during his 132 games for the club, joins Peter at the Mad Butcher's Lounge.

United in league. Kiwis captain Ruben Wiki and Kangaroos captain Darren Lockyer with Peter, by then Kiwis manager, and the Trans-Tasman Cup.

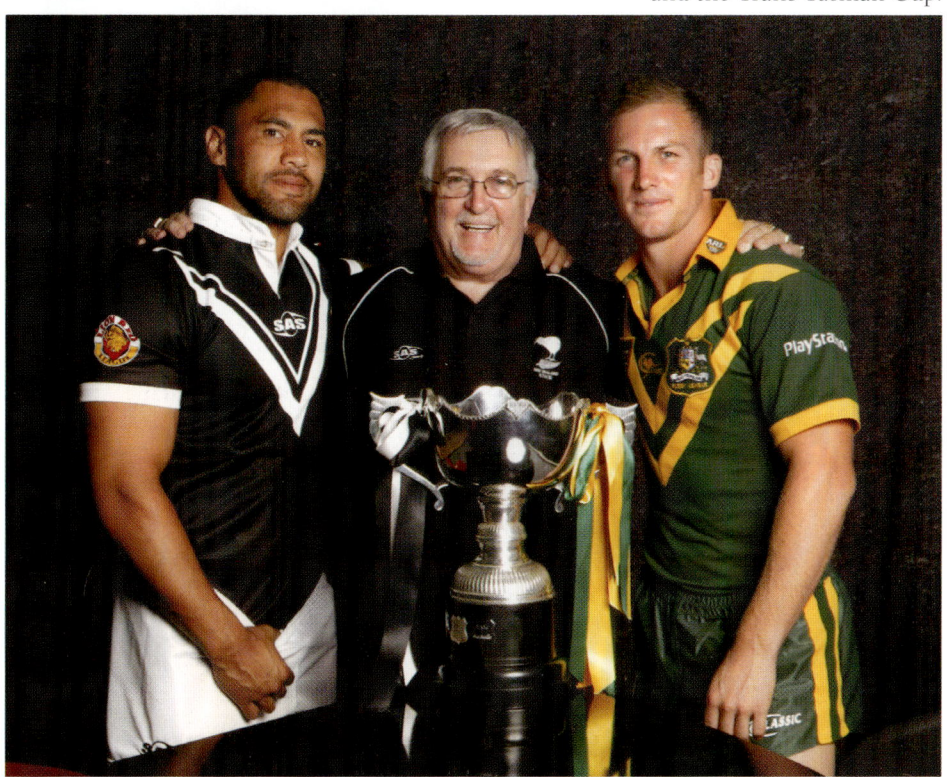

Peter presents great Kiwi league player Tawera Nikau with the 2004 Mad Butcher New Zealand League Personality of the Year Award.

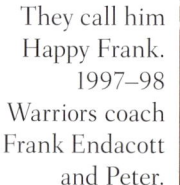

They call him Happy Frank. 1997–98 Warriors coach Frank Endacott and Peter.

At a sporting dinner in Auckland: Gordon Tietjens, New Zealand's world champion Sevens rugby coach; Peter; famous All Black fullback Bob Scott; and world squash champion Susan Devoy.

Peter and Janice today.

Always positive. Kiwis coach Brian McClennan and Kiwis manager, the Mad Butcher.

Old mates. Phil Gifford and Peter, in Las Vegas after a trip to Cuba, with Peter, as always, working the phone.

On Peter's 60th birthday he lives as Elvis, and is joined in celebrations by Warriors players Monty Betham, Mark Tookey, Stacey Jones and Awen Guttenbeil, and coach Daniel Anderson. Marilyn Monroe was pleased to see them, but didn't say much.

Could this be the most unnecessary kissing of the Blarney Stone in Ireland ever? On a 1995 Kiwis' supporters tour Peter performs the ceremony that, in legend, provides the kisser with the gift of the gab for ever.

Did we mention they call him the Mad Butcher?

What the Clear Ear campaign was about. Peter is joined by one of the 120 children whose glue-ear problems were solved with free operations organised and paid for by the Mad Butcher Suburban Newspapers Community Trust.

'All boys love trains, after all.' One of Peter's favourite organisations is the Manukau Live Steamers Club in Mangere, which offers free rides on a special family day to 600 families.

Peter raced this greyhound, Kedo's Rex, in a syndicate called League Mad. Warrior Mark Tookey (in black T-shirt on Peter's left) was in the syndicate as well as Warrior Justin Morgan, and former Kiwi Ron O'Reagan, who now cares for the dog in its retirement. The men in the white shirts are trainers David Schofield (left) and his father Denis.

In 2001 Peter was awarded the Ernst & Young Entrepreneur of the Year Retail Award.

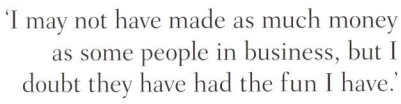

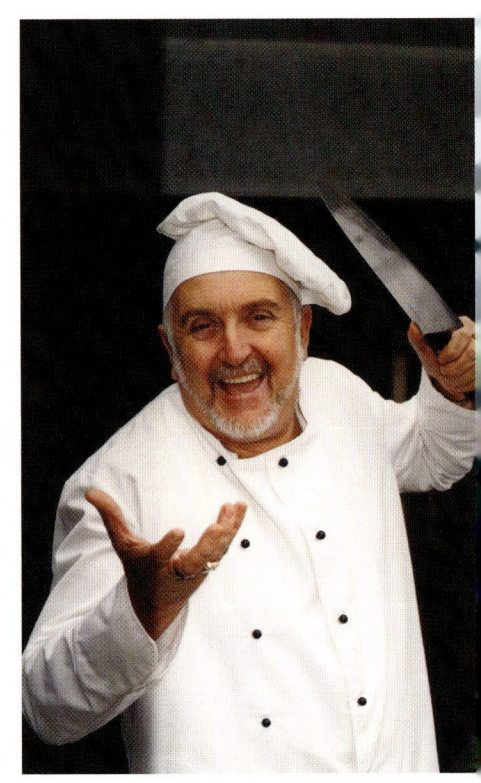

'I may not have made as much money as some people in business, but I doubt they have had the fun I have.'

Peter and his Kiwi mates took his book *The Year the Kiwis Flew* to the people, in this case the Manukau City mall.

'Slay the Dragon!' was the battle cry of the 2005 Kiwis when they beat Australia 24–0 in the Tri-Nations final.

If an army marches on its stomach, then Peter and former Kiwi Richie Barnett agree the Kiwis need to fly on their special Mad Butcher sausages.

Grand-daughter Kristin and Peter produced a very cheery Christmas card for 2007, featuring a pallet of Mad Butcher beer.

A beautiful vintage car with one of the world's worst drivers. Peter at the 2007 Crank Up rally in Edendale in Southland.

Prime Minister Helen Clark listens attentively to Peter's plan for red meat to be compulsory in all New Zealand schools.

final whistle the Sydney hoodoo was no more, the Kiwis winning 38–28.

Six days later the Aussies were scowling across the chalk at the Kiwis again, this time at Ericsson Stadium in Auckland. This time the theme was 'Welcome to the Jungle', a reference to Muhammad Ali's victory over George Foreman in Zaire in 1974, which Ali had dubbed the 'Rumble in the Jungle'. There was certainly rumbling. The Aussies were gang-tackled and smashed backwards, with their defences being pierced by big runs from Melbourne-based Jake Webster and Nigel Vagana off slick passes by Stacey Jones. At half-time the Kiwis were ahead 16–8.

But, as coach McClennan freely concedes now, 'the reason why we hadn't beaten them for 46 years in Sydney, or beaten them twice in one year for 52 years, is because the Aussies are pretty damn good at this game'. They did some rumbling of their own, and by the time the game was over, despite a late rally by the Kiwis, the Australians had won 28–26.

Initial judgements in New Zealand were harsh. In the *New Zealand Herald*, Chris Rattue wrote:

History called, but the Kiwis failed to answer, again. In a stirring test which further suggested that international league is on the rise, Australia and coach Wayne Bennett found a perfect reply to the pressure they had been under after losing the Tri-Nations opener in Sydney. Not that it was a telephone numbers victory, as cocky Aussie pundits like the great coach Phil Gould had predicted. Gould was at least 28 points shy in his pick, as Australia fended off a late Kiwi charge to win by two.

The Kiwis were brave, superbly aggressive in defence in the first half, and at times clever — you'd go a long way to see a better flick pass under pressure than Paul Whatuira's for a Jake Webster try. But this is the test arena, a hard place where there are victors, the vanquished and very little room for sympathy in between . . . A Tri-Nations victory still beckons the Kiwis, but for now, that seems a long way away.

The disappointment for Kiwi backers and the New Zealand sports public was immense, but there was little time for reflection among the Kiwis. The next day they were on a plane, flying to London.

As the team manager, Peter would see many examples of how much the Kiwi jersey meant to the players. He knew that it was club league that paid the big money, while being in the Kiwis basically only covered expenses. But he found that pride in the black-and-white jersey was still a huge issue.

A prime example was when Lance Hohaia and Clinton Toopi got on the flight to London with injuries that needed rehabilitation. 'In the air they were doing the exercises they needed to come right and get back on the field,' Peter says. 'The desire they had was amazing to see.' That desire was reflected in the delight from players when they were called into the squad. 'As long as I live I'll never forget ringing Willie Poching [while the Kiwis were in England] to tell him we wanted him to join us. He was so excited about being picked to play. When I asked him how he'd get there, he told me he'd walk there if I wanted him to.'

All went to plan at Loftus Road in London in the first game, the Kiwis beating the Great Britain side, 42–26, on 29 October. After the Aussies then kicked Great Britain 20–6 on Guy Fawkes' Day, the maths were very simple — if the

Kiwis won the test at Huddersfield against Great Britain on 12 November, they would go to the final. It looked simple, it looked certain. But it wasn't.

The preparation for the test was almost a shambles. Despite the Butcher's best efforts, the training ground provided was a muddy disgrace. The last run before the test was on a tiny, rain-swept, all-weather hockey ground in gym shoes.

About the only person who stayed positive during the Huddersfield test was Bluey McClennan, who told the players that the opposition would throw everything at them in the first 20 minutes. When half-time came and the Kiwis were down, he said, 'Look, I made a slight mistake. I said they'd throw everything at us for 20 minutes, but they've thrown it at us for 40 minutes. We can win the second half.' When the Kiwis came off after losing 38–12, his comment was, 'Well, we won the second half.'

'He's the sort of person you want to be around, because he's so positive,' Peter says. 'It was refreshing, to be fair. A couple of times I started to talk about something negative, and he stopped me in my tracks, telling me to look at what was positive in the situation.'

The Kiwis flew to Toulouse after the loss in Huddersfield, for a Friday-night 38–22 test win over France, a game that was really only for match fitness. At close quarters, Peter saw another example of McClennan's calmness under pressure. 'When we were in Toulouse he asked me to sit next to him in the box, and do the interchange,' Peter says. 'I made a mistake, and he just made a joke out of it. He wasn't being lackadaisical; he just had an ability to stay calm.' The next night in Hull, the Aussies did the right thing by the Kiwis, beating Great Britain 26–14 to put the New Zealanders into the final, to be played at Elland Road in Leeds.

Stacey Jones' path to the final involved as extraordinary a build-up as international sport has ever seen. Straight after the Toulouse test he flew to Auckland, arriving just in time for the birth of his son, William. There was barely time to hold the baby and kiss his wife Rachelle before, with her blessing, he was back at the airport, flying to Manchester, the nearest international airport to Leeds. He arrived in Leeds at 5 p.m. on Friday 25 November, the day before the final. About all he could remember was the slogan for the day, 'Slay the Dragon'.

If most of us had a vision of the Kiwis in the changing room before the Tri-Nations final it would be fairly grim:

fists smashing into palms, deep-throated grunts from the big forwards, furrowed brows in the backs. Talk to Kiwi forward Louie Anderson and the picture in reality was quite different. Music was playing. Jokes were being thrown around. Some players were even dancing. The scene was exactly what Anderson, about to play the biggest game of his league career, had wanted.

The night before he'd struggled to sleep. When the grey dawn finally arrived he had the sort of emotions a kid has on Christmas morning. 'I was so excited! I couldn't believe what was going to happen.'

Some coaches are unable to give players space, to allow the pressure at training and in team talks to ease back, so stocks of nervous energy are not burned up before the whistle even blows for a game. Coach McClennan was not one of the uptight breed. 'We had a lot of talks as a team,' recalls Anderson. 'Bluey would say really positive stuff about winning, and that really sunk in for a lot of us. There wasn't so much individual stuff. Away from the meetings, it wasn't footy for 24 hours a day.

'What sticks in my mind about him is his honesty and humbleness. He's honest to himself and to all of us. When you're honest and humble, it's easy to gain respect, and it's easy to listen to what he's saying to you, and to take it in.

He's a great family man, with good standards, and that certainly helped us along the way.'

It was the event itself that staggered his imagination, not the possible result. After the Kiwis' win in Sydney in the first test of the tournament, Anderson believed they could win the title. 'When I went into the final I believed we could win the game, but I never thought we'd win it by the margin we did. In the final I thought they'd come back at us after half-time, and put points on the board.'

His pre-game nerves started to settle down in the changing room. The graph of edginess shot up again when the team ran onto the field. 'After the national anthem we did the haka, and man, there was so much excitement. But I really took the time before kick-off to look at what was happening, and then I just went for it.

'We had a passion to win that usually came through when we needed to crank it up a bit. After that first game against Australia, we'd started to think, "Man, we can actually do it!" That fired the boys up and gave us an extra mental toughness to go up another level.'

As Peter Jessup wrote in the *New Zealand Herald*:

The Kiwis pinched the Tri-Nations final from under the Australians' noses, 24–0, in a match which rewrote the record books. The 24-point gap equalled the most put on the Kangaroos, but the fact the Aussies failed to score means it beats the 49–25 win at Brisbane in 1952. Only one other time have the Kiwis held Australia scoreless, the 18–0 result to Graham Lowe's team at Carlaw Park in 1985.

Kiwis captain Ruben Wiki was rightly awarded the Man of the Match in his 50th test, but not one of his side under-performed.

It was close to the perfect game from the Kiwis, whose enthusiasm to help each other drive their opponents backwards in tackles and to go for loose balls led to an early try and sustained pressure on Australia. The Kangaroos were ashen afterwards, perhaps many, including their coach Wayne Bennett, wondering whether they will be back in green and gold again because recriminations will surely follow across the Tasman.

'Doing the Bluey' might become a popular method of celebration, the Kiwis coach making a habit of marking his historic wins with fists held above his head as he leaps up and down, as he did on Elland Road.

Meanwhile his team were grouped, arms around

each other, also jumping up and down as they sang the 'Da Da Da' refrain from Dave Dobbyn's song, *Slice of Heaven.* The boys from Footrot Flats had stumped those from the top end of town, and they'd made history, something McClennan aimed them at all series. Captain Ruben Wiki cried as he was asked what it meant. 'History is sweet, mate,' he said.

At the end of the final, walking around the field, loving the moment, a beaming McClennan said to Peter, 'How good is this, Butch?'

The heartfelt reply was, 'It's fucking good, coach.'

On top of the world as the Kiwis were, it didn't take long for the curiously pessimistic streak that runs through many New Zealand sports fans to reassert itself. Heading into the 2006 Tri-Nations, there were those who felt the Kiwis' effort in 2005 had been some sort of fluke — one brilliant flash-in-the-pan effort that would turn to crap when the Aussies decided it was time to win again. In Australia the organisers certainly wrote the Kiwis off, booking hotels in Sydney for

Australia and Great Britain for the final but, astonishingly, not for New Zealand.

'There's no question,' says Peter, 'that a lot of people wrote us off after the 2006 Anzac test (lost to Australia 50–12) and another loss (46–14) in England in June. They don't understand that we only have the players for a few days and then we have to play the test. But in 2006, we were all actually more confident. I know that I certainly was in my job, because I'd done a year; Bluey was, because he'd been on a tour; and we were closer to home, in New Zealand and Australia.'

Personally though, it would still be a hard campaign for Peter. 'My wife Janice had been diagnosed with cancer some months before the tour started. I said I'd happily throw it away, I'd resign. But she said to me, no, you enjoy it, so go ahead and do it. What came out of that was that I learned how strong Janice is. She took a very positive attitude: that she wasn't going to die — she wasn't going to let it beat her.

'At times I suffered from a bad guilt complex, but luckily I was so busy I didn't have time to brood over it too often. Then my brother was very sick with bowel cancer in Wellington, and had a massive operation. I'm close to Gary, so that was hard to deal with, too.'

Inside the Kiwi camp there was a brotherhood, one that was forged over time, but still needed a push from management. 'The feeling we had last year was there, but it does have to be nurtured all the time,' Peter says. 'It's a combination of things. This year we got them all carvings on the West Coast — a koru — which we wore all the time. Every now and then we did a spot check, and if they didn't have them on they got told off. To be fair, they rarely had it off.'

Not every gesture was so fully understood. 'A couple of people criticised me because I went public on the radio and said, "If your company wants to support the Kiwis, send me some stuff." I got so much that when the guys came into the camp, they all got a bag full of goodies.

'But Nathan Cayless said to me, "When I got that bag, I felt important. It made me feel good." That was the aim of it. All those people who donated things — and there were so many I can't name them all — were supporting the boys. There were things like playing cards, sunglasses, muscle creams and T-shirts. The playing cards got hammered, and the good thing was, they had pictures of New Zealand on them, so whenever the boys were playing cards, they were thinking of New Zealand.

'All the people who gave something got something out

of it as well. It fired up their interest in the games — they felt they were personally involved with the team.'

For McClennan, so passionate when he talks about his theories on team building that it's obvious they come from the heart, not a public relations man's laptop, Peter was a vital figure in getting the players to buy into the idea that 'you have to be great off the field, if you're going to be great on the field'.

'Managing a team in England was a big job, being away,' says McClennan, 'but it's actually busier when you're in your own country. That 2006 tour was the most phenomenally organised one that we've ever had. It was so well planned, and every player would tell you that the 2006 tour, mostly at home, was just fantastic, and that's down to the Butcher to a huge degree.

'He worked incredibly hard, because he didn't just do the managing, he did the media side as well. On tour he carried three mobiles, and his mobiles go a lot.' McClennan laughs at the memories. 'On one trip I think they opened three or four Mad Butcher shops, so I doubt he could catch his breath between calls.'

You sense Peter's frustration at the lack of understanding that dogs the Kiwis when they don't perform early in the Tri-Nations. 'It's time together that helps make the Kiwis better. People forget that the Aussies play together in State of Origin. The English players are in Super League, and they had camps during the year. But our players are scattered around the world, so it's very hard to get them together.

'The tour for the 2006 Tri-Nations started slowly, but our week in Sydney before the final was high class. I'm not saying the rest wasn't good, but it really stepped up a gear in Sydney.'

The 2006 campaign began at Mt Smart in Auckland on 14 October with abuse, and a loss. The abuse came from New Zealand-born Australian Willie Mason, with a four-letter-word tirade at the Kiwi haka, and sledging to the media of Australian-born Kiwi Brent Webb in the build-up to the game.

In the *New Zealand Herald*, Chris Rattue wrote:

Willie Mason waited longer than most expected to enter the fray against the Kiwis after Kangaroos coach Ricky Stuart changed his starting line-up and sent Mark O'Meley out for the initial exchanges at Mt Smart Stadium. But Mason had already stepped over a line in the opening Tri-Nations test. 'What the f*** is that?' the Auckland-born Aussie prop mouthed towards the Kiwis' pre-match haka.

Well, those who have shed their lip-reading training wheels reckon that's what he said. But even a lip-reading rookie could tell you what Mason said next: 'F*** off.' There's a theme to this, and a speech coach might suggest to Mason that he needs more variety in his attack. Who knows what continually eats at Mason, the best go-to league bloke in media history. There is no such thing as a slow news day if Mason is in range of a voice recorder.

Mason's rantings didn't have a lot of effect on the Kiwis, according to Stacey Jones, who in 2006 was available for every game. 'We sort of brushed over what Willie said. Some players might have disagreed with it, some just said, "Aw, good on him, he's just pumping the game up."'

Mason got more than his just deserts, in the form of a sensational hit by Kiwi forward David Kidwell, who flattened and silenced him. But in the most important area, the scoreboard, there was no such joy. The Kiwis competed throughout, scored the last try, but trudged off the ground defeated, 30–18.

If that was disappointing, the second test a week later in Melbourne was heartbreaking. Ahead by seven points with eight minutes to go, Kiwi fans watched in horror as the Kangaroos manufactured two tries, and a remarkable 20–15 victory.

At Jade Stadium in Christchurch a week after Melbourne, the Kiwis slogged to a crucial 18–14 win over Great Britain, but the greatest demand on the team's unity was just around the corner with the bombshell of Australian-born Nathan Fein being ruled out of the tournament because it was his great-grandmother, not his grandmother (as the New Zealand Rugby League had claimed) who was born in New Zealand. For fielding an ineligible player, the Kiwis were docked two competition points.

Losing the points after beating England was gut-wrenching. Having Fein kicked out by the World Cup committee was a double blow. How did the Kiwis deal with it? 'We turned off the Nathan Fein issue,' says Peter. 'Because we were touring on the West Coast, we didn't actually get to see or hear that much about it. We did talk about it, but not a lot. Brian was very straight up with the team. But we had to deal with it and move on. I don't know that we got stronger, but we certainly didn't break up either.

'Brian talked to a few players individually about it, but I didn't really. My attitude in life is that everyone makes mistakes, and a mistake was made. But you've just got to get on with life, and cope with it.

'It was very emotional when Nathan left. He had to leave in the middle of our week in Queenstown. The boys liked him, he fitted in well, so it was genuinely sad to see him go. We all said goodbye to him, and spoke with him about how we felt.'

It was probably fortunate that one of the special periods for Peter during his three years in the Kiwis' management group occurred at the same time as the eligibility drama and its aftermath. 'We were in Queenstown when most of the drama was going on, so we were away from the media,' he says. 'The guy from AJ Hackett's bungy jumps really looked after us. He organised a whole lot of stuff. We had a beautiful couple of days there.

'Then we got a charter flight from Queenstown to Hokitika. It was an older plane, with big windows and plenty of room. There wasn't one guy on that flight who didn't enjoy it. It was a beautiful day, with great views of the Southern Alps. When we got to Hokitika, we went straight to Barry

Wilson's glass studio, and I'd arranged for him to give the boys a little gift. Every player got a paperweight with a Kiwi on it. Some of the boys had a go at glass blowing. The feel-good factor was really there.

'Then we stayed in Greymouth, and the weather was outstanding. People up north joke about the weather in the South Island, but in Queenstown and Greymouth it was sensational.'

To McClennan, having Peter by his side during the Fein debacle was exactly what he needed. 'As we went through what the media had dubbed "Grannygate", I was getting a pounding. That was when I knew that the Butch was a mate for life, when we really cemented our friendship. He was the one who really kept things solid for me, with advice and support. That was a tough week, because although we never entertained the thought, had we not won the next test in Wellington against Great Britain, the noose was ready. Peter was solid — he stuck it all right through.'

A game between the Kiwis and a Residents' XIII had been arranged in Greymouth, and in Peter's view it was the right place to be at a sticky time. 'There was basically a sell-out crowd at Wingham Park, and after the game we went back to the Railway Hotel where we had whitebait fritters like we'd never had before.

'They're great people down there. The mayor of Greymouth put on a reception for us. It wasn't stuffy, just a real nice bloke's thing. I joked with him that he didn't have any whitebait there. When we got to Wellington he'd sent up a whole lot of whitebait fritters, so we were able to have a decent feed of whitebait.'

Among the players, says Stacey Jones, 'as a group we didn't really speak about it [the Grannygate saga] too much. We just thought, "Well, these are the cards we've been dealt, we've got a game in Wellington [against Great Britain], and it's probably one of the most important we'll ever play, just to get some pride back in the jersey."

'The night before the game, a couple of us spoke at the team meeting, and I was one. I said, "This is a big game, because we've been made to look like a bit of a joke with what's happened." Our game was hurting. Really, the only way we could show what we felt was not to talk about it, but to get out on the football field and do what we do best.'

The Kiwis responded superbly, thrashing Great Britain by a record 34–4, which, when the Aussies whipped Britain 33–10 in Brisbane a week later, set up a Kiwis–Australia final on 25 November at Aussie Stadium in Sydney. That game is ranked by many as the best league test ever played. With the score locked up at 12-all after 80 minutes of pulsating action, it took a golden try by Darren Lockyer, conjured up by Jonathon Thurston, to break the deadlock after seven minutes of extra time and give the Aussies the win.

But the emotions weren't over with the end of the game. When the Kiwis returned to the changing shed, there was a surprise in store. All week before the final, Stacey Jones had been asked by the media if it was to be his last test. 'I just said I wasn't going to announce anything,' Jones says. 'I'd done that before, but then I returned, and I felt it made me look a bit stupid. But this time I was entirely settled on retiring. I actually found that knowing it was going to be the last time for the Butcher [as team manager] made it a bit easier for me to decide to stop. It wouldn't be the same without him.'

In the shed immediately after the final, Jones wasn't surprised to see Ruben Wiki get up to speak, but his captain did surprise him when Wiki asked Jones and Nigel Vagana to come up too. 'Ruben spoke very emotionally,' Jones says. 'There were a few tears, and he told the boys that that was it for him. Then he sat down, and Nigel said he was retiring from international league too.

'Everyone then looked at me. It was definitely my last game, but I didn't want to say anything because I had retired before. To me it was a special occasion for Ruben and Nigel more than anything else — I'd made my speech a couple of years ago. I'd told Ruben during the week that the final would be it for me too, but once I was called up I knew I had to speak. It was a pretty emotional time.'

Peter had put out a book on the 2005 tournament, called *The Year the Kiwis Flew*. 'While I got a royalty for it, I actually spent all that on promoting it, and we sold a lot of books,' he says. Then, after the final in 2006, Dean Lonergan was talking to Peter, and Lonergan said, 'That final was the best game of league I've ever seen.' It was all the encouragement the Butcher needed. 'I decided to put out another book; we called it *2006: The Year That Was*. An Aussie journalist, who wrote a piece for the book, thanked me for letting him be a part of history — that was what he said in front of people.

'I had decided to market the book myself, and I sold it through my shops for $10. I'll be lucky to break even on it, but I wanted the tour documented, because it had been a great series for the Kiwis. I made a big mistake by not putting it into book stores, just selling it through the shops. I'm man enough to admit the mistake.

'It was a magnificent journey. Pat Carthy [the Kiwis' business manager] and I got on well. We knew our jobs, and didn't cross over each other. Pat allowed me to concentrate on my job, because I knew I could rely on him completely. We had two very good doctors in Chris Hanna and then John Mayhew. I wasn't that keen on the idea of John at first, because he came from a rugby background, but he fitted in brilliantly.

'The experience as manager was fantastic. Being the manager of the team that won 24–0 was one of the greatest highlights of my life, because the Aussies have said many times they could field two or three teams to beat the Kiwis. I always saw myself as the facilitator — what Brian wanted I made sure it got done. My policy was, "Get it done straight away."

'I was a 63-year-old man, and he inspired me, got me fired up, which is not easy to do with someone at my stage of life. His enthusiasm rubbed off on us all. Players love him, but he doesn't piss in their pockets too much. With the right support and tuition I think he could have done wonderful things for rugby league in New Zealand.'

When the news broke in August 2007 that the New Zealand Rugby League was not going to keep Bluey and he was moving to the UK to take up the job of head coach for the Leeds Rhinos, Peter was gutted. 'I really thought he had something special, and I was devastated. In fairness to the other coaches I've known, I never worked with them as a manager. When Brian was dropped, I thought seriously about resigning as official ambassador for the New Zealand Rugby League, and of throwing my support for the Kiwis away.

'But then I realised that would be stupid, because it couldn't change what had happened, and all I'd be doing was hurting a game I truly love. I saw a pot of gold at the end of the rainbow with Brian. No criticism of any other coach, but Brian was special. I was so stunned when he was let go — it hit me mentally, even physically to a degree. It set me back — it was a sad ending. I have to say Brian being at Leeds and trying to coach the Kiwis wouldn't have been the perfect situation, but I believe he was worthy of one more shot at it.

'With Brian it was never about money, and I think that's been the case with most of the other coaches too. It's been about the pride of coaching a New Zealand team.'

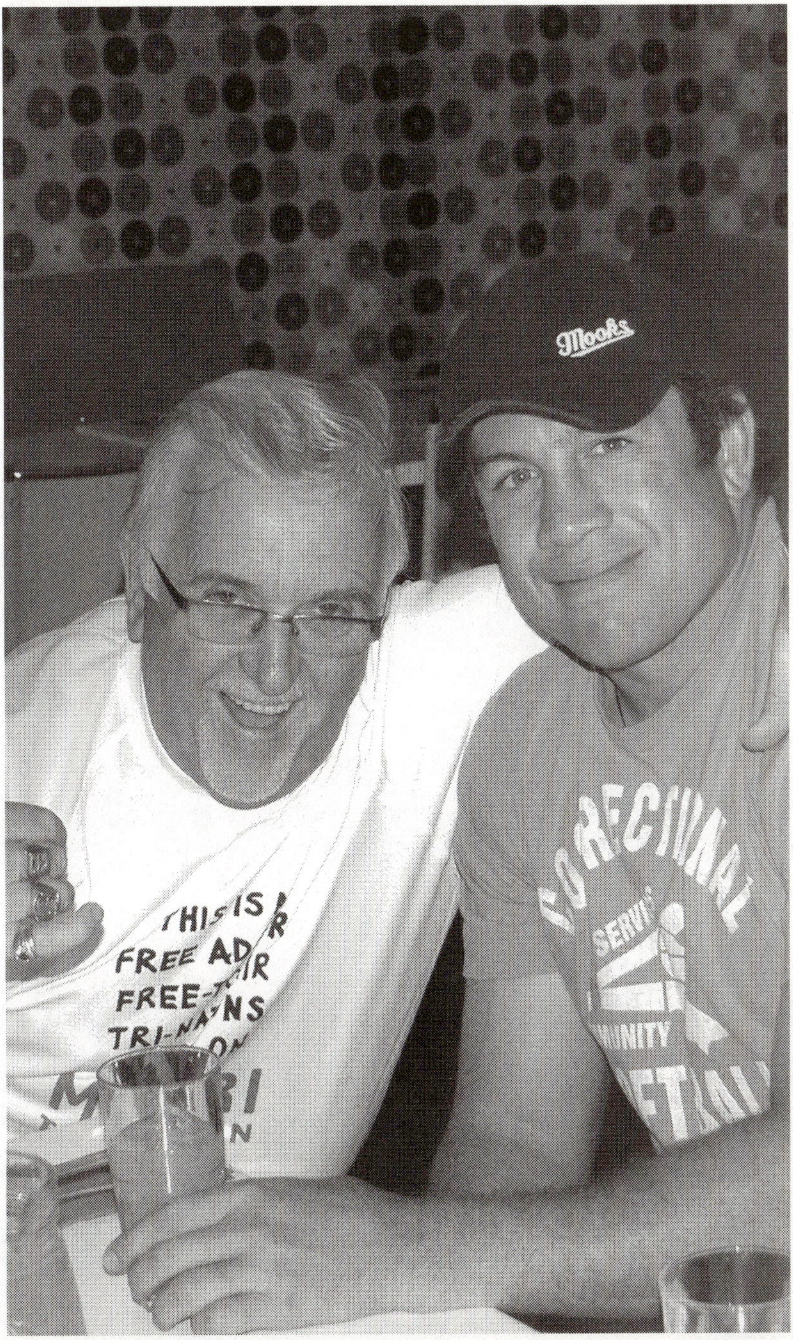
Mooks

14

Sell

From the time The Mad Butcher business took wings in the 1980s, the thought never crossed Peter Leitch's mind that one day he might not own it. And selling the business might never have happened if Mike Morton, a former Restaurant Brands New Zealand manager, had been spooked by what must be one of the most bizarre introductions to a new job in the history of New Zealand business.

It all began in a straightforward enough manner, eight years ago, when Peter decided someone with more extensive orthodox business skills was needed to manage the company. A leading employment agency was commissioned to find the person, a substantial amount of money was spent on advertising the job, and what Peter remembers as 'heaps of people' applied for the position. Some were hopeless. 'Believe it or not, there were some guys who honestly thought they'd get to go to all the Warriors games,' Peter scoffs.

Some were impressive, but one stood out. 'Michael [Morton] had no background in the meat industry as such, but it was obvious the job fitted him like a glove,' Peter says. But that's when it became unorthodox. Mike says the abiding memory he has of the key interview was going into the agency's boardroom, where Peter ignored the silver-service teaset that had been laid out and instead swigged from a bottle of Coca-Cola. 'He couldn't turn his phone off during the interview, because he had a couple of phone-outs to radio stations that he did while we were there,' Mike laughs.

A contract was offered, one that was so brief that Mike's subsequent amendments would be longer than the original. They shook hands, and agreed to meet at a later date to discuss any changes that Mike would like to make. 'Peter rang me,' Mike recalls, 'and asked me to meet him at the Powerhouse nightclub in Mt Eden Road. He was putting on a charity show on a Thursday night, featuring Guy Cater, the hypnotist. He told me to knock on a side door and ask for the Butcher.

'I arrived at about 7 o'clock, and his lawyer, John Ray, turned up. He'd come straight from the gym and was still in his sweaty T-shirt and running shorts. I said, "Here are my amendments."

'Peter said, "Well, what do you want?"

'I said, "These are the main things here."

'He said, "No problem. I'll give them to you, because if you don't like me, you'll leave, and if I don't like you, I'll tell you to fuck off. It'd cost me some money, but I'd tell you to fuck off."

'I drove away that night thinking, "What have I done? Have I done the stupidest thing in the world, or have I gone to work for someone who's incredibly honest and straight up?" I had to get that clear in my mind, going from a corporate type of environment to one of working for Peter. I was sick of the public company thing, where you looked at the share price every day, and that was the measure of your own worth.

'The next night, Peter rang and told me to meet him the following night at the Powerhouse again, to arrive half an hour early, and that, because I'd be in the VIP section, I had to wear a suit. So I turned up in a suit, and he said, "You look stupid, mate. You're the only one here in a suit." He made me go and put bowls of nuts on all the tables. That was my introduction to working with the Mad Butcher.'

Things were even less conventional in the days to come. 'The second week I was there,' Mike says, 'Peter did a press release to say he was going to issue a press release to announce a press release about something happening in league. I had to play a tape recording of it back for him, and I couldn't get the tape player to work. He said he was paying me all this money and I couldn't even make a tape recorder work.

'Then, I had to write a report for him, and having come from a public company, I wrote about a 20-page report on the position of the company. I waited for some feedback, but never got any. Eventually I asked him. The conversation went like this:

"What's the story, Peter? Are you happy with the report?"

"I haven't read it, mate. Are we making money?"

"Yeah, we're making money."

"Are we making enough money?"

"I think we can make some more."

"Good as gold, make some more money."'

Things could not have been more different for the ex-public company manager. 'He gave me total autonomy right from the start,' Mike says, 'which for a person who had built the company up over many years was really commendable.'

What Peter had recognised, and still does, is that Mike had the skills he didn't possess. 'We complement each other,' Peter says.

The new relationship would quickly be tested. After six months as CEO, Mike was offered a position in Dubai with Pepsico. The deal was attractive, with payment in tax-free American dollars.

Mike went to Peter, told him about the offer, and was immediately asked what would make him stay. 'I said I'd like to buy into the company,' Mike says. 'He came back to me the next morning with an offer. That's how fast he was to react, how nimble he was with a decision.

'I think you need to be a certain type of person to work

for him as well. I've found that his word is his bond. He works on the philosophy that he started out with, when he got the shop at Rosella Road on a handshake. He'd like all his business dealings to be like that, to be honourable, to look the guy in the eye, shake his hand, and say, "Yup, the deal's done." But he's been burnt a couple of times like that as well, so I think my key responsibility at the start was to firm it all up, and make it more commercial.

'Initially, I think it was his hard work that got the business off the ground, and then I think it was his nose for a bargain and a good deal. That carries on today. He never wants to turn anything down; he says anything can be sold if the price is right.

'His other great strength was that he was prepared to sell things on a much smaller margin than anybody else. He worked on a very simplistic model; he'd say, "If I buy it at $2 and sell it for $2.50, I've made a profit." He wouldn't have worked out the percentage of profit, overheads, anything like that. He worked on that methodology all the way through, on the sheer fact that if he sold it for more than he bought it for, it was a good job. When the volume got bigger, things like overheads came into play, but he still had a strong belief that he could sell basically anything.

'There was no real hierarchy within the business at all, which was good for me, having come from a corporate background where there was a whole political type of management — if one person was a level-nine manager, and you were only a level-eight manager, you couldn't question the other guy's decisions. Peter's whole approach of keeping it simple, making your word your bond, ran through the whole organisation. He was generous to a fault in many ways, but also wanted his pound of flesh, on the basis that if he was good to you, then you should be good to him in return.

'I think it hurts him personally when that burns him. We've had some incidents where staff who have been working for us for a long time have let him down. We're a cash business, and cash can make some honest people act in a dishonest way. Peter takes that very personally. If anyone questions his own integrity, that really hurts him too.

'What I say to people who come to work here is that when Peter asks them to do something, don't see it as belittling, but see it as being something he wouldn't mind doing if somebody asked him to do it. Whether it's "can you wash my car", or "can you carry this stuff out to my car", or "come and get something from my car", it's not that he's belittling their position in the company, it's just that he wouldn't think twice about doing it for someone else. The phrase "that's not my job" never applies here. If we do a fund-raising barbecue, he'll be one of the first ones there, setting it up, working, then picking up the rubbish at the end.'

When Mike Morton started at The Mad Butcher, there were 16 stores carrying the brand. At the last count there are now 34. There had never been a store in the South Island until Mike was on board. Peter has claimed in interviews that the only reason the company opened down south was because Mike wanted it to pay for him to visit his mother in Christchurch. 'I presume he was taking the piss,' says Mike.

In reality, the Christchurch store opening was a remarkable success, posting sensational figures from the first day, with sales never slumping. 'Peter was driven by the fact that people went to the shops. When we opened in Wellington, there were queues of people lined up just to get in the door. We did more than a week's worth of takings in just one day. People just wanted to come and see him.

'The fact is, he loves to talk to everyone, and I mean everyone. When we opened in Timaru, a lady brought down her miniature horse to see him in her car. He was outside talking to the horse through the window of the car.'

As the franchising has boomed Peter worried that he didn't know the franchise holders the way he did when there was just a handful of shops in Auckland.

But Glen Young, who has owned the Mad Butcher shop in Colombo Street in Christchurch since 2004, says the reality is that Peter's promise at conferences that he was always available for advice on the phone has never been broken.

'He's always been so approachable. You could always talk to him whenever you wanted to. I might have rung him on average every couple of weeks. You might have got a rark-up occasionally,' Glen laughs. 'But at the end of the day he was always right in what he said, so you've got to respect him for that.'

Glen took a real leap of faith to fulfil his desire to get a Mad Butcher franchise. After 20 years working for a supermarket, he dropped $30,000 a year in salary to work as a manager at the first Mad Butcher store in Christchurch, in Shirley.

The punt paid off when, after he had been working at Shirley for just a month, Peter offered him the chance of the Colombo shop.

'The store went better than I'd budgeted for,' says Glen, 'which was a reflection of what Peter brings to the table. Until the Mad Butcher in Shirley opened, to be blunt, meat in Christchurch, especially chicken, was overpriced.'

Although Peter was a true-blue Aucklander, Glen says Cantabrians were also aware of the amount of good work he did for charities. 'That went a long way to people here thinking well of him, that he wasn't just all about making money, he did a lot for the community as well. There was some negative feeling, just because he was from Auckland, but nothing like the amount of positive stuff.'

Helping to drive the business nationwide, says Mike Morton, is that Peter 'thrives on the crowds. He really is a man of the people. I think some people in the public eye pretend to enjoy that stuff, but he loves it.'

At first, Mike misread Peter's hesitation about picking

sites for new stores. 'He'd never make a decision. He'd go, "I'm not sure about that site, mate." I felt initially that he was covering his arse, but now I think it was more likely a deliberate ploy to force me to make a decision, basically saying, "If you believe in it, go for it," as part of giving me that full autonomy.

'Peter does tend to see anything that doesn't work as a failure, and he takes it very personally. But if a call hasn't worked that well, he's never come back and blamed me. We've thrown money at some shops that we probably should have closed, but he didn't want to, because he saw it as an admission of failure. One example was a shop in Papatoetoe that in the end I had to put my hand up and say, "Wrong site, not a great location." It was my belief that customers would walk from a car park at the side of the building round to the front. But it didn't work. There are basic things that make a store successful, like location and prices. But no matter what the prices are, unless you make it convenient for people they won't come to you.

'Peter's *never* gone and pointed the finger at me, saying, "That cost us so much money," or anything like that. He's more likely to say, "Aw well, learn by your mistakes." I'm probably harder on myself than he is if I get it wrong.'

What Mike has noticed with the years is a mellowing of Peter's volcanic management style, especially when it comes to handling people and staff. 'The old style of management — where you were very upfront if you were unhappy — can't really be used now.'

He has to laugh at how Peter now deals with confrontations. 'His analogy for me was, "Why have a dog and bark yourself?" He would wait for me to have the argument, but then, if he had to, he'd finish something off. He didn't want all the confrontation himself. He'd battled for years to make a dollar, and he was at a stage where he'd done it long enough.

'Peter hasn't been driven by money, but he does love the fact that the persona of the Mad Butcher is so big. He loves it when people come up and want to talk with him. That's what drives him.

'There are things Peter does that annoy me, and I'd think, "Why do you want to do this?" Then I have to stop and remember that it's what made the company successful at the start. I know we make a lot of work for ourselves that we don't really need to do — there are times when we could write a cheque, rather than do all the things we do.

'There are charity things that are tougher than they once were because of our size. If we sell a poster in the store and give all the money to charity, it appears as a sale, there's GST to be paid on it, and we have to pay tax. The days of being able to just take $5 cash and stick it in a jar have gone.

'He finds it hard to say no to people, and often he sends people on to me. Little things will hurt him. We raised tens of thousands for one charity and we got a thank-you letter with the signature stamped on it. We'd worked hard to raise the money, and Peter was so upset about that letter not being personally signed.

'He has very good manners, and will never forget anyone who has ever done something for him. He never forgets to thank them. Peter puts an incredible amount of pressure on himself. We were game-day sponsors of the Warriors, and he was tireless in promoting the game. I remember saying to him, "Pete, the people who are going to come will come. We won't convert people, no matter how much we advertise it." Then when we got there and saw the small crowd, you could see the disappointment on his face. You don't often see him deflated, because he's always up, so it's sad to see him like that.'

As well as league, his family and good causes, Peter is nostalgic for the way butchers were when he began, and is passionate about fighting for the 'good old ways'. An example of his fondness for butchery was when, during the filming of *A Mad Business*, Peter and Mike were driving through Milton in Otago, and Peter noticed a sign for the Butchery Museum.

On the way back Peter insisted they stop, and he met the proprietor, Rex Spence, a small abattoir owner who works in a local sawmill, who had gathered New Zealand's largest collection of antique meat cleavers, chopping blocks, photos and all things meat, including old recipe books. Rex had housed the collection in his garage, but when there wasn't room for his car, he built a new shed for it and decided to make it open to the public.

Peter was like a kid in a candy store, and promised Rex he'd make sure the whole of New Zealand knew about the museum. Back in Auckland, Peter organised an official opening, talked his old pal Rod Slater, from the New Zealand Beef and Lamb Marketing Bureau, into joining him in Milton, and informed TVNZ and TV3, who ran news items on the opening of one of New Zealand's more unusual tourist attractions.

Red tape is a fact of business life in the 21st century, but a sausage-eating contest sounds pretty straightforward. As Peter found out when he organised one that offered $10,000 to anyone who could beat the world record as stated in the *Guinness Book of Records*, it's nowhere near as simple as cook them, offer them, and watch them being eaten.

Before the first heat was held in a shop, with the final due to be at Carlaw Park, insurance was sought for the $10,000.

'Once the insurance company gets involved, it gets complicated,' says Peter. The indemnity policy meant not only did every sausage have to be checked for size, but more conditions were imposed, like having to examine the inside of the winner's mouth to make sure no pieces were concealed.

'You think it's a fun thing, but when that much cash is involved, you have to get very strict. If you get it wrong you pay out of your own pocket.'

The aim of the contests was to help promote league,

and the last one held was at Mt Smart, at half-time in a Warriors game.

The sausages, all pre-cooked pork that had been left to go cold, were stacked, and the contestants ('Not many of them huge people,' says Peter, 'it's all in the technique') had to eat as many as they could in 60 seconds. When the clock stopped a new record of 11 sausages had been set, a remarkable one downed every 5.5 seconds.

Moves to outlaw butchers giving cheerios free to kids in stores outraged him, and Mike recalls a long fight with the Ministry of Health over selling unwrapped brisket on the bone out of a bin in the Mangere shop. 'Peter was prepared to fight it all the way. We had meetings with them, because Peter had been selling it that way for 30 years, and he wanted to keep selling it that way. We had Perspex covers made for the bins, but the law is the law is the law, and you have to abide by the law.

'Peter would say to the ministry people, "Well, I'm going to go to all the food bars in Manukau and sneeze over all the sandwiches. What could you do about that?" He wanted to dig his toes in for tradition, but eventually he got his head around the idea that from a business point of view we could sell more if people didn't have to dig their hands into a bin. He eventually knew that he had to put business ahead of tradition, as loyal as he is to tradition.

'We often use chicken to drive the market, and while people believe chicken is chicken is chicken, they believe there are varying grades of beef. If people see you selling something cheaper than somebody else, they don't feel that the other guy is ripping them off. They believe you're selling a lesser grade of beef. They don't believe you're working on a smaller margin, so in the future we need to tell that story more. We changed the branding last year. We used to say, "We discount the price, but never the quality." Just by using the word discount there was a connotation that it was lower grade, so we changed it to "Best price, best quality."

'There's a snobbery factor that we need to get over. We need to let people know that our quality is as good as anywhere. We get a carcass and we do it the traditional way. We break it down and sell every part of that carcass profitably. We don't package it at a central point and gas flush it.'

Gas flushing, a common practice in the industry, is a process that increases the shelf life of meat. A mixture of carbon dioxide, nitrogen and oxygen is pumped into a packet before it is sealed. Carbon dioxide inhibits the growth of bacteria and mould, but oxygen, while it helps micro-organisms grow, is also needed or the meat loses its red colour. To the mix is added nitrogen, an inert gas that excludes air and prevents collapse of the packaging.

In basic terms, gas-flushed meat can sit on a shelf a lot longer. At The Mad Butcher stores, they bring the whole carcass into the shop just the way the old corner-shop butcher did. Chances are meat at The Mad Butcher will be fresher.

And while Peter may occasionally throw them at functions, the Mad Butcher sausages have an extremely good record for quality.

Five years ago the Department of Public Health did wide-ranging tests on sausages, and the Mad Butcher BBQ pre-cooked sausage emerged as the brand with the highest protein and the lowest fat levels.

Not long after, the beef supreme sausage received the heart tick for healthiness, the first sausage in New Zealand to do so.

In October 2006, Consumer NZ awarded the beef

supreme the title of New Zealand's best-tasting beef sausage.

Then, in 2007, on TV3's *Target* show, the Mad Butcher pork-flavoured sausage was judged the best pork sausage in the country for value, taste and meat content.

The road to Peter selling the business started the day when Mike said it was time for him to move on and do his own thing. Peter carefully considered his options. At 63 years of age, did he really want to go back to running the business himself again?

'Make no bones about it, I've done the hard yards,' Peter says. 'Not knowing the alphabet, not knowing my times tables — it was hard. So did I want go back? No. Should we advertise for another CEO? I doubted I could get another CEO who would be as successful as Mike had been. My advisers said I could, but I looked at a couple of companies that had recently put in new CEOs, and the companies had both gone backwards. So I could have ended up with a company worth $100, or a company worth only $50. Did I want that stress? Did I want to take that risk?

'When I looked back on the past year, Jan had had a

battle with breast cancer, my brother is battling cancer, and I had a health scare with my heart. So I thought, "No, I don't want more stress." I put a proposal to Michael to buy the business, and we negotiated, and he's got a very good deal.'

Mike says that the most sensitive part of the negotiations came when they were dealing with what he would do with the Mad Butcher name, and what Peter would be able to do with it. 'I tried to emphasise that he'll always be the Mad Butcher, because he's the persona it's all built upon.

'When we were doing the TV show, *A Mad Business*, we talked about the whole thing as we drove round, which helped build trust about the sale. I think he could probably have got more money selling it to someone else, but I think it would have been more onerous as to what they wanted from him. But there was also the element that I could reassure him he'd always be the Mad Butcher. About a year ago we started to symbolise Peter as a cartoon character, rather than using his face in the logo. We've been doing it as an evolutionary thing. For the first two years after the sale, Peter will remain with the company as a brand ambassador.'

Peter says, 'It won't be easy not owning the company, because I think until the day I die people will refer to me as the Mad Butcher. As much as I didn't plan to do it, I built one of the strongest brands in New Zealand, and it's directly associated with me, as the face and the voice of the company. So for me in the future there will be times that could be embarrassing when people talk to me, thinking I still own the business.

'One change will be that requests for sponsorship will go on Mike's desk, not mine. I won't be sorry to hand that over, to be honest. It's frustrating, how many requests you get for sponsorship. It's unbelievable. The sad thing is that it doesn't drive the business. People might think you're a nice bloke because you've sponsored them, but the fact is it's the hard-sell advertising of the specials that drives sales. They might like you, but that doesn't stop them buying their meat in a supermarket.

'I've had to turn good people down, and there have been many times over the years where I've come home very, very depressed. There were times when I just couldn't justify the sponsorship. The reality is that sponsorship in most cases is really just a gift. I've had 500 people and 36 franchises who rely on me to keep the business running, to give them a living, so I can't afford to have the business go down. I'll be relieved not to have to do that any more. I say that respectfully.

'I've been able to do a lot of good things. I've just had a Warriors poster done, that we sold through the shops. I went into Central Print to pick them up, and the guy, who had given me a good deal, asked what we'd be selling them for. I said, "Five dollars, and I'm going to give every cent to the Cancer Society." Chris, the bloke who owns Central Print, said, "You bastard. How can I charge you for them now?" And he gave us them for free. We raised $10,000 with the posters.

'There's some sadness too. It's been over 40 years of my life. I'd like to think that I've treated my customers fairly. With my hand on my heart, if someone hasn't been treated well, I've done everything I could to make things right.'

In the new stage of his life there's a healthier, fitter Butcher too. He's cut bread and potatoes out of his diet. 'I haven't cut meat out — you can't make life completely boring.' He's spending more time out with the Waiheke kayaking club he founded. 'I'll be due for the pension very soon. I'll be looking forward to that.'

Basically he's working to be around for as long as he can, especially to see his grandchildren grow and prosper. His attitude to life, as it always has been, is described by the message on his beloved mobile phone. 'You have a great day, because I'm going to have a bloody cracker.'

And this is how he sums up his business career. 'I've never had a mentor as such, but I followed my mum and dad, who shopped at Self Help. Why? Because it was no frills, and it was cheap.'